AWAKENING DARKNESS

Elgin State Hospital 1969–1972
A Rite of Passage

Ceremonial Memoir™
Amidst a Medicine Wheel
Part One of Four Directions–South

J. M. Seis

GREAT
MOTHER
PRESS

Tallahassee, FL

Awakening Darkness: Elgin State Hospital 1969–1972 A Rite of Passage
Ceremonial Memoir™
Amidst a Medicine Wheel Part One of Four Directions–South

Library of Congress Control Number: 2018901056

Printed and bound in USA

First Printing September 2018

Published by Great Mother Press, LLC, Tallahassee, FL
Cover Designed by J. L. Menzel
Cover photos © 2018 J. M. Seis

ISBN 978-0-9996960-0-2 (paperback)
ISBN 978-0-9996960-1-9 (digital)

Subjects: Religion & Spirituality, Shamanism, Goddess, Great Mother and Dark
Mother Archetype, Women, Healing, Transformation.

Gay and Lesbian History—United States, Coming Out in a Mormon Family.

Mental Health History—Elgin, Illinois, United States, Psychology, Coming of Age.

Visit: greatmotherpress.com greatmotherpress@gmail.com
www.facebook.com/ceremonialmemoir

"Your story is like those from the Jewish holocaust. Except your story is from our holocaust. I've reached my seventies hearing stories of lesbian and gay people who were forced into mental institutions by their families, but so far as I know, and I'm fairly familiar with much our literature, yours is the first one to reveal in detail the horrors perpetrated in those institutions to "cure" us. The photos you provide add all that much more visceral impact. There is no question that yours is a story that must be told."

Katherine V. Forrest, author of the Kate Delafield Series and editor at Naiad Press and Spinsters Ink.

"The memoir recounts a harrowing journey into psychic darkness. Sometimes excruciating, it exposes the raw underbelly of patriarchy, serving as a harsh indictment of US society in the 1960s. It is also an immensely compelling story of spiritual, sexual, and political awakening."

Lise Weil PhD, author of *In Search of Pure Lust*, founding editor of *Trivia: Voices of Feminism"* and *"Dark Matter: Women Witnessing,"* faculty of "Goddard Graduate Institute."

"In *Awakening Darkness,* J. M. Seis demonstrates how she overcame a painful world unknown to most. In the face of tremendous challenges as a young teen, her story is one of resilience and renewal."

Merle R. Saferstein, author, educator, and creator of Living and Leaving Your Legacy®

My love and admiration goes to J.M. Seis for her tremendous courage to claim and heal her past. It required a great love for humanity to share her deepest secrets and sorrows so others can heal. I am grateful that my dear sister/warrioress released this book. What I find most incredible is her ability to share her story so clearly without anger or revenge. Her love and dedication to her own healing is her gift to the healing of All.

Luzclara
www.luzclaramedicinewoman.com

TABLE OF CONTENTS

Foreword i

A Note v

Dedication to Teenager vii

PART I Inside 1

    God 3

    Doors 5

    Inside 8

    Seder 17

    Restraint 19

    Staffed 32

    Tests 34

    Outside In 36

    Chosen & Unchosen 38

    Girlfriend 41

    Puri 47

PART II Runaway 53

    Being Lesbian 55

    Family 59

    Tree 68

    Thirteen 70

    Spinning Wheel 81

    Leaving 86

    Minnie 95

    Shabbat 102

Midlife Prayer 107

    Summer 109

Pressure 123

Choices 128

Runaway 129

Promise 140

Pilgrimage..149

Moving 154

Sex 158

High School 164

Eli 166

Wedding 174

Marilyn 182

Discharge..187

Outpatient 194

Moving Out 202

PART III Wheel of Change 207

Center Building...209

Dream 217

Pact...219

Fairy Tale 224

Time 231

Arms 235

Wheel of Change 237

Farewell 243

Teenager Response 245

Afterword 249

APPENDIX 251

The Medicine Wheel..253

Dark Mother Archetype 256

The Use of the Word Shaman 260

Photos 261

John Johnson's Drawings 285

Jan's Poetry 293

Acknowledgments 303

Invictus 307

J. M. Seis Bio 309

Great Spirit,
Mother, Father, Creator,
Earth, and Sky,

I call on the powers of the Earth
from the South, the West, the North, and the East.
Bless the Child within us all.
Guide us home.
Blessed be.
Amen.
Kiyaya!

FOREWORD

By Sandra Ingerman

World-renowned shamanic teacher and author.

Santa Fe, NM

J.M. Seis is a great writer. I could truly immerse myself in the events she wrote about. Her book starts with a letter from her as an adult, communicating to her inner teenager. In midlife, Seis listens and acknowledges her inner child's harrowing story like a loving mother, but also as a shaman.

The focus of this book is on what happened from 1969 to 1972, when J.M. Seis, as a child, was put into a state mental institution in Illinois as an inpatient and then later as an outpatient. *Awakening Darkness* shares the story of J.M. Seis' life in the institution and how, through the power of awakening her inner spirit, she became the remarkable person she is today.

There are three sections to this book. The first is an introduction to J.M. Seis as a child in an institution. The second section is about what brought this child to the institution and the violent initiatory experiences that cracked her open to gain a new perspective on her identity and also on the world. In section three, Seis brings in the concept of shamanic community healing for individual and collective need. Brilliant strands of spiritual meaning are woven throughout the book. A greater mythic message emerges amidst the process of J.M. Seis healing and answering the call as a shamanic teacher and practitioner.

The topics covered within this book are diverse and yet timely. *Awakening Darkness* appears to be the only first person account of a gay child in a mental institution. Seis also portrays a feminist awakening by a young girl in a violent male dominant society where abuse of power is rampant. Along with the photos and drawings, this book illustrates a time in the history of mental health rarely written about.

J.M. Seis redefines how writing can become a ceremony of healing. She created a new genre, Ceremonial Memoir ™, where personal experiences are transformed by writing using ancient patterns from the labyrinth and the medicine wheel. Those who read *Awakening Darkness*, those who assisted, and even those who comment on it are, in essence, participating in a ceremony that is part of a larger vortex of healing.

I am so impressed by the work J. M. Seis is doing to teach others how to use shamanic practices to access deeper parts of their own consciousness. Ceremonial Memoir ™ as a writing genre includes involvement by a community in close proximity, as well as a larger community through publication.

Awakening Darkness demonstrates a different way of embracing darkness, both personal and collective. J.M. Seis' vision is to allow others to experience the beauty and power that is born in what we may consider our darkest experiences. It is a call for all of us to reach through our fear and shame to embrace the beautiful children within us that are waiting to come home.

I found this book inspirational. When J.M. Seis sent me a copy of *Awakening Darkness,* my deep respect and regard for who she is grew in exponential ways. I was deeply touched by all J.M. Seis has been through. I admire that she was able to rise out of the ashes like the phoenix and be reborn as a great teacher and healer. When you read this book, you will have no question that Seis awakened her inner spiritual fire and came through her initiation beautifully. Many who read this may be inspired to share their own history, transform their old experiences, and learn how to shine their light in the world as Seis has.

I have known Seis for at least twenty-eight years. I have experienced her as a person who carries deep wisdom. I was aware of some previous health challenges in her life. Over the years, I watched in wonder how Seis healed herself and how she became a shamanic teacher and healer who could bring so many deeply into the work.

In shamanic work, it is known that the greatest shamans are also "wounded healers." The key to being able to practice shamanism is going through deep initiatory experiences challenging both our body and mind so that our inner spiritual fire can awaken and connect with divine forces to help build "the spiritual muscles" needed to be in service to the community.

I feel this book will inspire anyone who reads it, for it is a true story of someone who journeyed into the underworld and immersed herself within the Dark Mother before being reborn. I know the seeds that *Awakening Darkness* plants will grow. Each of us must at some point in our lives go within and find our inner gifts and strengths, transforming through our own experience of darkness into light.

A note about the graphic nature of this story

There is violence in this story, including sexual violence. Please understand the context is intended as a healing story. I do not wish to disturb others or trigger anyone else's trauma by sharing my own. Instead, I invite those who read this to embrace whatever part of themselves might have been shamed or harmed for any reason. May my stories be a ceremony and memorial for those who never had an opportunity to be heard and loved.

This story is being told by a teenage part of myself for the first time in detail from visceral memory. The stories were divided into small parcels that were dropped into widely dispersed areas of my unconscious and into the very cells of my body. The story is sometimes raw and unpolished. Occasionally I used words from that time period that are not currently politically correct. At times I do not follow a linear order. I decided to keep much of this story in its original form in order to maintain the integrity of my child's voice.

The healing taking place between my younger self, who was silenced, and my older self, listening, required ultimate truth of what that child's experience was for her. That is the container that allowed this story to come forward. I would not have shared it publicly except for the strong encouragement from my mentors and friends who read it and told me, "This must be published." And so I've labored for many years rewriting and making tremendous changes within myself in order to become transparent, while bringing a part of myself home. *Awakening Darkness,* is my own soul retrieval.

To Jan, My Inner Teenager,

This book is for you; in fact, the rest of my life is now dedicated to you having a life and a voice. I celebrate your beauty and courage. I apologize for how, as an adult, I contributed to trying to forget about you because of what happened to you. I allowed my societal role to become a whitewash of credibility, adding more silence and invisibility to your experiences.

Dear one, who would not be crushed by unspeakable harm or injustice, you believed in love against all odds and stood strong and often alone in a war with no enemies. You endured insanity and yet did not lose your mind.
Thank you.

You wondered why no one ever came to rescue you. Now I understand that I had to find you, witness your story with compassion, and bring you safely home.

I understand what hurt you most was not so much the traumas themselves, as it was that no one seemed to care or even notice. No one asked. When you tried talking about what happened, you were silenced, shamed, blamed, or you ended up taking care of other people's feelings. You will never be that alone again. I promise.

I give you my love in a safe home within. To the best of my ability I will give you a physical home with supportive loved ones. I will tell your story and encourage others to tell their stories, embracing any part of themselves that has been forced into shamed silence and exile for any reason. It is time to believe in love again. This time a healthy, vibrant, spiritually-based love, rooted in the earth and ordinary life.

Come home, Sweetheart.
It is safe now.
I have listened and made record of your story.
I believe you.
I'm proud of you.
I love you.

Sincerely,
J. M. Seis

Whosoever survives a test,
Whatever it may be,
Must tell the story.
That is his duty.

Elie Wiesel

PART I

INSIDE

GOD

"How old is God?" I asked my father when I was around four years old. I remember this as clear as if it were just last week. He came to my bed to help me say a prayer before going to sleep. "How can there be no beginning and no end to God?" I responded to my father's attempt to answer me. I lay awake with dozens of questions I wanted to ask God but was afraid I would forget before I died and could actually talk to him. I was small and just learning how to write my name. "Does God know my name?"

"Are there animals in heaven?" I asked my father, who seemed to know everything. "I don't want to go to heaven if there are no monkeys there. I want to go where the monkeys are. I want to go to monkey heaven," I told him.

"Don't think about heaven or monkeys; just be a good girl and go to sleep," my father advised as he turned out the light and closed the door part way.

As a child at church, I was told and shown how people should behave and worship God. I watched as different adults stood in front of the congregation and shared how they believed God wanted us to be. Sometimes a man or a woman with trembling lips or tears dripping from the corners of their eyes, would stand up in the pews and tell stories about how God, Jesus and a prophet named Joseph Smith had changed their lives. I watched these people with a mixture of curiosity and discomfort.

One day, when I was about ten years old, I was alone up on the hill of our Pennsylvania ancestral farm. It was a rare occurrence for me to be by myself. Perhaps my siblings and cousins were off picking huckleberries. I found myself in one of those crystalline moments that pops up out of a blur of experiences and becomes a marker of awakening. On that summer day in a field edged by trees from a surrounding forest, I lay back on the grass under a large maple tree. This was the maple tree my grandmother often sat under, collecting coins from people who came to pick huckleberries on the land where she was born. But my grandmother must have been down the hill in the farmhouse, and all the others were somewhere else. I was alone and stayed there in complete silence and stillness.

As I lay with my back on the warm soft earth, I looked up to the sky and knew God was there, everywhere, as if the trees had all been holding this magnificent truth. The grasses bent over in gentle rhythmic waves. Brilliant white clouds crossed the azure blue sky and were not separate from anything else or from me. I could feel I was a part of this majesty of creation.

All my questions about God disappeared as I was held in great awe and cradled by wonder. I felt myself as one part of a much bigger story, all being told at once. I wanted to understand this story and was no longer as interested in the stories they told in church. For me, in that instant, I knew that God was in the living world not separate from me. That imprint remained a pivotal awareness, a foundation, and a loving mother within the earth itself that I would later return to in order to rebuild my life after it was broken.

DOORS

It was dark when my father drove us through the night. When I looked up, I saw no moon in the sky. We came to a stop at a large, sprawling brick building and went inside. It was nearly midnight when my parents left me in the care of the state. Tears fell down my mother's cheeks as she looked at me while a tall, thin older woman in a simple pastel dress took my arm and guided me away. I couldn't see the woman taking me or my mother clearly. A roar was sounding inside my head, a roar so loud it silenced everything. I was silenced. It was the death of everything I thought I knew, and yet it was also my entry into a great dark womb. At that time, it felt more like I was entering a tomb.

I remember the moment that the large, thick, heavy metal door, like those on an antique bank vault, began to close. It made a terrible creaking sound like a heavy groan from inside the walls, voicing through the lips of confused and bewildered hinges, "There are children inside these walls. They cannot go out." The door is closed. I heard the twisting of the long cylindrical handle come down, a metal tongue secretly extended into the wall, and stayed there.

Hands began touching me although I could not feel them. Voices made sounds which I automatically responded to, yet did not hear. Only the door was present, watching, keeping count of how many passed through and stayed there.

No one ever left this place even though eventually, they were all physically gone. The belly of this societal beast was bloated with the souls of children churning in its systematic wheels, frozen in time. They came in and were stripped down of everything they thought they were, when they might only be starting to understand and question their own individuality and personal path in life.

Here was the threshing floor, and the grain poured from my head as my sheaths were pulled off, examined, and taken away. Those clothes were my painter's brush strokes on the canvas of self-expression.

I was given an off-white, flower-printed nightgown, pale and stiff from too many washings and pressed flat by some mammoth machine. Then I was escorted down a hall to a room full of beds where I heard loud snoring. Soon I became aware of a foul odor of human origin. Eventually I got up and walked back through the darkened hall to the small room with a light on. "Something smells bad in that room," I told the woman seated at a desk facing the door. Her forehead wrinkled as she raised her eyebrows. She stood up from behind the desk.

"Well, let's get you a different bed then."

I was taken toward the other end of the long hall and directed into a room with an empty bed. It was a large room connected to other rooms filled with occupied beds. I climbed on top of the sheet and blanket that covered a thin mattress and stayed still for hours in the shadows waiting, watching, listening.

When daylight came, I got up and wandered from the dorm into the hall. There were a few girls standing by a door with the top half opened. A short plump woman in a green dress was handing over clothing to the girls outstretched arms.

"Whatda ya want?" She said eyeing me, while chewing gum. "You must be the new girl. Well, come on in here, and have a look over there. Your clothes won't be back from the laundry for a couple of weeks."

The clothing room attendant opened the bottom half of the door and signaled for me to enter. I felt myself float like a ghost into that small windowless room. Feet separate from legs. Torso separate from head. She closed the door behind me. There I saw two racks of faded nameless clothing. What would fit my tall, willowy body? Finding one small, faded and yellowed shift, I asked, "Can I see this one?"

"Of course! Take off that nightgown and try it on. Here's a bra. Looks like your size."

"Here?"

"Yes, here. Where else you gonna go? Hurry up. The other girls are waitin'."

I turned away from the attendant and toward the rack to undress. Pulling the stiff cotton sleeveless shift over me, I smelled detergent and bleach still clinging to the fibers. Quickly, I grabbed a brown cardigan sweater and pulled it around me, barely covering my bandaged left wrist. There was something alive in that wrist. Hidden flesh held the color of unheard voices, crying for life, telling the truth. I looked up and saw the attendant opening the door, ushering me out. As I reentered the small alcove, I heard sounds of other girls gathering, echoing through the long halls. Someone was crying.

6

It was springtime mid-April of 1969. The sun was shining. I'm sure birds were singing, although I did not hear them. Like looking through the wide end of a telescope, everything appeared narrow and small. Strange smells and sounds collided with the consuming silence engulfing me. My eyes blinked incessantly. I couldn't stop them from closing and opening over and over again. I didn't want to see. I had to see.

I had turned fourteen years old four months earlier. Although one rule of many endless rules in this place was to limit cigarette smoking to those fifteen years and older, I was given special treatment and allowed cigarettes. I don't know why. Maybe because I looked much older than I was. On the hour, the swinging top half of a door would open. A woman, often dressed in white, would hand out cigarettes to each girl. Personal items were held in a locked cabinet in the aide's room. It was a small space with a dark wooden desk and a big book on the desk. The "Incident Book" was something I would later become more familiar with.

A cigarette provided a smoky paradise. I watched a thick thumb roll the ridged striker in the metal case of a lighter. We turned and moved our little tobacco filled straws, like hummingbird beaks, into the flowering orange flame. Relief and restoration came with each inhalation of that delicious smoke. Exhaling, letting go for a moment, I felt something familiar I could hold onto. Quickly it burned away to ashes, and I fell through again into the moment of being inside.

INSIDE

Experience blurred. Moments turned inside out and upside down. Time didn't belong to me anymore. It belonged to these older people who controlled it and me. I had stepped out of time.

There were many things I was required to do that first day—or was it a week? On the inside is another world, with odd people, living different realities from those outside.

There were medical examinations of my body. Every new girl had to go through a battery of tests. I couldn't look directly at the older woman who led me from one building into another. I only remember her hands with the jingling keys moving, as she chose a different one each time before inserting it into a tiny dark opening in a metal circle on each door.

There was a man in a room with cold instruments who examined my still and silent body. He probed and made written notes. My eyes began diffusing and compartmentalizing every movement and sensation into hundreds of separate dulled perceptions.

Another man, old and with stale breath, peered into my mouth and poked at my teeth. He fumbled, and his hand shook so much that my gums bled from his sharp tool. I did not want to ever return to this man who was called a dentist.

The aide continued leading me around the grounds to different buildings, each having a specific name and purpose. We had just left the place where I had been assigned to live. Hanging above the door on the back porch was a small green wooden sign with, *Visitors, B1N*, painted on it. It looked like the word BIN, like "Looney Bin." *Was I only a visitor in this crazy place? Could I get out soon?* I wondered.

It was B-1-North actually, one of the children's units of Elgin State Hospital in Illinois. B-1-North was the intake ward, receiving girls into the institution. It had the highest degree of security for the most seriously ill and dangerous girls. All the girls admitted to the hospital passed through B-1-North, usually on their way to Halloran, another girl's ward that had less security and allowed the girls more privileges. Some girls came into B-1-North to be assessed and then were sent to other institutions or juvenile detention centers. I was never transferred. I stayed in B-1-North for one year, three months, and two weeks.

I didn't know anything that day. I just followed the close watch and lead of the aide taking me into the next building as she continued with her tasks. She said we were going to check out some girls from our ward who were in isolation there and bring them back to B-1-North.

"They had the clap," she said. "Been over there two weeks. Jus' now got word they're clear ta go."

"Oh?" I replied with a slight sigh.

I thought she meant that they all had a venereal disease called gonorrhea. I wondered how they all had contracted that illness while being locked up in Elgin.

The aide placed her key, hung from a crowded ring of keys, into the lock on the metal door with crisscrossed wire running through a rectangular glass window above the door handle. The sign on the brick wall next to the door had the letters, B-U-R-R and the numbers 790. I didn't understand what that meant or what kind of reality we were entering into when the door swung open.

My experience of stepping into what the aide called, "the Burr Ward" was immediately like taking my image of life and the world and placing it into acid. Mental film reels of how life should be and how it looks in the outside world curled up into distortions and melted away. New images suddenly recorded into my mind, imprinting deeply into my awareness, flickering with reflections of old WWII concentration camp footage. The smell was horrible. As we stepped inside the door, acrid odors of rotting human flesh, urine, and feces struggled with armies of disinfectant odors in hopeless conflict.

Bed after bed lined the floor in rows and blocks. Dozens and dozens of human beings or what might once have been called women were lying in those beds. Some of the beds were cribs where small curled-up fetal skeletal beings lay inside. They wore diapers. I had never seen such a thing.

The aide was pulling me through, but I was stunned, and something simply stopped in me. I couldn't quite integrate what I was witnessing. Hair on top of indefinable faces, vacant sockets once holding eyes now gone, huge open sores of rotten flesh breaking away down to the bone.

There may have been sounds, but I was again engulfed in silence, unbearably so. My eyes kept blinking as the aide pulled me through room after room of endless beds and bodies, some moving and some still. We went all the way to the back of the building where there was another locked door. Here were several young girls looking out of wire-laced windows from inside.

More keys turning in the locks released the girls from their prison in a prison. They jammed out toward us and to the doors we had come through. These girls seemed to know their way and hardly noticed me. They wanted to get outside. The girls had been locked up in there for too long. Maybe it was the aide or one of the girls rushing out who told me that all the old ladies in there were in the late stages of syphilis.

On the way out, I passed a woman sitting up in a chair who seemed almost normal. She had a nightgown on. An aide leaned down in front of her taking off a bandage, revealing a gaping wound along her shin. Our eyes met as the old woman looked up and smiled at me. "Hello dear," she said.

Maybe she directed her attention toward me because I was looking at her. I stopped. Suddenly, I couldn't hear her. I watched her mouth forming words. The wrinkled, smiling lady gave me the impression that she wanted contact and was grateful for my young presence there. She seemed hungry for life. Just a fragment of exchange with another was food she was starving for. I wanted to say something, but instead looked into her eyes and smiled. In that moment, I realized she was human and had seen and responded to the humanity in me. Something stirred in me, but I didn't want to wake up and feel. Not there. I turned my head away. We left and joined the others ahead of us.

Our small group of girls walked in stride with the aide back into B-1-North. The porch door closed and was locked behind us. After smoking another cigarette, we were all herded toward the other end of the ward. Keys jingled as the big metal door screamed open. We walked through it in a wandering line toward the cafeteria. As we passed a large open hall I noticed mostly male adult patients walking around. Many of them held cigarettes. Some were holding smoking butts in yellowish brown nicotine-stained fingers. Their lips were stained. Clothes hung on them like dry fabric on a dilapidated clothesline, faded, dull, and coarse from too much sun and wind.

Passing the commissary where small items could be purchased, we continued down another hall, passing a pay phone. My eyes lit upon that phone. I made a mental note of a mailbox against a wall earlier. I wanted to find a way to get to a phone to make a call and to a mailbox to send a letter. Winding to the left in a dark corridor with stairwells going down somewhere, we moved toward locked double doors that the aide pushed her key into and eased open.

We were guided into a big open room with high ceilings and many little tables, with one chair facing in at each of the four sides. The auditorium-sized room had other children seated at tables further away. There were boys sitting all together and behind them there were other girls. These groups were already eating.

The sound of metal and plastic echoed off tiled floors and reverberated around the cavernous space. An aide directed us into a single line on the left of a standing enclosed metal food-dispensing island with rails around it. There were plastic trays set on the rails as we entered. Each girl ahead of me took a tray and carried it around until the island opened up. There a strange looking adult patient slopped some food onto a plate or in a bowl that they then put on our trays.

I could not identify the food. All of it had the same unfamiliar greasy smell. I wasn't hungry. I was nearly 5'8" and weighed barely 100 lbs. I had no appetite for quite a while before coming to this place. The food and the manner of distribution spoiled any interest I might have had in eating it. I sat with the food on my tray, along with two other girls at a table. They ate ravenously. One of them asked, "Ya-eatin-dat?" She hardly looked up from her empty plate.

"Uh, no. You can have it."

Her tray of empty dishes was quickly pushed off to the side of the table. I watched as her small dark hands with uneven fingernails grasped the sides of my tray and pulled it in front of her. She ate my food. I'd never seen anyone eat like that before. More like a hungry animal than a person.

As the other groups finished before us, they filed out passing by our table. I heard exchanges of words and saw fleeting glances that added a rush of color and vitality to the lifeless, echoing room. The boys and girls were rushed through as though they were not supposed to communicate with us. Communication strained through the limits anyway. I was the new girl. They were looking at me.

"Check her out!" said one tall red-haired girl as she dug her elbow into another smaller girl's side. Laughter erupted as their eyes met mine and then they turned away.

"Where you from?" another called out to me.

"You girls git going. Now! Quit botherin' that girl," barked an aide from their ward. More laughter rose and fell as they followed her out the swinging doors.

11

Later in the evening there was a dance. It was a tragic comedy placing all those boys and girls with supervision in one room with a record player going. I was more uncomfortable with what I was wearing at that moment than seeing anyone else very clearly. I was taken to the "mixer" by the aide who led a small group of us down more long corridors, through locked doors and into B-2-South, a wing on the opposite side of Center Building.

My appearance had been very important to me in the outside world. I went to great effort to dress myself in a particularly creative way. I designed clothes in my sketchbooks using a pencil and colored pens. I normally wore make-up and curled my dyed-blonde hair on spikey uncomfortable rollers. When I was thirteen years old, I had trained at a modeling school in Chicago. I traveled to Elgin from New York City on a plane where the flight attendants offered me alcoholic beverages because they assumed I was old enough to drink. I looked eighteen. My favorite models were Cheryl Tiegs, Twiggy, and especially the tall Russian, Veruschka. Here I was standing in some old sleeveless shift of unknown origin. I felt awkward and uncomfortable being at a social function with other girls and boys. They were from different wards. No one was dancing. I kept a cool demeanor and said very little.

I stood there acknowledging the new world I had come to, unable to recognize myself in its contrast. I was radically severed from an external world that now seemed like drama and pretense. Here I was hidden inside society's dark secret, safely out of view. Some part of me understood that the great cauldron of psychic darkness I felt consumed by was more than just my own. It was a concealed world of collective pain and fear where one must focus on sheer survival. I knew I had to start learning fast. The dance where no one danced soon ended, and I began a different kind of dance.

An important part of the learning process on the inside was through those who were already there. It seemed to be part sport and part curiosity that drew certain girls to come up and talk to me on my first day. One of the girls asked, "Are you crazy? Ha, ha." I just looked at her. Then she got serious, looking straight into my eyes and said, "If you aren't crazy when you come in, you will be before you leave."

Another girl chimed in, "You might never get out."

That was a horrible thought that reverberated in my whole body like a sudden chill.

"Why are you in here?" one of them asked meekly.

"What did you do? Did you try to kill yourself or run away?" another chimed in.

A voice came from behind me. "Where are you from? Do you have parents?"

I began to distinguish from this mass of questions coming at me that some girls had more confidence and seemed to rule over other girls.

Later I sat down in one of the metal-armed vinyl-backed chairs in a larger rounded room off the long hall. A girl with medium-length red hair sat down next to me.

"Hi, I'm Ann." she said. "Don't let them bother you. They do that to everyone who comes in. They tried it on me a couple of weeks ago when I was admitted back inside, but I'd been here before and know more than most of them. I shut them up, all right. Showed 'em I know what's what in here. How old are you?" Ann asked me.

"Fourteen." I responded looking down at the floor.

"I'm fifteen." she beamed back at me. "Wow! How did you get the aides to give you cigarettes?"

"I don't know. I came in with a carton of True Menthols, and they just lit me up when it was time."

"Who got 'em for you?"

"My parents."

"That's cool. Can I try one?"

"Sure."

"Did your parents put you in here?"

"Yeah." I said looking down at the floor again.

"I wish I had parents that bought me cigarettes." Ann said as she looked out toward the closed windows at the curved end of the big alcove. "I don't know who my dad is. My mom is paranoid schizophrenic. She used to disappear for days, leaving me and my little brother alone to try and take care of ourselves. We got pretty hungry sometimes. Used the stove for heat. Not sure which was better, when she was home or gone. The state finally figured it out when we weren't showing up for school. They sent us both away to foster homes. My last home didn't work out, so I've got to stay here until they find me another one."

"You were here before?" I asked.

"Yeah, I got locked up last year and was waiting almost a year. I hope it doesn't take that long this time."

"I hope not too. I want to get out of here as soon as I can," I told her.

"Yeah, I know. But, you're in here now, so you better learn how to make it. Listen," Ann continued, lowering her voice, pulling up her chair and leaning

13

in closer toward me. "There are biters here. Watch out for that one," she said, pointing down the hall. She's thirteen but looks much younger and nicer than she really is." I looked at the tiny girl with almond shaped brown innocent looking eyes and short dark hair. She was sitting in a chair by herself at the end of a big green Ping-Pong table at the back of a long hall. "That's Sue. She doesn't give any warning before she bites and when she bites, she doesn't let go. She bites through. She even bites girls who are sleeping." Sue was Japanese. She sat quietly and often smiled or rocked. Later, I saw her parents come and visit her. They seemed like a polite, middle class suburban couple.

Ann turned my attention to another girl. Although she appeared younger, she was big-boned and taller than Sue. She had light skin and short, thin brown hair. She sat in a chair against the wall across from us. I watched her rocking back and forth while making a singsong sound.

"That's Julie." Ann spoke excitedly. "She screams and bites her own hand before she attacks, so you know she's coming. Her parents left her in here when she was two. Julie is twelve years old now," Ann spoke slowly. "She's a ward of the state. Those scars on her face and arms are from other patients. Sue has bitten her quite a few times." Ann's face narrowed as she frowned. "You know," Ann happily continued volunteering information, "Julie sometimes disappears for weeks. When I ask where she is, the aides say Julie is at the medical hospital for tests. I think they're doing experiments on her because of how she looks and acts when she comes back. There's no one to challenge them or check up on Julie."

I let Ann's words sink in. Julie could not speak for herself. She belonged to the state. They could do whatever they wished with her without question. I noticed the raw innocence of Julie's eyes and how she blinked her long lashes in harmony with her body's rhythmic movement. I wondered what she had experienced over the last ten years and what had originally brought her to Elgin. Who brings a two-year old to a mental institution and leaves her there?

There were three girls gathered together at a table nearby. One of them was thin and angular, almost boyish with her short wavy auburn hair. She moved infrequently standing still, rather than sitting with the other two. Another was taller and had shoulder-length blonde hair. She was quite attractive. Ann told me her name was Tracie and that she was sixteen. She seemed to take charge of the other girls. A shorter, heavier girl with brown wavy shoulder length hair and glasses was by Tracie's side. Her name was Doris. She didn't say much but seemed to have strong opinions when she did. Doris was sixteen years old too.

They formed a pack. Ann warned me to be careful around them. The blonde, Tracie, was watching me.

That evening after dinner and another cigarette, an aide opened the locked door that housed three shower stalls in a row side by side. They were set to the left of a narrow hall leading in, ending with a wall that had a tiny window high at the top. Modesty was impossible in this place. There was no privacy.

The bathroom was beside the water fountain, across from the main alcove. It had a door only the aides could lock and unlock. When you stepped inside, the open room had four toilets set on cold gray cement along the left wall. There was a metal plate covering an open drain in the center of the floor. On the right were four ceramic sinks with a long mirror on the wall above them. At the end across from the door was a large white painted window with wire running through it. That window was closed and locked. A large utility sink was to the right of the window after the line of four smaller sinks.

There were no divisions or stalls for the toilets and there were no curtains on the showers. There was no way to get in and out without seeing others and being seen naked. This was not comfortable for me. I didn't want to undress or go into that narrow shower room. At some point, I had to. I acted as though I didn't care.

As I went into the shower, I tried to figure out how to be invisible. It seemed to be working at first. I was feeling the fall of water on my torso, being careful not to wet my hair because I didn't know how I would set it again. Flashes of other girls' bodies went by. Suddenly there were three girls in my stall, hands pressing hard on my chest and body, my back against the wall. The tall blonde pressed her naked body against my body.

"You're mine!" She said as she pushed me hard, then pulled me forward. The three of them held my head under the water and then ran out laughing. Tracie had claimed me; I got out of the shower and dressed.

Before I arrived at Elgin, I had already learned to not feel my feelings. If I wasn't okay, I had a way of editing my reality by pretending it wasn't happening. I escaped my body and the present moment by taking refuge in my head, where creativity could paint a picture as I needed it to be. I didn't dare show any response to what happened in the shower.

Ann had been keeping an eye on me. "You were lucky." She told me. "There was a girl in here last year who was attacked in the shower. Those girls put a broom handle up her snatch. She had to go to 'gynie' and didn't come back."

I had noticed that the quiet boyish girl in the pack walked strangely, with her legs wide apart. Uncharacteristically, she wore a skirt. I asked Ann about her.

"Doris picked Heddy up and slammed her down on a metal chair arm between her legs! That happened last month." Ann told me. "She's been walking like that ever since." I didn't want that to happen to me.

The aides opened the dorm doors when it was time to go to bed. Otherwise the dorms remained locked during the day. There were three dorms connected by open doors between them at the far end of the unit across from the big metal vault door. On my first night, I was assigned a bed near the open door of the middle dorm. There were six other beds in that dorm room wedged against the walls and a short distance from one another. Sue, the silent night-biter, was in one of those beds down and across from me. There were two girls in the small dorm to my right. The bigger dorm to my left held about ten beds, all close together with aisles to walk through. There were windows on the opposite side of my dorm. The big dorm had another side of windows too. These windows were sealed. There were offices and another dorm at the other end of the unit. Some of the epileptic girls were in cribs and a large "mentally retarded" girl named Karen slept there. Perhaps there were six girls in that room.

When it was lights out, I lay in the bed with my eyes open, afraid to close them. I stayed alert to any motion or sound. I didn't move. Every couple of hours a flashlight would shine in on the beds as an aide came by to check on us. That was the first night I began learning never to fully sleep.

SEDER

I take a moment to reflect before returning to the storm of memories gathering around my childhood experiences. It has been thirty-nine years since that first day in Elgin. I have rarely been able to talk about it, except in fragments. The stories have been buried alive. They come out now still breathing.

There was a psychologist at the hospital who became a significant influence in my life during that time. She told me that I was "the only one who survived Elgin." I remember when she said that to me on an outing when I was around sixteen years old. It felt like a burden to have survived when the others didn't. I wondered what happened to the girls and boys she was talking about. Eventually I learned that even that psychologist, as well as the other staff, didn't make it out of Elgin without being injured in numerous ways. They too were internally marked and emotionally dismembered by what took place there.

People who currently know me cannot imagine what I lived through. The silenced stories have become unhealed ghosts of children whispering in the dark. The stigma of being cast out is powerful and lasting.

I went to my first Passover Seder last Sunday. During the Seder, Jews all over the world remember the enslavement and exodus of the ancient people of Israel from Egypt. The woman who invited me and organized the event added some of the mystical aspects of the Kabbalah to the ceremony. The Seder is a night when individuals can experience a transformation freeing their own inner limitations, the slave within.

My friend said, "Liberation can happen suddenly like an eruption." In that moment, it occurred to me that I am free. All my life I have been aware of my bondage, both literal and figurative, to situations, to beliefs, and attachments of which I am not fully conscious. I've lived a life chasing freedom yet kept rediscovering the cage I was running from within me. Seductive snares have followed me everywhere morphing into deceptive traps, which I have repetitively fallen into.

Now I see there is another reality coinciding with loss. There is an inextinguishable light at the core of my being. I am guided even at times when hope is swallowed by misfortune. I've had to stand still at times, trusting a way will open, and it has.

At the Seder, I could suddenly see my life differently. As I sat sharing a ceremonial meal with a group of lovely people, I had a moment of knowing— something right beside me, but slightly out of reach. How fortunate I've been in my journey to fall out of limiting societal beliefs, even though it hasn't led to comfort or ease. In my moment of realization, reality flipped around so I could understand everything differently. I have come to appreciate the benefit I've gained through disadvantage and the freedom I developed inside me while being imprisoned.

During my time in the abyss, I discovered a thread to my original wilderness, and through that, my innate connection to everything and everyone. Being stripped to the core can reveal what lies at the core.

I am sitting still. Finally, I am remembering being in the place that was called "Elgin." By realizing that some part of me was never able to get out of there, I can also see how another part of me slipped under the door into the sensual embrace of nature and began to dance to a different rhythm.

By witnessing these ghosts as if it were yesterday, a truth enters my life through the back door. In this truth, the silence finally ebbs.

My life as it has been, my worldly identity I worked hard to create, has fallen away recently. My success and struggle to be someone, to have a meaningful, respected persona, and to do something of value have ceased. I am back in the time of Elgin with the ghosts. Paradoxically, I am experiencing a kind of liberation, a freedom born out of terrible and beautiful darkness giving birth to new light.

RESTRAINT

Restraint can come from inside or from outside. When I was first admitted to Elgin, I kept a constant level of tightness inside my body to hold everything together and to keep myself from expressing or showing any emotion. Poise and flow of movement, elegant stature, grace, and perseverance during difficulty had become part of my social strategy before I arrived.

I was extremely self-conscious, even of how I held each finger on either hand. My left pinky partly curved and positioned a little higher than the rest of my fingers. I controlled every movement, every word and every silence. Once admitted to Elgin, I could not relax and did not sleep much because of my physical vigilance. My gift for language came from books and from growing up with intellectual older siblings. I articulated with decisive clarity by accessing an extensive internal vocabulary.

Femininity was important to me. My manners and posture were impeccable. Every morning I applied black mascara with a tiny spiral brush onto my eyelashes and painted navy blue eyeliner on the edge of my upper eyelid, coming out just a little further than the end of the lid beyond my eye. I never let anyone see me without my makeup.

I kept my hair dyed blonde until just before arriving at Elgin. Originally, I was told that I would be going to a girls' school and would not have access to as many conveniences. After I arrived in Illinois from New York, my parents told me the truth. Anticipating that it might be difficult to dye my hair, I had most of my hair returned to a light brown color with a dash of blonde left in.

I was uncomfortable with people touching me, and I didn't touch them. With my training as a model the year before, I maintained an aura of distant elegance that stood in contrast with my drab and barren surroundings. However, during my first interminable month in Elgin, my ability to maintain my distance and poise was broken.

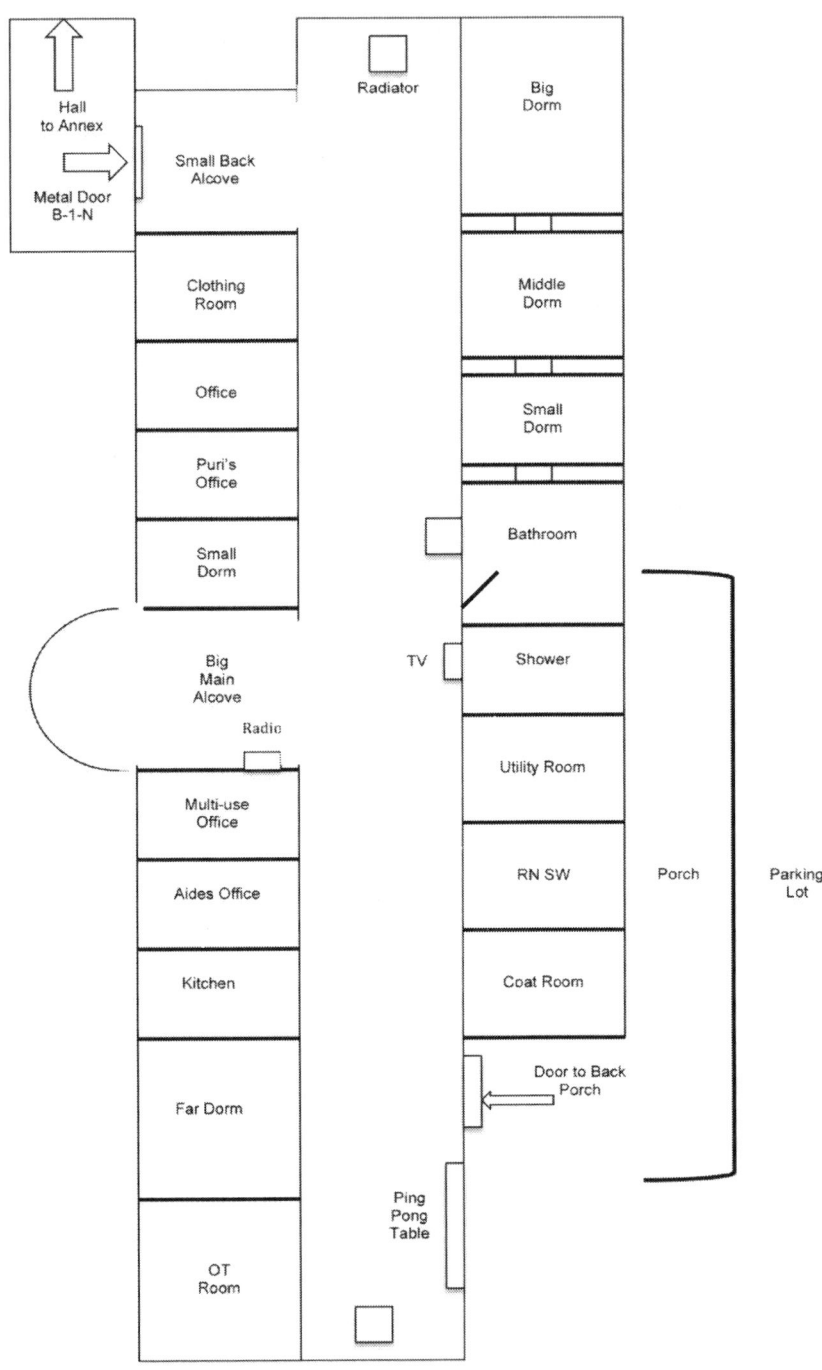

Floor plan of B-1-North, Elgin State Hospital 1969, from memory. © 2008 J. M. Seis

The space I was contained in consisted of a long wide hallway with a small alcove at one end. The locked metal door in the small alcove connected to the "Annex," a central part of the greater building called "Center Building." Center Building stood as a megalith to mental health on an eighty-acre compound with many other smaller buildings on the property. Center Building was the oldest part of Elgin State Hospital. The metal door with peeling paint that I originally came through was in that small alcove. To the left of the locked metal door was the door to the clothing room, which was usually locked, except in the morning when we dressed. The clothing woman in charge of that room took her keys out and called us to come each morning before breakfast. She would usually stretch her arms over a half-door shut beneath her to hand clothes out to the girls waiting in line. Sometimes we could go in and pick out our clothes for the day.

Clothing brought in from the outside was taken away on admission. Garments deemed appropriate were sent to the laundry facilities where they had labels sewn into the cloth with the patient's name and the initials of the hospital and ward printed on them. Eventually some of my clothing showed up in the clothing room with labels that had my name printed along with B1N, ESH, (Elgin State Hospital). My identity was being smeared and seared by the institution. I was internally branded to a place that was originally called the Northern Illinois Hospital and Asylum for the Insane. My clothes no longer felt like my clothes. They were hospital clothes now.

A couple of heavy metal chairs stood in front of the windows at the end of the long hall. Between the two chairs there was a big radiator with a wood and wire mesh cover over it. A small shelf with fewer than ten books was attached about five and a half feet up on the wall to the right of the radiator. The books were old dilapidated paperback novels that no one ever seemed to read. Across from the back alcove were three connected dorm rooms called the big, middle, and small dorms. Along the long hallway were offices with closed, locked doors. Those doors rarely opened. When they did, adults you didn't see very often would disappear inside. Some of the girls would go behind those doors with the adults.

A tall, narrow rectangular metal water fountain stood just before the bathroom door. This water fountain was an important fixture that provided a place to visit during the day. Girls would wander over and turn the hard, yellowed plastic knob on the top right corner until a stream of cool water leapt up to be watched, played in, or lapped up by outstretched tongues. There were the showers, followed by the utility room with its long stringy mops in rolling buckets emanating strong disinfectant odors into the hallway. Across from the shower door was another larger alcove identified as the main alcove. This central alcove had a rounded end with windows facing toward the front of the hospital grounds.

Cars and trucks would come in from the outside world, driving around the hillsides before coming closer to the Center Building. We could not see the outside world through the trees and hills of the grounds. I felt separated from life as though captured inside a terrarium with specified dimensions. I could see nature, yet I was in an unnatural habitat, disconnected from it. I had fallen from grace with the outside world.

B-1-North was one long wing extending from a large central core of the main building that first opened in 1872. It was part of the Kirkbride Plan of buildings designed to have a curative effect on mental illness. Hanging in the Center Building Annex was a large plaque with words raised in metal proclaiming the noble mission of the state mental hospital as a place of hope to care for the insane.

B-1-North's long hall contained a coatroom. Heavy metal posts with bars between them held an array of miserable looking outerwear. Torn, oddly-colored slickers and coats of varying thicknesses hung side-by-side from wooden hangers. Just beyond the coatroom was the back door to the porch. It was kept locked.

There were a number of chairs in the main alcove, but not enough for all the girls to sit in at the same time. Pacing back and forth, sitting or lying on the floor at the ends of the hallway distracted some of the girls from their need for a chair. A chalky pink colored wooden table was set off to one side. It was big enough for four girls and sometimes an aide to occasionally play cards. I couldn't understand the card games they played. I had not been exposed to playing cards much. Some of the girls played gin rummy over and over again.

"Come on, y'all. Lez play," the older aide Magee called out as she swung the double-hung door to the aide station closed. "You can play too cain't ya?" she asked me with her twangy southern accent.

"No. I'll watch. Maybe I can learn." I sat down off to the side of the table as other girls eagerly pulled their seats closer.

We didn't play cards in my family very often. Occasionally I played games of Go Fish and Old Maid with my childhood friends and younger siblings. Generally, my parents didn't play with us.

Once in a while, my parents would include a game called I-Spy at the end of a church program called "Family Home Evening." After we read from the

Bible and said a family prayer, someone would hide a small bright red top from a saltshaker. The saltshaker top had to be placed somewhere in plain sight, while the other family members hid their eyes. It could be placed anywhere as long as it could be seen without moving anything. The person who saw it first would often walk away from the location and then call out "I-Spy!" The others would have to see if they could find it, paying attention to where that person had been.

Perhaps I had become the symbolic red saltshaker top of my family, hidden away in plain view in the state mental institution. I wasn't sure that anyone was looking for me or cared that I was there. If anything, they looked away and didn't speak a word.

Sometimes music would play. High up on a wall at the edge of the main alcove on a small ledge was a breadbox sized plastic radio. Its cord hung down and plugged into a wall socket, all above reach. Only the aides were allowed to stand on a stool kept in their office and adjust the radio.

Popular music would reverberate through the halls when the aides decided to turn the radio on. One day I was pacing back and forth through the hall. As I approached the main alcove, I heard The 5th Dimension singing *The Age of Aquarius*. My reflexive muting of sound opened to receive a message from this song wafting over the din of children's misery and chaos. I felt my skin tingle with awareness and my heart beat stronger to the possibility of entering a new time for all humanity. I felt called by that song as though by destiny, to be part of a time of love and peace, with "harmony, understanding, sympathy, and trust abounding." I needed to let the sunshine in. I knew it could heal me.

Hearing messages from the outside world was precious. Between the shower door and the utility room was a bulky black-and-white TV with a medium-sized screen set on a small table pushed against the wall across from the big alcove. The TV was usually turned off during the day. I liked watching TV.

Across from the coatroom and the door to the outside porch was the aides' station, around the corner from the big alcove. There was another small examining room between the aides' station and the alcove. The door to that room usually remained closed. The aides' station was the area of the most activity. The aides were our surrogate parents and keepers of the ward by day and night. Usually there was one aide on the ward at night and sometimes two during the day.

Next to the aides' station was a small kitchen with a door that was rarely opened. Another dorm was further down the hall. That's where I was told the most "mentally retarded" and non-functioning girls were placed. I asked to be relocated when I was placed in that dorm on my first night.

At the far end of the hall was the door to the OT, or occupational therapy, room. This door was rarely opened. When it was, I saw tables and some small boxes on a row of shelves that had different kinds of art supplies and other items in them. When I went into that room, I felt a fragment of peace. The blonde-haired woman, who was younger than the aides, occasionally came onto the ward and opened that door. She was kind and helpful. It was almost as though she carried some sunshine from the outside world in with her. The OT woman appeared to care. I often sat on the floor by that door as a source of comfort during the long hours of the days spent on the ward. Eventually the OT woman stopped coming to the ward and that door remained locked.

Across from the OT room was the Ping-Pong table. No one ever played Ping-Pong there. The table was used for sorting laundry or other tasks. That's the table Sue liked to sit by at the far end of the ward, away from the other girls.

At the end of the hall were two more windows and another radiator with a wooden and wire mesh cover over it. Sue could not tolerate those radiator cages or the two throw rugs on the floor being off center. She would walk all the way down the hall to the other side just to straighten the radiator cover by an inch or two or straighten a rug. Bored and restless girls would sometimes play the "Sue game" and kept bumping the radiator cover after Sue sat down at her distant table. They watched her get up and do the same action over and over again. There were not many rugs on the tiled floor; there was one by the door to the back porch and one by the shower.

Patients kept the linoleum floor clean. Girls were expected to sweep and mop the floors every day. Mopping restriction was given as a punishment, so sometimes one girl would have to mop the entire ward. That could take quite a while. It was a form of humiliation meant to subdue unwanted behavior.

After returning from dinner, the aides would turn on the television. Girls who were interested would pull up a chair and watch. There was usually a semi-circle of chairs set in front of the TV at night. One night I noticed a show was starting that I wanted to see. I stopped and sat down. Forgetting for a moment where I was, I lessened my vigilance for a fraction of a second. A loud voice came from behind as someone grabbed me by my hair. Up out of the chair I flew and was slammed to the floor with some human thing on top of me. I couldn't see through the flailing arms and legs. Loud yelling rang in my ears as sharp words I could not understand scratched at me and were muffled by kicks and punches. She was holding on. I was trying to get away.

Everything was happening so fast while my body became mixed with this other body in violent communion on the floor. Girls gathered from all over the ward in a circle around us. A wisp of hope rose in me when I caught a glimpse of an aide coming out of the office. My hope vanished when I saw her take a place in the circle and watch the fight as though we were the evening's entertainment. Eventually I pulled away from the girl who attacked me, leaving her holding a hank of my dark blonde hair in her brown hand. I felt my head and drew back bloodied fingers.

Though I may have walked, I felt as though I crawled down to the end of the hall and lay on the floor with my head by the OT room. Bleeding, I huddled there terrified, as dark silence hung thick under the door. I wanted to slide through that tiny space and curl up onto the floor beyond the locked entry to somewhere else. I couldn't catch my breath. My heart was pounding. My eyes kept blinking so fast I could barely see. Tears started as feelings rose up into my face, but stopped still. Everything became mute inside me.

The next day I found out that this girl was angry because I sat in "her chair." I didn't know there were reserved seats or that I had to ask to sit down to watch TV. There were rules made by the staff and rules made by the patients. There was no formal instruction about these rules. Occasionally there seemed to be some agreement about the rules. Aides would look away and pretend not to notice, and girls would collude with the aides in unspoken pacts. I was learning that favoritism and special treatment could be bartered for and arranged. The rules could change at any time.

I later had a conversation with the girl who attacked me. The attending aide recorded the fight in the "Incident Book" that night. Wanda was twelve years old from the south side of Chicago, a black ghetto. Chicago was one of the most racially divided cities in the United States at that time. Wanda already had given birth to two children that her grandmother was raising. She had gotten pregnant by an uncle. Eventually I developed an understanding with Wanda, and we got along better. She didn't even seem to realize that she had hurt me. That was just how life was for her; sudden violence could explode at any time. It was impersonal.

I didn't have much direct experience with black people or black culture until I was in Elgin. I had lived in white suburbs all my life, outside of New York City and later Chicago. I would see black people when we drove across

Manhattan to Brooklyn to visit my father's parents on weekends. I was somehow naturally drawn to and comfortable with black music since early childhood. My older sister used to mock me for playing a radio station with jazz, soul, and rhythm and blues. She called it "nigger music." When I developed a dark tan one summer, my sister told me I looked like a "nigger." I had never heard that word from anyone else. I didn't like it or the contempt and mockery with which it was thrown at me.

As a freshman in high school at the beginning of the school year in August 1968, I bought *Ramparts* magazine at the local head shop. I read about the Black Power movement. Hanging on my bedroom wall, I had Black Panther Party posters of both Huey P. Newton and Bobby Seale. I was greatly affected by reading *Soul on Ice* by Eldridge Cleaver and Sammy Davis Jr.'s autobiography, *Yes I Can*. I stopped saying the *Pledge of Allegiance* in high school because I no longer believed there was freedom and justice for all.

The civil rights movement was close to my heart. I was shocked when Martin Luther King was assassinated in the spring of 1968. Bobby Kennedy, a great advocate of the civil rights movement, was murdered in June. The whole country was numb with grief.

So much happened in 1968, the year before I was locked up. I remember watching TV when the violence erupted at the Democratic Convention in Chicago. It was like the whole country had gone crazy. The Vietnam War that I had grown up watching on TV became even more horrific in 1968. Anti-war protests became wide spread. Society was in upheaval.

There weren't many authentic black lives portrayed on TV or in the movies at that time, but I was curious and sympathetic to those I saw living in the ghettos in New York City and in Chicago. Feeling oppressed myself, I identified with those who supported the civil rights movement in the increasingly tense political climate of our country.

Black girls from Chicago were admitted to Elgin, where a form of segregation continued. They were treated differently. Quite a few of them stayed only briefly and then were tossed into other places that I was told were worse than Elgin. Some of the girls tried to keep that from happening by working consciously to remain in Elgin. I could hardly comprehend the idea that there could be places worse than Elgin. I felt I had descended into a hell on earth.

I remember one moment of fragmentary rage bursting to the surface when I stood in the early morning brackish glare of the girls' bathroom. Seemingly out of nowhere, I suddenly waved my fist at the ceiling crying out from my hissing depths, "I hate you, God!" I let all that pent-up pain fly out of me at that moment, immediately wondering if I would be punished. Where was the lightning strike? Wasn't that what God was about? I didn't really believe that, but religion's influence on me had been strong. I was angry with God and the world for what I was seeing and experiencing. I felt as if I had no control outside, so I tried to control my inside.

By crashing through the bottom of society's structure, I had a different vantage point of the world. In some ways, I learned more about the outside society from being rejected by it. Peering through the cracked glass at the parody of reality everyone seemed to be struggling to believe in or make sense of in the outside world, I realized I didn't really want to be a part of that. So many people on the outside were acting as if everything was okay, but I knew there was something terribly wrong with humanity. Early on, I knew I wanted to find a way to create change and new awareness in myself and others.

You can learn a lot about a culture by looking at its garbage. We were considered trash, and Elgin was the area of disposal. I held no illusions anymore about that outside world. I didn't find my way or place in it. I was tasting the underbelly of the beast crushing me. This was a blatant writhing truth that no one seemed to know or care about, yet it was the world I was in and the one I had to find my way through.

I did not realize then that the world had once cast a glance toward Elgin. In 1948, Olivia de Havilland starred as a mental patient in the Academy Award winning movie *The Snake Pit*. Actual footage was made on site at Northern Illinois Hospital and Asylum for the Insane in Elgin. Now it was my turn in the snake pit, but it was not a movie set. It was my life and it was real. I had to wake up and face it in order to survive. I also had to let parts of my inner self go into hibernation or die.

A group of black girls were hanging out in the hall just in front of the main alcove, first in a close huddle, then dancing and chortling together. One of the white girls laughed at their movements, which were rhythmic and sensual. The radio was going strong, playing song after song. I walked closer to the group. I'd made most of the days pass faster by pacing up and down the long hallway. I carefully watched how they moved their bodies. One girl who had just been admitted was showing the other girls a new dance movement. They were following her. Soon they were all making the same low undulating movements to the music. I was fascinated. "What you lookin at, girl?" one of them asked me.

27

"How do you do that?" I responded. Soon I was copying their movements and leaning down low to do the camel walk along with them. I smiled. They laughed as I felt my body moving with completely new sensations.

"Braid ma hair," one of the girls demanded with a tone of some affection mixed with threat. She put a container of *Vaseline* into my hand and a hair pick into the other. She sat down in front of me and I slowly braided her hair. Other girls walked by and offered their instruction on how much grease went into what amount of hair that was then braided and tied up with a rubber band. I picked and pulled her fine jet-black curly hair into braids along her head.

During that time there was momentary peace. Thelma was one of the new black girls on the ward. She had ebony skin, was tall and wide with extremely short jet-black hair. She looked quite masculine. The other girls mocked her. I spoke with her and helped her figure out how things worked at Elgin. She seemed to like me. Once, while I was getting into the line forming to go to the dining hall, a girl jumped off a chair onto me with her fists flying. Thelma grabbed her and pulled her off me like a flailing rag doll. She threatened the girl, instructing her in coarse, harsh terms to never touch me again or she'd have to deal with Thelma. From that time on, Thelma walked by my side and no one touched me violently in her presence. I had a bodyguard. I could relax a little bit.

Ann had a sense of humor. She was smart and knew clever things. She was careful about who she hung out with and protected herself by being an authority and behaving as though she had most everything figured out. The aides respected her. I continued to listen to what Ann told me and learned about the people who worked at Elgin and how the system ran. I wanted to get out of there, and asked Ann how to do that.

"You need to be staffed first." Ann said

"What's that?" I asked.

"You are staffed when you go before a group of hospital staff and they ask you questions. Depending on what you answer and how you look, act, and dress, they determine what will happen to you. They decide if you get out, if you get transferred and where, how long you stay, and if you are allowed home visits or not. You do have a home to go to, don't you?" she asked.

"Yes. I have a home and a family." I said. That was a special thing in there. I had somewhere to go. Even if I didn't feel safe with my parents in their home, it was something many of the girls did not have as an option.

I was afraid of the staffing but also wanted it. I longed to get out of that place. The aides recorded my behavior in the Incident Book. Everything I did

28

was watched or so it seemed. I was quiet and I tried to get along. I watched how other girls were treated and what happened to them. After being there a couple of weeks, I was integrating into the system.

There were long times between meals. Wandering around in the hall was all I could do. Sometimes I'd sit by the main alcove window if no one else was there. That was a prime spot because it was one of the only open windows that could be raised about five inches, but no further. There was heavy metal wire on the outside. Sometimes I would place my face close to the opening and breathe in the outside air. I watched the trees open their buds and begin to leaf out.

I sat and watched as industrial looking trucks and vans came and rumbled along the driveway in and out of the institution. Visitor's cars drove cautiously by. I could hardly stand it. There were times when I felt as though I might explode from the inside and not exist anymore. I wished that. Every hour there was a brief interlude when I could smoke one of my menthol-filtered cigarettes. I shared my cigarettes with some of the other girls who didn't have enough money to purchase them. I let Ann smoke my cigarettes.

The sound of girls' talking, screaming and wailing was a constant racket echoing through the halls. Karen, the short, fat, "retarded" girl, could be sweet and happy and then turn cloudy and start crying loudly for no apparent reason. There were two epileptic girls who were required to wear helmets on their heads all the time.

One of the epileptic girls seemed pretty normal and didn't want to wear the helmet. I wouldn't have wanted to wear it either. The aides made her put it on anyway. She'd slip it off whenever she could. I remember seeing her eyes sink back into her head and her body go limp, then the violent shaking and jerking would begin. The aides' voices would rise up, and one of them would grab a bite stick and shove it into her mouth. They would roll a bed out into the hall and take hold of her jerking body, physically forcing her arms and her legs out as the other aide took canvas straps and tied her limbs to the metal bed frame. There she would lie after her seizures and eventually come back and want to get up. They wouldn't let her up right away, and she often missed meals. I think she felt embarrassed to be tied up in a bed in the hall like that. We would all walk by and look at her. It was bizarre to see her tied down, yet I would soon learn it was a more common experience on the ward than I realized.

Other workers would come onto the ward during weekdays. There was an office across from the aide's station that was called the nurses' station. Two women had desks in that room. One was a nurse named Wertheim, and the other was a social worker named Reynolds. Those were their last names, but that's how people were titled there. All the aides were called by their last names, not their first. Although they were like parents to us, we did not know their first names or anything about their lives. Reynolds was soft spoken and rolled across the hall in a wheelchair. Sometimes one of the older girls would help her get into her car at the end of the workday. That was a privilege. I only did that once, after I'd been there a long time. Reynolds seemed gentle in her nature but was a broken woman, not just because of her paralyzed legs from a recent car accident. She seemed broken in other ways too, as if she had no power and was just there doing paperwork. She hardly ever came out of her office and when she did, she rarely looked up or spoke with anyone. It was as if she wasn't really there. I began to forget that she was. Wertheim, on the other hand, seemed to hold all the power. I noticed the aides would behave in a certain way around her so as not to cause conflict. That was their hierarchy.

One day an important-looking man wearing a suit came onto the ward. It was an unusual event for any man to come onto the ward. This man motivated a quick adjustment from the aides, who tried to get everyone up and looking better than they did, but it was too late. Dr. Vico saw all the girls who were lying on the floor and put the whole ward on restriction. He did not want to see anyone lying on the floor, but there weren't enough chairs, and the dorms were locked during the day. Most of the girls had been given daily medications that made them sleepy. There was nothing to do.

Soon there were male guards in uniform like military men coming onto the ward through the metal door in the back alcove. They grabbed the frightened girls. Some cried. Others screamed as they were handily tied down to a bed with canvas restraints. I could hardly believe what I was seeing. I stayed in the main alcove trying to get out of the way as girl after girl was grabbed and thrown onto a bed and tied down. The aides had opened the dorms. One of the aides ran by holding a syringe in her hand as a girl struggled with the guards, protesting being captured and not wanting to be tied down. "I didn't do anything wrong." She cried. The girl's pants were pulled down and the syringe was injected into her hip. I later learned that it was Thorazine, an anti-psychotic medication. The male guard's hands held the girls arms down as an aide tied them to the bed corners with canvas restraints.

They came for me. I had hoped to escape their notice, wishing that maybe they were only tying some girls down, but they came. I was taken into a small dorm room. I didn't fight. I wanted to cry as they roughly pulled my small wrists into the white canvas cuffs and pulled them tight. The canvas straps were looped around the bottom of the bed frame and pulled until my arms stretched out to either side. My legs were moved toward the ends of the bed and my shoes were taken off. My feet were then pushed through canvas loops. The straps were pulled tight enough to hold my ankles and then were stretched and tied to the opposite sides of the bed.

I was in the small dorm that only had two beds in it. It was located across from the bathroom. I felt like crying as I lay there but stopped myself. I couldn't remember who was put in the bed next to me. I only felt my own terror in that moment. These men in uniforms had stretched and tied my body onto a bed and left me there. Everything inside me was shaking, but I kept still. I could hear the guards outside the doorway talking with an aide. They decided not to inject me with Thorazine. I was spared that. I stayed quiet as I heard other girls crying while they were being tied down. Footsteps pounded on the hard floor as the men walked down to the small alcove. Keys jingled as the handle of the big metal door squealed open. The door shut and the latch squeaked back into the wall. They were gone. I turned my head toward the shadows on the wall as a tear escaped from the corner of my eye.

Within a week after being tied down, girls were lying on the floor again. There was nothing else to do. The aides got better at knowing and preparing us before Dr. "V" came onto the ward. Fortunately, he didn't come very often.

STAFFED

I can barely remember when I was staffed. It was a terrible day I wanted to forget. It started in the clothing room, where I wasn't able to find anything I wanted to wear. My clothes that had been sent to the laundry were not back yet. I had to choose from clothes that were things thrift stores would throw away. I was terrified to go into the staffing room in front of those adults who held my fate in their hands, yet I wanted to get out of there so badly I pushed myself to prepare as best I could.

I walked through the big metal door in the small alcove shadowed by an adult leading me down the long corridor into a little dark cave where people with big heads and little bodies looked across at me. I sat in a chair feeling tiny, while watching their mouths move and flash like sharpened rat teeth chewing on words about my life. They asked questions I did my best to answer, while feeling like a little bird trying to chirp before its beak can open and its head could raise up. I felt weak and naked, shorn outside and bloodied inside by what I heard them saying and how they scrutinized me.

When I was brought back to the ward, I dropped down under the little bookshelf across from the small back alcove and hung my head. I could feel that I had not said the right things in response to all the loaded questions they asked me. The entire scene ran across my mind, melting into distortions of meaning. They had the power. Even though they read sections from my diary my parents had given them, the stories they told about me were not my stories. My story had not yet been told or heard.

After my staffing, I was told that I was not going to be released. I would be staying on B-1-North. It had been a month since I'd arrived, and now I got the news that I was going to stay. A stark cold terror began an icy journey through my veins toward my heart. Sadness was a luxury I could not afford.

Later I learned that I was judged to be a severe case and that they planned to keep me in Elgin until I was eighteen years old. Until that point I had not spoken to a therapist about what was going on with me. I was only housed on the ward with the other girls. After my staffing the aides started giving me a daily medication that caused me to become extremely drowsy. Etrafon was a new tricyclic antidepressant drug introduced in the 1960's. It has recently been shown to increase suicidal thinking and behavior in children and adolescents, along with a greater incidence of other side effects. It interacts poorly when combined with other drugs such as Thorazine and the use of tobacco. Etrafon had not been tested on children when it was first introduced. Perhaps we were the test subjects in Elgin.

TESTS

There was an old trailer that was used as a school for children in Elgin. It was located down a road, behind one of many brick buildings beyond Center Building. An aide took me to this school. A man in the trailer handed me some papers with questions on them. I sat down and began filling in answers to the questions with a yellow #2 pencil. After a few minutes I handed the completed test papers back to the man.

I can't remember all the tests and papers they had me fill out because I was only a ghost floating through the doors and into the rooms they took me to. My mind reeled back on itself as I continued to process the information that I was not leaving and didn't know when I would get out of there. Some part of me receded into a deeper place inside myself where I could hide.

One afternoon a woman I hadn't seen before came onto our ward. I was taken with a group of girls through the main Center Building to an upstairs room on the other side. We were going to group therapy. There was a mix of boys and girls from different wards who were funneled in together. Talking began as they joined our line moving along the corridor. The woman leading us through the maze-like halls and stairs was in front of the large group of ten to fifteen boys and girls. She didn't notice when one of the larger black boys grabbed me from the back of the line and pulled me into a stairwell.

He dragged me halfway up the stairs and then tried to force his penis into my mouth, pushing my head down hard, poking and jamming his thing against my face. I turned my head and felt the semen hot on my cheek, dripping. He moaned and let go of me enough for me to pull away from him. I ran down the stairs, wiping my hands across my face and blinking my eyes so wildly everything seemed to go black and white. The film playing in my mind of what was happening seemed to get stuck, suddenly flickering and clicking incessantly.

I don't know how I found the group again, but I was chastised for showing up late. "I got lost," I mumbled. Then I was silent, deadened. A man and a woman tried to get the group talking, but I couldn't hear them. It was just a background hum that I could not decipher.

When we were brought back to the ward, I went to the water fountain right away and pushed the cold metal knob on top. I pretended to drink but carefully turned my head so that the water washed my cheek. I didn't want to go into the bathroom and wash my face because that would make it more real. If I did nothing, it was nothing. Nothing happened. I was getting a drink of water. That's all. Slowly and carefully I spit some back out. I went over and sat by the alcove window, looking out.

If I looked long and hard at that tree across in the yard, perhaps I could will myself to be outside. If I concentrated and felt every living fiber of the tree completely inside me, I could be there and not here.

OUTSIDE IN

In May after the staffing, I was told that as a result of my intelligence tests I would be going to public summer school in June, "Not the hospital school. They think you're too smart for that," one of the aides snapped at me with a half-smile, half-sneer. "You're going to Elgin High School." The tests I had taken included an IQ test. Doctors I had not seen or talked with decided to take a chance on me and created an experimental program. They would try sending institutionalized children to an outside school. At first, only two of us were chosen to go – a new tall girl with long blonde hair named Stacy and me. She came from a suburban family in the same area as mine.

There was quite a turnover of girls on our ward. They would come in and sometimes only stay for a few days or a week before they went somewhere else.

Tracie, who had grabbed me in the shower when I first arrived, stayed for a while on B-1-North ward. She was sometimes quite kind to me and would give me make-up or introduce me to new music on the OT room record player. One day she led me to the back window at the end of the hall where a young boy was waiting on the other side of the brick wall. He reached over and pressed a white paper cup against the window screen. The boy held it low where the window had been lifted to let warm early summer air sift through. There was a straw in his cup that he had managed to push through a small hole in the screen Tracie had rounded with a pencil. She bent the wires into the perfect shape and size needed. "Drink some of that," she told me, smiling.

"What is it?" I asked, never quite knowing whether to trust her.

"Wine," she said, as the boy on the other side of the screen looked pleased with himself.

Glancing around and then bending down, I pursed my lips and pulled the sweet fiery liquid into my mouth through the straw. The boy disappeared as soon as any sound from an adult was heard. When questioned later, I denied any knowledge of it.

Tracie would often call me to her bed at night. I was assigned to the big dorm for a while. She would tell me to put my finger into her. There was nothing romantic about it. I would run my hand under her blanket as I sat on the edge of her bed and find the place between her legs where she was warm, open, and wet. My finger slipped inside her as she writhed in pleasure. She'd tell me she wouldn't need me if she was on the outside with her boyfriend and that I was not as good "as a real man."

Although uncomfortable, I felt some sense of pleasure in a confused way. This was not exactly how I wanted to be with a girl, but something about it was okay. Tracie held a position of power on the ward. Being in her good graces provided me with some privileges and some safety. If I was willing, she couldn't force me, so I was willing. At least I thought I was. I hadn't chosen to be with her. She had chosen me, mostly as a plaything for her own amusement.

As I lay awake at night, I wrote poetry on small pieces of paper by the light of the red EXIT lamp. The lamp hung above an emergency exit that was always locked in the back of the big dorm room. Eventually I learned to write in complete darkness so I could release words onto paper to help me process my experiences. I didn't dare write in a diary. Keeping a diary had caused some of the trouble I was in.

My parents discovered and read my diary. They gave it to the doctors they took me to, which eventually led to my going to Elgin. Since then I learned not to write down exactly what I was thinking and feeling anymore. Instead I wrote poetry, where I was able to use abstract language and metaphors. Scraps of dreams and bits of longing combined into a cadence of words that became the story of what my life was at that time, and what I wanted it to be. Each night I wrote a little more. As the pieces of paper began to multiply, I spread them under my mattress so they would not be discovered and taken away.

CHOSEN & UNCHOSEN

Right after my staffing, certain privileges were bestowed. Staffing was a milestone. It happened only once for each patient, usually within the first month of being admitted to Elgin. I was deemed cognizant enough to navigate on my own for short periods of time. This new policy allowed me to go to the commissary in the afternoon for a specific length of time. It might have only been twenty minutes, but it felt luxurious to walk out of the ward by myself. I took my shoes off to feel the grass in the yard between the buildings. New green grass crinkled between my toes and infused the sweetness of earth into my being. For a moment I felt free, joyful, and fully alive. Being barefoot felt so good I wished I didn't have to wear shoes at all anymore.

The commissary pass was given as a privilege when I behaved as expected. It was restricted as punishment when I was deemed inappropriate or in violation of the rules in any way. Eventually my barefoot rapture was halted after another girl saw me and told one of the aides.

Money was kept in the aide's station. My parents had left an allowance for me. I would be given a small amount of money and let out the back door by the porch to cross over into the Center Building. Often there were female adult patients from the ward above ours sitting in metal chairs on the back porch. These old ladies became gargoyle-like fixtures in my mind as I ran or walked past them on my way to the commissary and the dining hall. There was one old woman in particular who would catch my curious eye. I called her "the walrus." Her jowls hung down on either side of her sagging lips like long white tusks. She was missing some teeth that allowed those still left in her mouth to protrude unpleasantly from her parted lips. I hated looking at these old ladies sitting there with their eyes glazed over in utter passivity. Their fate was repugnant to me.

"Why don't they run away?" I questioned the aide named Magee one day. She fumbled with a large round ring of assorted keys to find the right one for our door as we approached the back porch. "Do you have a key to open their doors?" I asked, looking at all her keys and then peering up into her green eyes. "If I had the keys, I would let them all out so they could be free."

"Oh, really?" Magee laughed at my suggestion. "You could leave all the doors wide open and those old gals wouldn't go nowhere. They don't know what freedom is and they wouldn't want it if they did. This is their home," she remarked confidently. I was stunned.

"What about that one?" I said pointing to the walrus woman.

"Why, Miss Mably? She's been housed here for more than forty years. I know her from her younger years. She ain't going nowhere!"

Later in my life, after I moved to Chicago in early 1973, I began to recognize some of these same old ladies I had become familiar with. They had been let out of the institution. Many were wandering the streets, homeless; but in 1969 the adult patients were as much a part of Elgin State Hospital as the mortar and bricks.

I loved stepping into the commissary. It was a small room down a hallway from the large main entrance in the Center Building. The doorway opened onto a crowded array of items for sale. Packages of bright orange, yellow, red, blue, and purple mingled together. It was the only vibrant place to be found, crammed with abundance.

Behind massive wood and glass displays, I saw paper and pencils, pens, playing cards, stamps, batteries, and envelopes. Tobacco and cigarettes stood out prominently with bags of loose tobacco and rolling papers along with pre-rolled and packaged cigarettes. There were containers with condiments on the counter, catsup, mustard and relish. Newspapers were stacked, books and magazines aligned. Shelves climbed the walls. A plethora of color stampeded in an otherwise drab grey colorless environment. Excitement filled my senses each time I entered this carnival of products for sale.

The commissary provided an alternative source of food from the indescribable mash and lumps given in the cafeteria. I ate candy and ice cream. The smell of hot dogs occasionally wafted out into the hall. Coca Cola and popcorn were available. Adult patients wandered around looking at nothing in particular, smoking or asking for a cigarette. Those who wandered into the commissary may have wanted to revel in the visual and visceral sensations that emanated out into the vast emptiness from that small space.

I began to recognize certain adult patients I saw day after day in the hall and in the commissary. There was one small thin man who looked both very old and very young. He repeatedly talked aloud in different languages. I noticed that he had many scars on his head. He seemed gentle and harmless. The man behind the counter told me about this patient. "What is he saying?" I asked.

"Nothing and everything. Ole Joe was in a concentration camp in Europe and thinks he's still there," the commissary man explained. "They spoke all different languages over there in the camps. That poor soul can't tell where he is. He's talking to the past."

I watched the slender man each time I went to the commissary. He was middle aged, about 5'6" with hints of short light-brownish hair on the sides of his balding shaved head. His brown eyes appeared to be looking inward, reflecting back a history that was unceasing for him. He seemed to be playing a recording over and over again, gesticulating with his arms and hands, his head slightly bowed, telling stories wound into a tight, garbled, unending circle. I tried to understand what he was saying by watching him. I greeted him when I passed by, but he didn't notice me. The reality inside him was much louder than my voice and more present than my presence.

Having a commissary pass provided me with an opportunity to secretly mail letters in the Center Building mailbox and to make phone calls. The connection I attempted was with Jane, my forbidden obsession. Jane was my girlfriend on the outside. Instead of keeping a diary, I began writing about my life and sending it to her.

GIRLFRIEND

Jane caught my attention from the earliest moments I saw her in junior high school. It was when I was twelve years old, after I moved from New Jersey with my family to a suburb of Chicago. Jane was pretty and popular in junior high. At that time, she would have nothing to do with me. Once she gave me an acknowledging glance when I got my courage up to say "hi" to her as she passed in the hall. Usually she either ignored me or didn't notice. In eighth grade, she sat at the desk in front of me in algebra class. I could not concentrate on the algebraic formulas being written in chalk on the board. I just stared at the back of Jane's neck and felt myself grow warm and flushed in a way I didn't understand at that time.

A representative from a modeling school in Chicago came and did a presentation to the eighth grade class at the end of the year. I wanted to go to modeling school and convinced my parents to let me attend. Jane wanted to attend too but didn't have a ride to Chicago. I seized upon the opportunity and offered Jane a ride with my mother and me. That was an innocent beginning to a miserable triangle of love and battle that lasted for many years. Jane finally spoke with me during that summer before high school when we drove down and attended modeling school together. I was winning her attention and her trust.

During the summer of my thirteenth year, I turned myself from a plain awkward shy girl with mousy brown hair and ill-fitting mismatched clothing into a fashionable blonde-haired, seemingly sophisticated young woman. When I entered high school in August of 1968, the social playing field turned around and I became much more noticed and favored by others. Jane lost some of her status in the bigger pond with so many kids who did not know of her previous reign. She had more reason to associate with me as I began to climb the popularity ladder. We had established a beginning friendship in the summer and gradually continued our association once school began.

In 1968, during my freshman year of high school in Center Lake, Illinois, I cracked out of my shell and came out as a lesbian. I didn't like the word "lesbian." I didn't like any labels. I first heard the word used when I was at church summer camp the year before.

In the summer of 1967 when I was twelve years old, I had a best friend from church named Kathy. Together we had a wild time at Mormon camp, goofing off and talking about everything. Kathy was athletic and could dive into the swimming pool flawlessly. I could barely swim. She was an experienced horsewoman and convinced me to gallop away on a horse alongside hers as she directed both horses. We disappeared for two hours on our own horseback adventure and didn't care about the trouble we got into when we returned.

We had both just begun our menses and Kathy thought it would be funny to tie menstrual pads on the bushes around camp. My older sister, who was our camp counselor, did not find it funny. One night in the big tent Kathy and I were joking and telling stories. There were five girls lying in sleeping bags in the tent with us that night.

Once the lights went out, Kathy and I decided it would be fun to strip naked and get into the same sleeping bag together. I really didn't think much about what we were doing. We were drunk on silliness and feeling adventurous with our new changing bodies. It felt liberating to be naked. Once I was in the sleeping bag with Kathy, everyone became quiet. I began feeling strange, unfamiliar sensations in my body. Kathy and I just lay still, but Marianne cried out loudly from the dark saying, "I can feel the Devil in here. You two are being lesbians!"

I knew Marianne was accusing us of something horrible, but I didn't understand what. I made a mental note to remember that word so I could find out what it meant.

Camp time shifted to not being much fun as Kathy and I suspended our uninhibited behaviors and conformed to the demands and expectations of church leadership and peer pressure. My new glasses fell out of my back pocket into the outhouse hole. I spent many horrible hours with a long stick trying without success to retrieve them. It was an appropriate metaphor for where my view of life was about to go. My childhood was ending and a descent beginning.

What might it have been like to experience an innocent blossoming love with another young girl in adolescence? My affections toward certain girls led to complications with them and with the world around us. I didn't understand what I was feeling and being drawn to explore.

Visiting Kathy and trying to maintain a close relationship did not last. She had been diagnosed with diabetes as a young girl. One time she chased me around her house with a syringe, threatening to inject me. I was scared. I felt sorry that she had to inject herself with insulin every day, sometimes into her stomach because her thighs were so hollow and bruised from the constant bombardment of needles. I suppose it was her way of trying to show me her pain and share her fear. She locked her door and separated us after that.

Kathy's mother kept a steady supply of codeine cough syrup around as her own strategy for coping with the challenges in her life. Kathy had shown me her mother's hidden stash located in a low wooden cabinet in a room not often used. They were considered good church members. Kathy and her parents soon moved away and I never saw her again.

In 1968 when I finally had a chance to befriend Jane, I discovered she was a chronic liar. This might have thwarted me except that I was used to being treated rather poorly by others I cared for. Intermittent affection and attention followed by anger, mistreatment, or being ignored had become normal. I couldn't be sure of what Jane really meant or rely on her to call or do what she said. She could be completely present and attentive to me in a way that made my heart fly, but in the next minute I was invisible and non-existent to her.

I would often call Jane to arrange getting together with her after school. It was almost impossible to coordinate what might have been a simple meeting. Then in late November of 1968, Jane actually let me come over. I told her I was going to be in the school building next to her house. I could hardly believe it when I heard her soft voice over the phone say, "Why don't you come over? I'll leave the side door unlocked."

I slipped out of a Wednesday evening church "MIA" meeting and found Jane upstairs in her bedroom. No one else was home. She lived there with her mother and two sisters, one younger and the other older. While in her room alone we started talking. I told her about a dream I had that summer. In it one of the witches on the TV soap opera "Dark Shadows" was chasing me through a city street. I ran into a building, climbing up the stairs to get away. I ran all the way to the top of that high-rise into a storage room filled with old office furniture. Seeing the witch fly up, open a window, and step into the room made me realize there was nothing I could do to stop her. I hid under a desk terrified. She was completely confident and knew right where I was hiding.

The beautiful witch came over to where I was crouched under a desk and saw me cowering there. I didn't know what she would do. I was afraid. She reached over and unbuttoned my blouse. As I froze, spellbound, she revealed my new young breast. I could not move. She crouched down and surrounded the small pink nipple of my left breast with her sweet lips, drawing me into her mouth. In that moment, I exploded with a most powerful sensation that rocketed me right out of the dream.

Jane listened to me and understood. We were standing by her dressing table. I could see myself reflected in the mirror behind her. Courage flamed through my veins. I curved my body toward Jane and placed my lips on hers. Soft tenderness and movement deepened our mutual embrace. My arms came up and wrapped around her. We stood like that for a long time, soundlessly. Pleasure filled and expanded into every cell in my body. My heart awakened and bonded to hers.

The next day was Thanksgiving. I floated around my family house on the constant unending kiss that I didn't want to wake from. Everything else paled in comparison to the new inner reality that shone like a sun through each pore in my body and sang praises through my heart. I invited Jane to sleep overnight a week later. My parents allowed it because my mother knew Jane from the summer modeling training in Chicago. I had twin beds in my bedroom. When she was in my room, I invited Jane to climb into bed with me. She did. We began a curious tender exploration very slowly and carefully in the dark. We didn't sleep but for a few hours with intertwined arms and legs, breasts, and lips together. This began my first real love affair. I wrote about it in my diary.

From late November of 1968 until I was admitted to Elgin in early-April of 1969, my entire world as I knew it came to an end. I had reached out for Jane's love and soon found I had to fight for access to her. Access was allowed, then denied, by my parents as well as others in authority. I found ways to reach her anyway. I was willing to risk everything for one phone call. During my time in Elgin, I continued to secretly mail letters to stay in steady contact with Jane. Discovery could be dangerous.

Being chosen to go to school from the hospital gave me privileges and access to more information and contact with the outside world. I was increasingly respected by other girls on the ward. Some of the aides began giving me special treatment. Many girls acknowledged me differently. During this time, I was able to release some of my constant vigilance. I felt little sprouts of self-esteem begin to grow inside me.

One day in Elgin I was sitting at the end of the hall by the big dorm across from the locked metal door. I was reading the *Inferno*, an epic poem from Dante's *Divine Comedy*. Immersing myself in Dante's fourteenth century prose, I sensed a deep internal truth. It stirred my own creative cauldron suspended above the heat of Elgin's flames of suffering.

While engrossed in Dante's book, I carelessly turned my back to the ward, facing the light of the window so as to illuminate the pages as I read. Suddenly my head was snapped backwards with another girl's face directly over mine. Water pulled from the water fountain spewed violently from Doris' mouth onto my face. She was pulling my hair and holding my head back while spitting on me. I couldn't figure out what was happening or why. I soon learned that this action was retribution for telling my parents something I shouldn't have. It had somehow gotten back to the ward. The aide who was in charge was reprimanded because of me. She was one of the nice aides who tried to make life easier for the girls, but now she was being transferred off our ward. I was blamed for that.

The slip occurred when my parents came to visit me at the hospital. Quite often we would argue. I grew angry when my mother said that one of the reasons they had to put me in the hospital was to control my behavior and to stop my contact with Jane. In my defiant response, I foolishly let slip that I had called Jane. Someone in authority pursued that scrap of news and determined that the nice aide had been too permissive with me. I was careful not to let any information pass from my lips again to my parents about what happened in the hospital.

When my mother and father first began to visit me at the institution, I had just experienced my first episode of being tied down in restraints. I desperately wanted to get out of the hospital, but my parents refused. They met with the hospital staff. I was diagnosed as having a behavior problem, promiscuity with homosexual tendencies. The hospital tried to control my behavior through confinement. Shortly after being staffed they used drugs to subdue me. Eventually I was able to expand a bit out of Elgin's constriction when they decided to send me to public school.

It was a most confusing sensation to be taken out of the hospital by bus with the other girl, Stacey, to Elgin Public High School for summer school. I attended two classes during the day. The only class I remember now was biology. We learned about nature with captured, pickled frogs. I refused to cut into the dead amphibians. It felt like a desecration. There were sharp instruments, glass vials, and a small ceramic mortar and pestle in the lab.

I became so fascinated by the mortar and pestle that I returned to the institution one day with a set in my purse. What purpose it could serve was unknown to me. Perhaps it was the symbolism of a mortar and pestle that brought me some kind of comfort or meaning. I felt that I was being crushed and ground down by a gigantic social pestle into the mortar that was Elgin. Obtaining this instrument made me feel as if I was in control, even though I didn't quite know how to use it or understand how its transforming processes might become part of me.

On another day, I went to a store by the school before the bus came and purchased a packet of Gillette razor blades. Gazing at these cool blue-grey slips of steel gave me a sense of safety and comfort. I taped them to the underside of a dresser drawer in my dorm. They waited quietly for me there.

Stacey ran away from school within the first two weeks and was discharged to her parents' care. I passed my classes and didn't get caught with any of my forbidden purchases or other minor violations, including that theft or being late for class. The so-called doctors I rarely ever saw deemed the school experiment enough of a success to register me for the fall classes at Harkley High School. Because of the success of my school experience that summer, other children were registered to attend public school in the fall. Most of them would be going to the elementary or middle school. I was the only one who would be attending high school.

PURI

In Hindi the word *puri* means bread. It's a popular unleavened bread that puffs up in hot oil and turns a delicious-looking brown. In the stark harsh reality of Elgin State Hospital, Puri was my bread, without which I surely would have starved and become another nameless vacant ghost lost in life—or dead.

Prahba Puri was a small statured, dark-skinned young woman from India. Ann told me she was twenty-three years old and was still attending college in Chicago to be a psychologist. Whether or not she had her degree, I was told that she was the only psychologist for all six children's wards in Elgin. She used one of the offices on our ward. I would see her walk through that large metal door only on certain days of the week.

Puri wore a close-fitting short-sleeved knit blouse with a flowered cloth wrapped around her slender frame. Ann told me that her dress was called a sari, the traditional clothing from her home in India. She had a lovely smile that she offered to the girls, while gazing at them through thick-lensed glasses. Her dark eyes sometimes nearly crossed but sparkled with flashes of inner light. Crooked front teeth poked out of her mouth, pushing her top lip up a bit. Smiling easily, she spoke quietly with a thick accent.

Ann and the other girls laughed about how they interpreted swear words for Puri. There were many slang words used on the ward that she did not understand, so she asked the girls to explain.

It was a privilege to see Puri. Since she was the only working psychologist with so many children, she chose only those with whom she felt she might be able to make a difference.

I was not chosen originally, but after my staffing and intelligence tests came back, Puri called me to her office and invited me to participate in group therapy. Once a week I went into her room with five or six other girls. Puri would try to get the girls to talk about their feelings and what was going on in their lives. I wasn't able to say much. My mind would rattle around and reverberate with unpleasant associations. I was trying to adjust to the whole situation and find my place. My first experiences with group therapy had not been therapeutic. I didn't know if I could trust Puri and wanted to see what she did and how the group interacted. At that point, I didn't trust communication or interactions with any adults.

Puri occasionally took a small group of us in her car on outings to town. We felt our self-worth begin to re-inflate when we were treated like real human beings. One afternoon we went to Burger King. Unlike hospital food, the fish sandwich I bit into was alive with flavor. I put extra catsup on it. Ann joked. She told funny stories that made Puri and the other girls laugh.

Ann and I discovered a photo booth. We jumped inside. I had some quarters. Lights flashed. Black and white strips of images flopped down from the side of the booth into a little metal holder. The other girls wanted to have their pictures taken too. Puri gave them quarters. For the moment, we felt like children without any cares.

Puri began to meet with me for individual sessions. Only a few girls were chosen for that opportunity. Trust came slowly in tiny increments. A chasm was crossed when I told Puri my secret of having purchased razor blades at the store by the high school. She convinced me that she would not violate my confidence, but that I must give her the packet. I did. This did not prevent my habit of cutting myself. I had a small silver cross that a boy had given to me when I was in New York. I was allowed to wear it on a chain around my neck after I first arrived at Elgin. Using a nail file, I managed to grind the bottom edge of the cross, sharp enough to cut flesh.

It is difficult to explain the need to inflict wounds on oneself to someone who has no understanding and can only see it as a grotesque form of self-mutilation. I was not asked why I was cutting myself when I was thirteen in the fall of 1968. I was told that I did it to gain attention and that it was manipulative behavior. I was too busy trying to survive my constantly challenging and changing environment to self-reflect about the meaning or purpose of my cutting. The need would erupt from deep within me like a burning necessity I could not ignore. If the original cuts had been a cry for help, the attention it brought was not safe or helpful. Instead, I learned to cut more secretly, high up underneath my left arm where the soft skin could be folded out of view.

When I cut open my arm and saw the blood, I felt relieved of pressure that had built up to an unbearable point. I would bleed myself so I could continue to function. It was a form of self-healing and self-care at a time when normal expression of my inner reality was impossible and extremely dangerous. I witnessed my own pain in this way, acknowledging and validating how a part of me was being severed by devastating experiences. My left arm expressed what I could not cry or talk about. Instead, I bled. Blood was truth.

Puri questioned me about my relationship with my parents. She was working with them separately. I shared my impression of my father and mother at that time. I had not experienced physical affection from them or my siblings since I was about five years old. Touch was functional or a punishment. Most of my experience with physical touch had been primarily sexual, violent, or both.

My mother sometimes touched me when I was ill, to detect a fever or look into my ears or throat and feel my glands. I was often sick. She took me to doctors before I could talk because of chronic pain in my knees. Several doctors examined me but could not determine the cause.

When I was four years old, one doctor told me he could not see my pain. I was shocked. How could a doctor not be able to see pain? I could. I wanted to show him how. I could sense my own and others' pain vividly. There were colors in and around my own and others' bodies that communicated how they felt—a wordless communication. Couldn't he see and feel that as I did? Later, I sought ways to dull that sensitivity along with my pain.

Puri began teaching me to become more aware of my feelings and to hug my parents. She taught my parents to hug me. It was a weird, unnatural configuration that my parents and I awkwardly attempted during their visits to the hospital. They would hug me when they first saw me and when they left. I couldn't feel anything other than discomfort during the hugs, but I continued to engage in the new foreign routine.

Puri was trying to get my parents to tell me that they loved me. This was unusual for them. My grandparents had not hugged my parents or told them that they loved them. As stoic, hardworking religious people they did not express vulnerable emotions. Love went underground. Puri was trying to pull it up to the surface. My father struggled with the therapy he and my mother went to. He was deeply unhappy and frustrated with the process. They were angry with me. My behavior had been the focus of the problem that needed to be fixed. I was in Elgin to be contained and repaired. It was hard for my parents to look at or realize their own part in the bigger picture of our family struggle.

Visiting days were on weekends. Family members could come onto the ward and sit with the girls. Not many girls had visitors. In the beginning, only my parents visited. They came on Saturday because Sundays were always reserved for attending church. After my staffing, I was allowed to go to a park in the town of Elgin with my parents and four of my six siblings. My youngest brother and sister climbed on the playground equipment, laughing as they went down the slide over and over again. No one mentioned where I was living or the fact that I was not home. My father made home movies of our picnic in the park and my return to the back porch of the hospital. In the movie, I am visible under the *Visitors BIN* sign while a door opens with an aide appearing followed by a gaggle of girls. There I am seen waving goodbye to my family as though everything was perfectly normal, before I turned to catch up with the other girls.

One Saturday my parents arrived and sat down in some chairs lined up against the wall in the hallway. My father gave me a book wrapped in tissue paper inside a box that fit it perfectly. It was a book of poetry written by Elizabeth Barrett Browning. My father knew I wrote poems and liked poetry. Inside the front cover, in my father's handwriting, was a long heartfelt letter to me about his love and his hope for me as his daughter. This unusual display and expression of caring opened up my pain about losing my father's love and respect early in life. I had given up on love with my father, and he had seemingly given up on me. But the book with his letter in it was real.

Through my father's writing, I could sense a part of him that I had quietly longed for and hoped could be what I wanted and needed from him. I was aware of his positive affirming attention and affection, something I had mostly only witnessed him give to others. I kept the book but did not know how to have a relationship with my father, nor did he with me.

Although my father seriously considered it, my mother refused to give me up to be a ward of the state. After my staffing at Elgin, when it was determined that I would need long-term care, the institution suggested this option, perhaps to save my parents money. If I were a ward of the state, my parents would no longer have to pay for the cost of my being institutionalized, although their insurance paid most of those costs.

Even though my mother was confused, angry and tired, she held on to her legal right to me as her daughter. She was forced to take a stand and not always yield to my father's perspective. My parents agreed to persevere with therapy sessions. My mother was trying to understand how to make things better. She trusted and respected Puri.

Puri continued reaching out to me. I must have given both my mother and Puri some ray of hope because they remained actively involved in my life at that time. They each offered possibilities and attention that I desperately needed, although I didn't know how to respond to them. My father soon stopped attending therapy and became withdrawn and distant.

As my time lengthened at Elgin, my mother usually came alone to visit. Sometimes she brought my three-year-old, tow-headed brother. My other siblings resumed their lives as normally as possible and perhaps experienced more peace in the household with my absence. They never talked much about my departure or asked what actually happened to me from my perspective any time during or after my Elgin experience. It became a taboo subject everyone was aware of, but no one ever spoke directly about. Their silence continues to this day.

PART II

RUNAWAY

BEING LESBIAN

In 1968 being a lesbian was considered a sin by religion and a crime by law. It was believed to be a form of mental illness and deviation from a normal heterosexual way of life. For me at that time, it was about love and discovering myself and my identity. From the start, I believed I had a right to love who I loved and how I loved. That was my deeply-held conviction. How could love be wrong? How could I be punished for genuinely loving another, while those in positions of authority violated trust and abused their power in unloving ways? What gave them the right to disallow and minimize my expression of love?

I was angry. I could see and feel the injustice occurring in my life, but I could do nothing to change it. My only recourse was to superficially adapt while covertly attempting to resist, escape, and undermine what I experienced as a corrupt system. I shattered, looking through fragmentary jagged pieces of myself trying to discern my own truth, apart from what was happening to me.

From the time I was very young, I felt that I could love anyone no matter what they were like. I recognized this bond with every face I saw in *Life* magazine, *National Geographic*, the characters in the stories I read and in the movies I watched. That's how I would be or what I would do if I were in their life, not as me, but as them. I sensed that deeper down in the pot we were all born out of the same stew, boiling up in our own private bubble of that particular reality in that moment. I imagined a matrix we were all created from, not in my mind or thoughts but felt in my heart.

Because my birthday was late in the year, I started kindergarten at age four. Unlike other children who cried when they had to leave home and clung to their mothers at the beginning of school, I happily went to school that first day and went home with another girl afterwards. My mother had to search for me and go to the girl's house in order to bring me home. I welcomed the opportunity that school provided for growth and new awareness beyond the limits of my family life.

I was eight years old in fourth grade. There was a red-haired girl in fifth grade that kept showing up in my dreams. I had strong feelings for her, so strong that I would pray every night that I would wake up in the morning with her in my bed. I didn't understand why I wanted that to happen or what I would do if she did. This girl seemed perfect to me in every way.

Jessica was beautiful. When she smiled, my heart took off like bird's wings beating in my chest, trying to break free. I couldn't speak to her. I only looked at her from a distance in the hallway or when all the classes would go to the assembly hall. I watched her after school with other children and wished she would talk to me. I was too shy to let her know that I hoped to talk with her and gain her attention. It seemed as though I did not exist in her eyes.

I began writing Jessica's name on a piece of paper, folding it into a small flat square and wearing it in my sock every day. That way I could feel close to her and silently express my devotion. One day the paper fell out and my best friend Joyce saw it. She grabbed it and said, "What's this?" I demanded she give it back to me. She didn't. She opened the paper and read out loud, "I LOVE JESSICA." "Why did you write that?" She asked.

"I don't know," I said, feeling my face burning red.

"That's stupid!" Joyce said and crumbled my paper and threw it on the ground. I thought I saw a hint of hurt flash through her eyes. I picked up the little piece of paper and never mentioned it or wore it in my sock again.

I watched as my sister Pearl was crushed by high school. She was five years older than me. Every day after she came home, I went to her room and sat on her bed listening while she talked for hours. Over and over she purged her pain while telling me about her uncomfortable social experiences at school. I determined not to let it crush me when it became my turn to go to high school. The year before I went to Elgin, in the late summer of 1968, I entered high school like a warrior.

A boy I knew in junior high had a difficult time. The other kids were cruel and mocking toward him. Jay had an unusually large head for his tall, thin body and wore black wide-framed glasses with extremely thick lenses. His mother probably picked out his clothes for him. He stood out in a crowd of teens. I liked Jay. He was gentle and kind.

One warm sunny morning, I walked into Center Lake High School as a new freshman. I could see the backs of a closed circle of teenagers standing in the front vestibule. "What are they doing?" I wondered out loud. I heard jeers and laughter and plinking sounds on the linoleum floor tile. As I walked up, I could see Jay standing in the center of the circle looking scared and confused. I immediately understood the feeling Jay expressed through his sad eyes. I knew what it was like to be singled out and hurt by others.

The kids were taunting him and throwing pennies at his slowly turning body. He didn't know how to get out. When he tried, they threw more pennies at his head, chest, and back. He finally closed his big brown cow eyes and stood still, clutching his books to his chest. I looked into the faces of the boys and girls surrounding him, not recognizing any of them. Finally, I stepped into the circle and stood next to Jay. "Stop hurting him!" I shouted. "Do you really like what you're doing?" They stared at me as though I'd just stepped off a spaceship; then they gradually turned away and dispersed into the halls. Jay went to his class.

Jay lived in my neighborhood. Donald, my middle school boyfriend was a friend of Jay's and was usually protective of him, but high school was a different world. Donald couldn't keep up with what was happening to Jay. In his sophomore year, Jay died. I was in Elgin by then. The fit and muscular male gym teacher disciplined the boys by making them do laps around the field. Jay wouldn't have done anything to upset the teacher on purpose. Donald told me that the gym teacher regularly mocked and demeaned Jay with the other boys.

Jay had an enlarged heart and suffered a heart attack on the track during his forced extra laps. I was given special permission to leave Elgin State Hospital to attend his funeral. I had not seen anyone dead before. Jay lay in his coffin like someone set him up to do it as a bad joke. He didn't wake up. The neighborhood and school community seemed to be asleep. No one said anything. His family moved away. Jay's experience emphasized how dangerous being different could be.

I hated gym class freshman year. I wasn't any good at sports. It was a miserable requirement. I began to miss it on purpose. I was especially uncomfortable undressing in the locker room and seeing other girls naked. I had seen babies with no diapers on; and once on a camping trip with my family, I saw two women coming out of a shower with no clothes on. That was a shocking yet informative experience.

My family was scrupulously modest. My best friend Joyce, who lived next door in New Jersey, had once shown me her father's Playboy magazines hidden in some books under his night table. We stared at the naked women's bodies with rounded breasts from the vantage point of our own pre-pubescence. It was like looking at the Grand Canyon for the first time after living in a sandbox. I was in awe, frightened, and excited.

How could I have even begun to imagine that I might have a sexual self? I had no idea. It was impossible for me to understand the messages that warned me and yet compelled me to search beyond the limits of who I was expected to be. In those early experiences, I began to unravel a powerful passion nothing and no one could stop me from experiencing. Not even myself.

FAMILY

As is typical in a large, exceptionally religious family, there is often a designated scapegoat, a child carrying the shadow. Someone must take on what the rest of the family disowns, so they can maintain a presence of unquestionable goodness. I was in the middle of seven children and that became my role as a child.

In the privacy of our home, my outwardly friendly, benevolent father could explode, banging his fists on the table, shouting and sometimes throwing a utensil through the air. He carried a deep anger laced with toxic shame that could simmer into eruption at any time in various ways. There were abrupt departures. Doors slammed.

My father often needed someone to mock and belittle perhaps to feel more confident. It seemed to be his way of transferring his insecurities onto someone else, so he didn't have to feel his own vulnerability. Feelings were dangerous in my family. I remember being asked by my father in a low accusing voice at the dinner table if I was *intelligent*. Still young enough not to know my vocabulary, I looked up at him and saw his frown and decided to say, "No." Peals of laughter erupted from my father, brother, and sisters. My siblings called me stupid. I sat confused and hurt. My mother, always in motion doing something in the kitchen, was silent and kept her back turned to me. Being mocked and made fun of for not knowing something was a regular occurrence.

I longed for a place in the family discussions and activities centered around the dinner table, but my difference in age and communication skills prevented that. My three older siblings were close in age. I was five years younger than the next oldest. They had already arranged their pattern of behaviors and roles, clamoring for my father's attention while my mother hovered around serving everyone without much to say.

My father broke my heart when his attention toward me shifted. I was around five years old. He was comfortable being physically affectionate with me until I reached that age. Then he suddenly turned on me and literally pushed me away. I was not allowed to sit on his lap anymore even though my younger brother was my father's 'blanket' and would lie napping with him on the sofa.

Sometimes I ran to the corner of the block when my father got off the bus after working in Manhattan. I was so excited to be with him, holding his hand as we walked home. Perhaps my father in his own unconscious way was trying to protect us both from incest. His father was the only one in the extended family who was not devoutly religious and was an active alcoholic.

My father told me about his life as a young boy. His father returned home after many years away. My grandfather tried unsuccessfully to get him interested in what my father described as "filthy pictures" of women. I think he was about eleven years old when that happened. My father refused and essentially rejected his own father, focusing more on his mother and the Latter Day Saint, (Mormon) church as his primary influences.

My two aunts later shared with me that their father had sexually molested them when they were children. My oldest aunt read my grandfather's diary after he died and told me she was stunned when she read his pondering about why he "preferred to sleep with children rather than women." I know of several grandchildren who were exposed to my grandfather's lewd behaviors. I was, although I wasn't conscious of it at that time in my life.

I believe my grandfather was the first predator to strike my innocence. Blood in the water draws more sharks. In 1968 and 1969 other rapacious men came to feed on my susceptibility when I arrived at the threshold of puberty.

My father was spared some of the effects of his father because my grandfather left him and my grandmother when my father was about one year old. His father went to work in the Northwest timber industry during the Great Depression.

As a young boy, my father was raised with my grandmother's family on sharecropped land in Texarkana, literally barefoot and picking cotton. He had a caring uncle who was like a father to him, dozens of cousins, and an adoring mother. Although it was a time of being exceptionally poor, he told us he was happy then. His sister was born ten years after him when my grandfather returned, and they moved to "Hell's Kitchen" and later to the lower east side of Manhattan.

My father made use of every opportunity he was given to grow beyond the lives his parents lived. He worked hard and continued to help his mother, father, and sisters financially when he could. In his own way, he was a great man, yet the pain and struggle I went through with him was endless.

When I was a little child, I tried to find ways to be closer to my parents. When I was five or six, my father would make me sit next to him at the dinner table and teasingly call me *Lobster*. I didn't like that name. I knew he was tricking me and later told me he chose that pet name to be less obvious than his first choice of *Crab*. My older brother and two sisters laughed at me. My younger brother learned to laugh along too. I painfully felt the difference between laughing with others and being laughed at, being in on a joke or being made the joke.

My father called my younger brother *"Pumpkin"* with obvious endearment. His favoritism toward my brother and permission to take out aggression and frustration on me was contagious. The mocking would escalate. If I said anything in my own defense or tried to stop the teasing, he would thump me hard on top of my head. If I cried, I was sent away from the table. During my innocent years, I cried easily. That would begin a typical evening drama. Tormented and rejected, I would go upstairs and cry, sometimes loudly. Often I would lie in my bed kicking my heels against the wall in my converted attic room, hoping someone would care, while the family ignored me and went on with their meal. I could hear them laughing and talking.

I desperately wanted and needed to feel like part of my family. It has become obvious to me now that it was at this point in my history when I first lost my sense of having a home, before we moved to the Midwest and before Elgin. Recently I read the results of scientific research demonstrating that being ignored releases the same chemicals in the brain as being physically injured. As a young child, I felt severed from the body of my family, unsure of how I would survive. My soul was wounded.

My mother rarely made enough food for all of us, except on Sundays and holidays. It was a competitive situation at the dinner table. All eyes would watch as a small casserole emerged from the oven, or some other entrée along with vegetables, salad and bread. We all knew that there was not enough, so we each tried to get our portion before it was gone. Although my mother developed a habit of storing large quantities of food for a future time of need that never arrived, she didn't seem able to offer an amount matching the hunger of her family at mealtime. Even though Mormons are instructed to prepare a food storage, I later wondered if this behavior was my mother's way of indirectly telling us there wasn't enough of her nurturing to go around. She gave the minimum, while quietly attempting to stockpile her own resources.

Often when I was sent away from the table without dinner, my mother would save a small portion of food for me. Later I would come down to sit alone at the table and eat while my mother cleaned up the kitchen. I rarely saw the front of her at home. She was perpetually doing housework, preparing food, cleaning up, and doing laundry. So busy serving, she couldn't sit still with others eating at the dinner table except to perch briefly at the edge of her chair during prayer.

I can understand how my mother developed an identity of self-sacrifice and service. By the time my mother was five years old, she was already cooking, serving her father and younger brothers, and cleaning up the kitchen. My grandmother could be loving but also stern, training her daughter with firm discipline. My mother strove to meet the expectations of her parents, her church, and her husband. She was constantly aspiring to be a good girl and to please others in authority.

My mother was pregnant three times after my birth, and her babies needed care. Sometimes my older sisters assisted. I helped take care of my youngest sister and brother. It was only in church that I would see the front of my parents along with the congregation. My mother led the music, and my father participated in the service from the pulpit. Both of them held top leadership positions at our church throughout my childhood. My father became the bishop of our "ward" while we lived in New Jersey. I felt as though the church was causing me and my siblings to be orphaned during that time.

I couldn't seem to stay out of trouble in my family. When food was missing from the refrigerator, my name would be called. Sometimes I didn't come in from outside soon enough. I left toys on the floor. My mother screamed, "What's wrong with you?" I didn't know. Most of what I did wrong wasn't anything I could remember or associate with the present. My father hit me or thumped me with his big hands, but my mother often punished me with a wire-handled fly swatter. She whipped my bottom and bare legs with it. Being hit with a fly swatter was diminishing and humiliating. Punishment was a constant theme where guilt and shame compounded. I can't remember her hitting my brothers and sisters like that.

I know my grandmother whipped my mother as a child with "a limber stick," which my mother was forced to go outside and find for her own punishment. Perhaps I was singled out because I was the easiest one to ridicule and blame in our family. Being the youngest girl, I was sensitive and reacted quickly to teasing and taunts. I wonder if the treatment toward me as a child was because they sensed I was different and my difference was not welcome. One time when I was forty, my mother and I stayed up late talking in the kitchen. She confided that she felt fear about me as her baby. She told me she could tell I was different from her other children and she was afraid of what might happen when I began walking and talking on my own.

Shame is a stain that is difficult to remove. Shame began fusing with my identity at a young age. Some part of me began to think I was being hit because I was bad, a "bad girl." My siblings also appeared to believe this about me. Undoubtedly, they too carried their own hurt and shame that was ambient in our household. When I was a child, my brothers and sisters seemed to be having a completely different family experience than I was. I wanted to be accepted and loved but didn't know how to in my family. I attempted to gain attention and understanding. I waited for my turn that did not come. Getting negative attention became normalized. As I watched my parents interact with my siblings and others at church, I wondered why I didn't fit in. I used to cry when my mother yelled and hit me. Her high-pitched screaming was unnerving. My mother could be yelling in a loud shrill uncontrolled way, yet if the phone rang, she would answer in a meek, polite voice. Her radical change in presentation to others disturbed me. Who was she?

When I was eight years old, I had a moment of awareness that changed everything. I realized I had a choice not to cry anymore. It was my way of defying the stinging humiliation accompanying my mother's punishment that I couldn't make sense of. Silent and still, I took my mother's thrashing. My lack of reaction enraged her more, and she beat me harder at first. Even though it hurt, I pushed my feelings deep inside, out of view. Eventually my silence caused her to retreat. She continued to take out the fly swatter to hit me until my teens, but not as often. I also stopped crying when my father and siblings teased me. They too found other ways to amuse themselves at the dinner table. I withdrew and became invisible.

At nine years old, I knew I was unhappy and asked my mother if I could see a psychiatrist. She laughed at me. I don't know where I got information about what a psychiatrist was, but it stayed with me. I asked for help, but was not taken seriously. I was often unseen and unheard when not being negatively focused on.

I wanted to run away. I planned it many times but wasn't sure where to go or how to get there. My oldest brother had run away as a child of seven years old and actually made it to our grandmother's house. He walked six miles across town and up a steep mountainous road. I was impressed by how he took charge of his own destiny that way. An angry neighbor had yelled at him for kicking a ball into her yard. Instead of turning to his own mother or father, he ran to his grandparent's house where he was raised from birth until two years old. Sometimes I thought about running away to grandma's house too.

There were times I pretended to be dead, hanging my head on the car seat by a window hoping another passing car with a concerned family would notice and come rescue me. I practiced that ploy when my father drove our family out to California when I was four. I didn't understand how to express the need to have a compassionate adult save something precious I felt dying inside me.

I thought of dying as an option when I was around eight. I imagined falling down stairs, off a cliff, or from a high building. Disembodied thoughts urged me to jump. I imagined hanging myself and tied a rope around my neck once at eleven, suspending myself from the bedpost until I turned blue. My heart remembered being loved before I was born and wanted to return to my spiritual home. I felt I belonged somewhere else.

At ten years old, right after my father became bishop, I tried smoking and drinking, which were strictly forbidden in my family's religion. A clear list of what not to do became an easy roadmap to rebellion.

My cousin told me that four aspirins in a Coke could make you drunk and eight aspirin could kill you. We both drank Cokes with four aspirins and tried to imagine that we were tipsy. Drinking Coca Cola was against our religion at that time, as was alcohol and coffee. Later I tried taking eight aspirins quietly in the bathroom alone with the door closed one night. I didn't die or get drunk, but I did have a strange time looking at myself in the bathroom mirror, watching to see what would happen after I tried Tina's death recipe. I don't know if my cousin secretly tried it too. During those years she was chasing boys and in a lot of trouble at home, especially with her father.

My father was loved and respected by family members as well as by church members and co-workers, but I could not discover his love and care. I had lost him almost completely before we moved away from New Jersey. He worked a full time job as an electrical engineer, was the bishop at church and went to school to get a master's degree, going far beyond anyone else's educational level in his family.

My father picked on me when I was young, but after we moved, I turned it back on him. I confronted his patriarchal privilege, his hierarchic rule, his self-righteousness, and the way he ordered my mother around expecting women to diminish themselves and serve him. I refused to comply. I did not want to be a subservient martyr like my mother. I considered her unstable and ineffectual. I was angry. When I was thirteen years old I began an overt battle with my father that lasted for many years.

There was stress in my family in New Jersey, but something happened to all of us in 1967. My father took a job in Illinois and we moved away. Only my parents and four of their seven children moved with them. Pearl stayed and lived with our grandmother to finish high school. June started college in Utah and my oldest brother, Brian went on a mission to England for two years. Suddenly becoming the oldest child at home added to my disorientation.

We no longer had regular access to our extended family of friends, cousins, aunts, uncles, and grandparents. The church that knew and loved us, and where my parents were an essential part, was over a thousand miles away. The new church didn't care much about us. My parents were not welcomed or given jobs in the church as they might have expected. It was culture shock for all of us.

After we moved, my father made a list of the "family's bad feelings" that had become unmanageable, but the items he put on the list were about behaviors related to chores not being done on time and tools that weren't put back where they belonged. He didn't realize then that a vital thread was torn from the fabric of our family that might have held us together during the storm about to ensue. Nothing was ever the same. The family fragmented even more than it already had.

In my freshman year of 1968 at thirteen years old, I was sent to the school psychologist. I told him about my family life and my struggle with my parents. I explained my experience of being the middle child of seven who spanned twenty years from the oldest to the youngest. He asked personal questions about my relationship with all of them.

My older sister had extreme mood swings. Pearl was five years older than me and was the one who primarily raised me. She taught me to tie my shoes, read to me, and was like a surrogate mother. She told me after we were adults that my crying as a child upset her. When I asked her why I was crying, she told me our mother was often yelling at me. One time Pearl took me to the bathroom and taught me how to brush my teeth to stop my crying after my mother yelled at me to get ready for bed.

Pearl was usually my roommate. She could become threatening and lash out at any moment, yelling, scratching my arms until they bled, saying the most terrible things she knew would hurt me. Later she would be kind again. She was the only person in my family who paid much attention to me and seemed to care. With her erratic behavior, she inlaid a confusing pattern of love and pain, isolation and interdependence within my heart that continued to replicate in my subsequent relationships.

My oldest sister June, who was eleven months older than Pearl, had a refreshing sense of humor. She kept the family laughing. Her primary interest was in boys and her social life, which drew her focus out of our home. I loved to sneak into her room and play with her collection of small painted ceramic horses. When she lived at home, her room was clean and organized. It felt like another world different from the rest of the house. If I was caught, I got in trouble for going in there.

As a child, my older brother either teased or ignored me. When I was eight years old, Brian was eighteen and already initiated into higher levels of the church's patriarchal priesthood. He performed my baptism by total immersion in the waters of a baptismal font with my family and other church members present.

At the age of eight, I looked up to my oldest brother. Brian had a love of folk and classical music that I found inspiring. As a child, I danced to the music of Gershwin's, *Rhapsody in Blue*. I heard it as a divination that I felt symbolically described my entire life. I knew just what part of the score I was living, while dancing passionately the life I was yet to live. For me, music was an energy I perceived in color as well as movement through space and time. Brian gave me an album from the play about Don Quixote. I listened to it over and over again. *The Impossible Dream* became my theme song. I felt called on a quest to discover love, real love. I believed I could attain true liberty through love.

Brian had dark brown hair that was shaved close to his head with a tuft on top. He wore thick black-rimmed glasses and read a lot of books. He talked about what he found interesting in them. When Brian left for college and a mission, I read some of his books. Although I admired my brother, he was a mystery to me. It wasn't until we were much older that we had an opportunity to become friends and loving supportive siblings to one another.

When I was in my twenties, my two oldest siblings apologized to me for how they had treated me as a child. My brother apologized for teasing me and not saying or doing anything when others in the family targeted me with anger and blame. My oldest sister confessed that she had picked me up when I was four years old and had thrown me into a wall. She told me that she had lost her temper because I came down the stairs in my pajamas and emptied some tinker toys onto the rug she had just vacuumed. She apologized. I didn't remember. That was life in my family. Attention was focused on how we looked at church and to the outside world. Inside our house, our interactions were disjointed and chaotic. Sudden eruptions could happen at any time. Family members were stressed and operated out of individual need. We were all alone, together.

When I was eleven years old, I used my imagination to write postcards to myself from an imaginary mother. Art and writing provided a way to soothe my pain and express myself. I created a story and drew pictures on index cards from my "real mother" who was a magical witch. These cards showed her riding on her double-handled broom, actively involved in making the world a better place. She lived as an artist in Greenwich Village, New York, with her black cat alongside her. In the story through each card, she told me she loved me and that she would come back for me someday.

This mythical mother was mysteriously dark. She symbolized my nascent awareness of being held by something larger than myself, a presence both benevolent and fiercely wild.

In my imagination, I surmised that I had been mixed up at birth or had been adopted as my older sisters sometimes teased me. Maybe they both sensed something was innately odd about me. I hoped that when my real mother realized I was with the wrong people, she would fly back to get me, and bring me home.

TREE

There was a maple tree in the backyard of my childhood home in New Jersey. This maple tree appeared to grow at the same pace as I did. For many years, I was able to leap up and grasp the familiar outstretched lower branch and pull myself up, locking my legs around it. From there I would climb high into its branches and cling there, feeling the texture of the bark with my fingers as I gazed out over the houses into the distance. The sky seemed closer. This maple tree felt like it was holding me as I held onto it, rocking slightly with the breeze. My tree was a stable comforting presence.

Early one evening I ran from the house and climbed up my familiar maple tree just as a storm was approaching. Clouds rolled in, darkening the landscape. Winds pulled at the leaves and shook them restlessly. Instead of climbing down and running back into the house, I made a decision to climb up farther than I ever had before. I clung to the smaller branches extending up out of the sturdier limbs. My cheek pressed against the smooth light-colored bark. I closed my eyes when a big gush of wind bent the high limbs over. I dipped down and swung back in its embrace. I was not afraid. The tree held me. Rain fell like tears. My eyes were sky and my limbs were branches. No more pain, just rain. Lightning struck the hillside behind me. Thunder and flash. Wind.

I held on. I had a choice to get down and go inside, but instead I held tightly to the tree that was dancing in the wind. I felt safer there.

"You can go this way or that way, here or there. You can choose to go to the center and know the depths of human experience or remain on the edge and go the way your mother and father, sisters and brothers, grandparents and great grandparents have. You can choose."

Was I imagining, remembering, or hearing voices? Another flash and crash of thunder. I was dripping wet, holding tightly as the tree danced my potential life before me in a mirror of rain and wind.

"Yes" I said as though I already knew what I was agreeing to. "I will go to the center." Swaying down, the tree almost threatened to drop me on my head.

"You will be lost. You will be found. Remember to make a map of your way home." Suddenly I was cold and shuddering with my lips pressed into the bark. I climbed down out of the tree and went back into the house. At that moment, a vow was seeded deeply within the fertile darkness of my fierce wild heart.

THIRTEEN

Memory is imperfect. Some experiences make an indelible mark on the body of being and wait timelessly to reveal themselves. The events that occurred during my thirteenth year have tangled together in an unrecognizable order. They fall now into a cascade of words, becoming story.

After we moved to a suburb of Chicago, I struggled in my budding relationship with Jane. There began to be intrusive influences from those in authority. My relationship with Jane was complicated by her mixed feelings about me. In some ways, she seemed to feel as interested in me as I was in her. Then she would flip and act like she didn't care and didn't want to be seen with me or for others to know about us.

Jane challenged me to get a boyfriend; she would not let me get close to her until I did. I decided to say yes to two different boys who had been trying to give me a ring and a bracelet to go steady. I showed Jane the ring and the ID bracelet asking her, "Are you satisfied?"

She laughed and said, "Well done! Okay then, yes."

I developed crushes on two other girls in my classes but couldn't express it to them. Jane was the one I wanted to be with, but her attention and affections toward me often seemed transitory and fleeting. I visited Jane whenever I could. One time she was lying on a couch in her home, talking on the phone to some boy who was interested in her, while unbuttoning her blouse and revealing her breasts in her bra to me. Any resistance evaporated as I found myself beside her on the floor, reaching my arms up with my hands sliding into the opening she gave me to caress her.

If I could get away, I stayed overnight when Jane would let me. She would invite my attention and embrace, but as soon as I became more intimate with her, she would appear to be asleep. I assumed that she was pretending to sleep so that she could act like nothing happened. She would wake up sometimes in ways that let me know she was aware of what I was doing. I tried to wake her by whispering sweet words of love. Sometimes she would declare her love for me and return my affection; but later she would tell me I was the one with those feelings and that she liked boys. It was all very confusing for me, but I felt it was worth it to be close to her. Obsession took hold.

Shame began to tear away at my confidence. There were times when I felt as though I was molesting Jane. In the dark, she would take my hand and place it between her thighs near her wet warmth and then appear to be sleeping. Thinking she might actually be asleep, I would stop touching her and lie still while burning up with desire and confusion about what to do. Passion welled up in me. I was willing to do almost anything for her affection and attention.

It was on and off with Jane. I never knew what to expect. She would ignore me, acting disinterested and then smile and kiss my lips. After going through tremendous sadness and my own distractions from it, I was all hers again. She let me take responsibility for our romantic relationship while she was free to be straight to the world and popular with boys. I didn't blame her. We were both confused. I just kept loving her while ricocheting back and forth between highs and lows, depending on how she treated me.

In the fall of 1968, at the age of thirteen, I began cutting my left inner forearm. My right arm would punish the left for desire, and the left arm would release the pain of that desire by bleeding quietly into bathroom tissue. A razor blade pressed down slicing across fair skin allowed bright red beads of ambiguity to break free through the linear incision. These were superficial wounds. At that time, I cared so much about my appearance, and yet I could not control myself from injuring my own arm and making scars. It didn't make sense, nevertheless I couldn't stop. Eventually someone noticed in gym class, and I was sent to the school counselor. I spoke with the counselor, a middle-aged woman, about being attracted to girls and my mixed-up feelings about it. She was kind and listened to me. I can still remember her caring, clear blue eyes. I don't remember any other adult looking directly at me or listening to me until that time. I felt I might understand myself and feel better if I could talk with Miss Fasel again.

Another woman, fierce and masculine-looking, was the head of the counseling department. She looked like a hawk with short black hair feathered with grey streaks. I would later learn that she and the counselor I was speaking to were closeted lovers. The kindly Miss Fasel did not continue to talk with me. Instead, she sent me to the school psychologist.

Dr. Carter was a forty-five-year-old man who was partially crippled. He walked with one leg shorter than the other, so he had a thicker, higher shoe on that foot. I was told that he had been born with a clubfoot. I was familiar with my mother's father having a short, bowed leg from a sled accident in his childhood. He wore a tall shoe on one foot. I loved and trusted my grandfather. It was not unusual for me to be around someone who walked differently. This psychologist took great interest in my case and saw me regularly over a period of months. He gave me passes to get out of my classes, which I appreciated and used. I didn't have to go to gym class anymore.

Over time, Dr. Carter gradually encouraged my trust and tried to get me to confide in him. He began treating me like an adult. I enjoyed that. During the same time that I began seeing Carter, the school counselor Miss Fasel called my mother. Miss Fasel must have mentioned that I had expressed lesbian tendencies and was cutting myself. My mother had never heard of lesbianism.

I remember clearly when I went home that day. My mother was prone to erratic emotional outbursts. I never knew when she might blow or how bad it might be when she did. Arriving home from school, I walked in the front door through the hall and into the kitchen. There she was at her usual station, standing at the counter by the stove preparing food. She was cutting vegetables with a knife more methodically than usual. Looking up at me, there was fury in her eyes. She opened her mouth strangely. "The school counselor Miss Fasel called and told me you have been truant." My mother's voice steadily grew higher and louder. "She said you haven't been attending gym class."

"Oh?" I muttered, starting to back up.

"She told me that you are having sexual feelings for girls and cutting yourself!" My mother was beginning to shake and her rigid body began almost robotically to lift the knife higher and higher and stab the vegetables more emphatically.

The next thing I knew, my mother's voice turned into a shrill scream as she raised her knife and looked directly at me. "If you want to be cut, I'll cut you!" she screamed in a high wavering voice as she lunged toward me with the upraised knife.

"No, Mom! Stop! Stop it, Mom!" I cried out as I turned and ran in the other direction. Fortunately, I was faster than my mother. I ran around the hall into the living room and back again to the kitchen with my mother chasing me, holding the knife up in the air, threatening to cut me. Eventually I ran upstairs to my room and locked the door behind me. My mother was quickly behind me, banging on my door.

"Open up! You open this door right now!"

I held the door lock tight in my hand so she could not shake or turn it open. Eventually she returned downstairs.

Soon I heard the sound of the garage door automatically opening and then the door to the garage from the house creak open and close. My mother was speaking to my father in a muffled voice. After a brief silence, I heard his footsteps ascending the stairs. His broad fist began banging on my door. "You open this door right now or I'll break it down," he demanded. "Come out. You hear me?" I opened the door and looked into the angry red face of my father. He brought me into their bedroom to sit on their bed and have a talk with me.

There were many talks that ensued following that confrontation. My parents would question me about my behavior without any possibility of understanding it. I didn't understand myself and could not open up to them. We had a strained relationship that had worsened over the years.

In high school, Dr. Carter gave me a lot of attention. He spoke to me of things I was curious about, like sex. He asked me questions and listened to me. I was trying to figure out my life and my feelings. He offered to help. I wanted to trust him.

"How do you know you're a lesbian? Have you been with a girl?" He asked with his wide eyes waiting. "You can't tell just from a dream."

"I've been close to a girl." I ventured.

"Oh really? And who was that?" He inquired. I stayed silent and looked down. "Well, that doesn't mean you're a lesbian. You're just confused."

"I know how I feel and who I want to be with. I want to be with a girl, not a boy."

"You wouldn't know what to do if you had the opportunity to be with a girl," he countered.

"Oh yes I would." I demanded.

Carter laughed and then steadied himself, speaking more slowly. "You're too young to know about such things. You need to learn about boys. I'm sure you will discover your true feelings if you do. I'll help you learn about these things."

Nothing he said could convince me that I was not a lesbian. I wanted to understand more about sex so I could be with Jane. I didn't tell him about that. I felt protective of my relationship with her. I'm not sure whether my more intimate interactions with Jane began before or after Carter's continuous intrusive influence.

73

I had to meet with Carter regularly. He sat behind a wooden desk with books and papers on it. When I came in the door, I'd sit in a chair off to the right, facing his desk. Sometimes he would come around to the front of his desk.

He started teaching me about the meaning of love from Greek philosophy and mythology. I had already become familiar with Greek myths from books I had read in my home. He talked to me about the difference between *agape, philia,* and *eros*. He seemed to know a lot of information and was teaching me as though he was a philosopher and I was his student. I told this doctor my own ideas, beliefs, and dreams about love.

During these preliminary visits, Carter was also doing psychological testing on me. I answered questions, filled out paperwork, and took the Rorschach inkblot test. At one point, he asked me to look at a blank piece of paper and tell him what I saw. I was upset when I actually did see an image appear. I drew it onto the paper as he asked. A face emerged from the pencil tip onto the page, becoming a woman with sharp pointy teeth and a frighteningly open smile. She had wild eyes and hair like a demon, similar to the serpents of Medusa!

One time Carter told me to kiss him. I was shocked. He said something like, "How do you know that you don't like boys unless you try?" He made it sound like part of my therapy.

I told him "No. I don't want to kiss you. I have kissed boys and didn't care for it."

Carter continued with shrewd confidence. As an authority, he said, "Young boys don't know anything yet. You should kiss a man. That's how to learn and get well."

I couldn't imagine kissing that old man. I didn't understand his laughter and constant pressure on me. I was having more trouble at school. I'd begun drinking. Although I was thirteen, it was not difficult to acquire alcoholic beverages and cigarettes. My growing confusion and pain required stronger methods to numb myself so I would not feel my uncomfortable feelings.

I found a whole stash of tiny bottles of liquor at the bottom of one of my father's desk drawers. He must have saved the dozens of samples he was given on his many business trips. I don't know why he saved them, but I was glad he did. He didn't notice them missing. After that, I stole liquor and wine from the neighbors when I was babysitting. Sometimes I would drink before I went to school.

Once I was called into the principal's office because my skirt was too short. Mini-skirts with go-go boots were popular then. He was called out of his office for a minute, so I immediately jumped up and opened all his desk drawers and located two small bottles of liquor that I shoved into my purse. I was forced to go home and change my clothes. The lengths of skirts were monitored. I stashed the alcohol for later use.

Girls began talking about me in school and saying that I was a lesbian. One afternoon when I walked into the cafeteria, a stocky muscular blonde girl named Pam stopped, looked at me with fire in her eyes, and launched her fist into the pit of my stomach. Her mouth wrenched out the word, "Dyke!"

As my body bent forward involuntarily, my eyes stayed steady, looking into hers. When I pulled myself back up and caught my breath, she pulled her arm back to hit me again. I kept staring at her and finally said, "Why are you hitting me for loving someone? Haven't you ever loved anyone? What if you weren't allowed to love your boyfriend?" She stopped. Her eyes filled with tears and she walked away never bothering me again.

I'm not sure why, but rumors spread. Some girls threatened to beat Jane up after school. I don't know how they discovered any information that put us together as lesbians. Jane was handling it with humor and defiance. One day at school, she threw her arm around me, and we walked arm-in-arm with happy faces through the halls with other teens and teachers staring open-mouthed. It was thrilling but dangerous. There were moments when we were able to push the wave of hate into awe and bewilderment. It was empowering, but it didn't last. Jane would go off on another one of her own social escapades, and I would go on my way.

Teenagers in our family's religion were expected to attend "seminary" (religious training) each morning before going to high school. My mother made sure I woke up at 5:00 a.m. to be ready to be picked up to go to church. A small group of us would suffer through an hour of religious doctrine before going to school each morning. Beside my own discomfort at waking up before dawn to attend what felt like insidious indoctrination, I was completely baffled by how to handle the strange drama erupting there. Brother Arnold was the seminary teacher and drove me to church and afterwards to school each day. He was highly respected and considered a brilliant religious teacher in the church. Brother Arnold was married and had two young sons.

For some reason, Brother Arnold began to confide in me. Maybe my parents told him that I was expressing lesbian tendencies. I'm sure he knew something. During the dark of predawn as his hands gripped the steering wheel and his eyes froze forward, he spoke in a low voice about his disturbing temptation to get into the pants of a young handsome teenage boy who was also attending seminary. I'd watch as beads of sweat formed on the top of Brother Arnold's bald head as his lips trembled while confiding his dangerous secrets. I felt sorry for him but was also repulsed. As soon as we arrived, he would jump out of the car smiling and behave in the charismatic way he habitually did with others.

Mike, the object of Brother Arnold's affections and strangling lust, was trying to get to me. Once while waiting for Brother Arnold to come out and drive us to school, Mike quickly ran his hand up my dress and twisted a finger around in the elastic band of my underwear, trying to gain entry. I was relieved when Brother Arnold jumped into the driver's seat, slamming the door. Off we flew to school, me sitting between the two of them.

I tried taking drugs that were being offered by some of the kids in school. I felt better when I was drinking or on drugs. I was hurting but found momentary relief when I was high. Music carried me away, art and poetry flowed out of me effortlessly. I made friends with a group of kids who were known as "long hairs" or "heads."

At first I chose Tony for a boyfriend since Jane insisted I have one. He was a "greaser" or "hood" is what we called them in New Jersey. Tony and I were hanging out with a group of kids when five of us jumped into Sam's car. Sam was a tall thin boy with longish light brown hair. I sat between Sam driving on my left and Tony on my right. After being with Sam, I decided if I needed a boyfriend, I might as well pick one I actually liked. After that ride, Sam became my boyfriend.

Cheryl was a girl at school who hung out with me and was also friends with Jane. She liked Sam's best friend Bob. The four of us began going out together regularly in Sam's cool 1968 gold Chevy Impala with a black vinyl top. It was a two door with black interior and a bench seat. The radio only played AM.

Sam and I would sit in his front car seat talking and listening to music while our friends chatted or made out in the back seat. I felt safe with him. He was a nice guy. He liked me too, well enough to stand up to Tony's threat to beat him up in the lunchroom for taking his girlfriend. Sam was a sixteen-year-old junior when I was a freshman at thirteen. He was quiet and gentle by nature.

Most often he wore a suede jacket that had long brown fringe sleeves. I loved that jacket. Sam loaned it to me. I spilled cough syrup down the front and apologized to him after unsuccessfully trying to clean it. I had discovered over-the-counter bottled codeine when I could not readily acquire alcohol.

Sam frequently drove us to the only places teenagers could hang out. We visited a mall that housed some department stores where we could walk around talking and laughing together. One evening I strode out into the parking lot with a light, close-fitting brown suede jacket. When I showed Sam my stolen prize, he told me to return it. I went back into the store and left it there. Sam was an honest boy who wanted me to learn his values instead of stealing and acting out against my parent's rules. Now I understand I was behaving that way because of an inner sense of powerlessness and rage. Stealing provided me with a strange sense of justice in a world where I felt fairness was lacking. Sam had a way of calming me, inspiring me with his integrity.

A few days later for Christmas, Sam gave me that jacket. He had purchased it for me knowing how much it meant to me. It wasn't long until my father sternly confronted Sam and forced him to take the jacket back insisting, "If my daughter needs a jacket, I'll buy it for her!" The engulfing authority of my father eclipsed Sam's efforts to shine his light on me. The value of Sam's gift to me was not lost with the returned jacket. He saved it for me in his car to wear every time I went out with him. I was warmed by his caring and generous heart.

Breaking free of what I felt was a hostile home, I often ran off in a haze of reaction. Sometimes I called Sam to come get me. Once in March of 1969, after a series of incredibly painful events, I called Sam late at night and ran off to his room. Sam never pressured me to kiss or be sexual, yet a spark of his love for me grew effortlessly between us that night. With uncanny clarity, I remember a moment of sudden unexpected bliss while in his intimate yet innocent embrace. Joy lifted me briefly from my cloudy confused quagmire that was growing even more dismal and dangerous. I chose Sam, not Carter, to learn about feelings of love with a boy.

During November of 1968, Carter was trying to get me to kiss him in his office with the door closed, offering me passes out of class and other things. It felt like a fly kept landing on my face. I don't know if it was his persistence or pressure, perhaps it was my own confusion and pain that blinded me as I continued to plummet down emotionally. Maybe the attention he continued to feed me finally swayed me. I gave him a kiss. I hated it. He told me I was being cured. I told him I didn't like it.

Carter used his influence and power to draw me in as I slid further down with my own struggling identity. He pretended to be an ally helping me. The sessions I was required to go to became increasingly more bizarre with complicated interactions. Carter was building me up as being much more mature than other girls at the high school. "You're special," he said as he continued to make advances toward me in his office. I avoided his attempts.

Carter's conversations included telling me about sex and how a woman's body worked. He asked me about my sexuality all the time, acting as though he was the expert. He was a doctor and behaved confidently as though he knew me better than I knew myself. Perhaps he did in some way, but he used that knowledge to manipulate and control me for his own desires.

I wanted to learn about sex so I could be with a woman, and Carter said he wanted to teach me to be with a man as part of my therapy. He used persuasion and coercion to show me how. The sexual material he spoke of was mixed with psychology, myths, and biblical passages. He instructed me on how to masturbate by explaining what female anatomy was and the purpose of a clitoris. He explained orgasm. I didn't respond in his office to what he was telling me, but I listened and later at home looked in a mirror to see for myself. I began experimenting. Gradually, I discovered that what he said was true, but it was not the way I wanted to learn. Although I felt a surge of sexual energy that was pleasurable, I also felt emotional pain with deepening confusion. With Carter's insidious intrusion into my personal life, my sexual exploration could not be innocent. It was tainted by the doctor in charge of my care.

Carter made up a code name and began calling me at home. He often phoned after school to talk with me. It was a new experience to receive so much personal attention from a man in this way. I didn't understand it or know what to do about it.

One day in his office Carter said, "Your test results have come back." He spoke in a slow voice as though he was thinking carefully before saying more. "I haven't turned the results over to anyone else yet. I thought you might want to know and keep that from happening."

"What do you mean? Were the results bad?" I worried.

"These psychological tests can be read in a number of ways. I understand you and know how mature you are for your age, but others may not see it that way." Carter frowned.

I listened and wondered what he was talking about. Wasn't he the doctor that did the tests and wrote the results? "Who wrote the results?" I asked.

"Oh, it's a psychological testing facility for detecting mental illness and deviant behavior," he replied, shunning the notion that he had anything to do with it. "I'll call you after school and tell you more. Remember, I'll call you using the name Roger, okay?"

"All right." I said and turned to leave his office. Later that evening Carter called using his code name.

"It's Roger," my mother said, holding the yellow phone receiver out toward me. I looked at her knowing she had no idea who was really on the other end of that line. A moment passed as I stood staring at the long cord spiraling down to the floor and up again to the yellow phone box with its rotary dial.

"Oh, thanks," I replied, picking up the phone from my mother's hand and heading down to the basement stairs, shutting the door behind me.

"Listen," Carter began. "I was able to get your file out of the office. I can meet you somewhere and show it to you. You'll see. It has damaging information that could go on your permanent school record and haunt you for the rest of your life. It could affect whether you get into college."

"Well, what can I do about it?" I asked him.

"I'll give it to you to destroy." He offered. "Will you meet me?"

"I don't know if I can get away. My parents are really watching me closely."

"How about tomorrow night? I'll come by on the road behind your house and pick you up. Meet me at 6:30 p.m."

"I'll see what I can do." I told him and hung up. Was he really going this far out of his way to help me? I wasn't sure, but I was worried and wanted to find out.

The next evening I snuck out of the house. No one noticed. Carter picked me up a couple of blocks away in his little VW bug. He began to tell me about many problems developing at school. He said that the counselor, Miss Fasel and the department head Miss Wright, were secretly a lesbian couple. They were afraid of being found out because of me. He suggested that they were trying to get me kicked out of school as a decoy. I was stunned. He told me he needed to drive me to his apartment in Chicago to get the files. Although he said he would, I never did see the damaging files he warned me about and had offered to give me.

Once we arrived, I was waiting for the files, but instead he gave me a glass of wine. Unable to refuse easy access to alcohol, I drank the wine and listened to him talking about the conspiracy against me at school. He put some terrible old-fashioned music on the record player and made a fire in the fireplace.

After sitting down in front of the fire, he asked me to come sit with him on the rug in front of the couch. I didn't at first, but eventually I gave in to his coaxing and sat on the couch. He told me the story of Adam and Eve. I felt dizzy. Gazing up, I noticed some pictures on the mantle of the fireplace. There was one girl's face that I could see as he reached up and began trying to take my clothes off. The girl in the photo had a pleasant face and kind eyes. She looked smart. Her hair was light brown and shoulder length, the way mine was in junior high. He was pulling at me and telling me things I couldn't understand. "Stop," I said at last, while pushing him away.

This girl on the mantle was looking at me. She was the same girl in another picture with an older woman beside Carter and another young boy. Was that his son?

I told him I didn't believe in the bible stories the way he was telling them to me. I wanted to be with a woman. Then he pulled me down onto the floor and leaned over onto me. His breath stank of garlic and wine. He was holding me tightly, talking about biblical passages while poking his crooked little penis toward my vagina. "This is the way it's supposed to be. You have to learn for your own good," he said while he was hurting me.

I wanted to get away, but suddenly froze, not fully in my body anymore. It was like a dream I couldn't wake up from. Part of me struggled to gain control from inside a body that no longer functioned properly. Flashes of myself immobilized and silenced as an infant slid sideways into my mind and paralyzed my body.

The girl in the photo on the mantle was looking at me. The frame was gold. She was older than me and seemed to know something about what was happening, as though she might almost start speaking.

Where were his wife and children? Why was I there? I was on his living room floor. How was this happening to me? My mind reeled back and disappeared as though I was no longer present, then I became aware again. I felt sick to my stomach and wanted to get out of there. It was only moments, a blink of time under his weight, until my body unfroze and wriggled out. "Take me back," I demanded.

Carter drove me to the suburbs through the murky night and let me out of his car a block away from my parents' home. I walked toward the dull yellow house, letting myself in quietly. The sound of the TV blared. I glanced at my father as his perception hung on the sounds and images he sat vigilantly in front of. I climbed up the stairs to my room and closed the door.

SPINNING WHEEL

Little pieces of this story flash and swim up in random order as I recall how the spinning wheel of events at that time began turning faster. I wasn't okay. I was slipping further away into endless pain, desperately trying to rewrite the script of my life into a love story, not a descent into hell. My consciousness edited out what I could not comprehend or metabolize. I had learned early in life from those around me, to minimize and ignore what was difficult. That method of coping wasn't working too well.

My oldest brother had come back from his mission in England and was going to be married to his fiancée at the temple in Salt Lake City. My father drove my mother, my three younger siblings and me to Utah from a suburb of Chicago, Illinois. We barely fit into the blue wood-paneled Ford Country Squire station wagon. My parents sat in the front bench seat and my three younger siblings sat in the middle seat. Sometimes my mother would hold my two-year-old brother in the front seat with her.

I lay in the very back of the car in a sexual haze mixed with anguish. All I could do was think about Jane. My body felt on fire with passion for her, but then the intrusive advances of Dr. Carter seeped into my thoughts, causing revulsion. Most of the time, I couldn't focus clearly on anything or anyone. The contents of my shattering life were falling onto everything else, while I kept attempting to keep it separate and myself safe.

Along the way, we stopped at a lone gas station off the highway in a dusty dry desert area, perhaps in southern Wyoming. A cowboy wearing a big cream-colored straw hat went out to pump the gas as everyone fled into the bathrooms. For some reason when I got into the small building, I walked over to the counter rather than the lavatory.

I noticed an old-fashioned western style cash register that looked like it came from a saloon on the TV show, *Gunsmoke*. My right hand pulled down the long metal arm with its smooth wooden handle. The drawer popped open. Everything in me became automatic. On the right side of the drawer there was a pile of twenty-dollar bills. I took five of them, leaving the rest. I was thinking that I would ask Jane to marry me. I wanted to buy her a diamond ring. The big-bellied cowboy came in from pumping gas. There I was standing at his register, unable to close the drawer. His face grew alarmed as he looked at me. "What are you doing there?" he demanded.

"I'm sorry," I told him. "I was curious to see if this was a real antique and how it worked."

"It's real," he said, as he looked inside at the money and closed the drawer. "Okay, get out of here and don't do that again." I went to the bathroom with the hundred dollars folded into my pants and then returned to the car. My father drove us away as I resumed my submersion into foggy sexual obsession about Jane while in the back of the family vehicle.

When we returned from the trip to Utah, I went to Montgomery Wards department store and purchased the best diamond ring I could find for Jane. Later in the week I went to her house and got down on my knees and asked her if she would run away to England and marry me. For some reason, I thought it was legal for us to get married in England. Marriage was firmly rooted in my mind as the ultimate act of love that could last forever.

Jane looked at me with her mouth partly opened and took the ring box into her hands. As she opened it, her eyes got big and she started to laugh. She asked me, "Did you find this in a *Cracker Jacks* box?" "No," I assured her. "It's a real diamond in gold." "Where did you get the money to buy this?" She tried it on her finger and it fit. She left it on and opened her arms to me. I could tell the ring touched her heart even though she joked about it having such a tiny diamond. She did not say yes to my proposal, yet she continued to wear the ring.

I tried to avoid Carter, but that was impossible. He continued his siege. I was called out of my class to go see him. He challenged me when I told him I didn't want to meet him for sessions or go to his apartment again. He explained that I would be kicked out of school if I didn't come to his office regularly. I didn't want to be cut off from my friends, so I continued to meet him in his office, where I was subjected to his version of reality. He pretended to be my ally and tried to prove that he was protecting me from other malefic influences, like the other counselors, the principal, and my parents. I didn't trust him, but I took the extra passes he gave me to get out of class. Some of what he told me seemed to be true, but he painted a different picture than what I was experiencing. Although his reality was not my reality, I stumbled amidst the contrast.

I was completely overwhelmed by what was happening in my life and how complicated it was. I drank more. I was caught stealing liquor from the neighbor's house. I accidentally cut my toe on a broken fish bowl that was hidden under snow on their back porch where I'd stashed the bottles to pick up later after babysitting. I was taken to a clinic to have my toe stitched. The bottles were discovered afterwards when the neighbors cleaned up.

My father slammed the front door on my hand and didn't seem to care. Later I told my father I hated him and swore at my mother. My parents and I began fighting more and more. My father punched me in the face with such force that I flew across the room and hit the wall. I locked myself in my room. At night I tried to sneak out to be with Jane whenever I could.

My parents took me to a psychotherapist who was a church member. He lectured me for five minutes and spent over an hour with my parents. We went there several times. Each time, the therapist would talk with them in a closed room while I waited. He suggested that they consider putting me in an institution. They discussed the possibilities of controlling me by putting bars on my bedroom windows and a lock on the outside of my bedroom door.

I was forced to go to church each week but forbidden from taking part in the sacrament where young boys offered blessed bread and water to the congregation. They were instructed to pass over me because I was deemed unworthy. Other church members looked at me and then turned away in disgust. This began a more radical severing of me from my church culture. For a Mormon, life is interwoven with a family that is entwined with the community of the church. My primal survival needs felt threatened without that relationship.

Clearly, I was breaking rules and expectations of how I was supposed to be. There I was, drinking, smoking, and being sexual with a girl by choice. My rebellion against impossibly rigid thinking and violent structures of control was an attempt to gain space to simply be and discover who I was. Although I was by nature, a kind and loving person, I was truly out of control.

I could not have understood then how emotional, spiritual, and sexual violations can cause children to act out, and or, act in. There was no way for me to clarify my own newly forming sexual identity out of the chaos of intrusive sexual encounters. Nearly any form of natural sexual exploration or expression was impossible. My understanding of how sex and power dynamics operate between people became distorted.

The method of treatment by my authority figures was to subdue and dominate my behavior and my body through anger, rejection, punishments, and isolation. This attempt to control and shame me fueled even more fury in my warrior heart. I was motivated to blast through any obstacle in order to discover and claim my right to feel and express love with who I chose to love.

During this time attention came toward me from many directions. It gave me a strange feeling to be noticed in seemingly positive ways after being a scapegoat, getting negative attention, or being an invisible child that no one appeared to notice at all. The attention toward my new adolescent body was both exciting and frightening. It felt powerful, but this kind of power was dangerously unfamiliar to my adolescent mind.

I walked to school through quiet suburban streets, on sidewalks in front of nondescript houses set on orderly lawns. As I strode along carrying my books, I would often see one man after another leave their house, get into a car, and drive away. The women would stay home while the children went to school. One morning I witnessed an adult woman press her naked body against the window I was passing. I felt confused by seeing a naked torso like that.

On several occasions, an older man dressed in a suit would slow down his car and then stop on the road beside me as I walked to school. He asked me questions and offered to give me a lift. I could tell there was something sleazy in his eyes. I told him, "No, thank you," and continued to walk. Courtesy was my default. I was taught to be polite to adults, especially men. That man persisted day after day to try and pick me up. He looked like he could be somebody's father. He probably was. I did not get into his car.

Earlier in the year, one afternoon while I waited by the curb in front of the high school for a ride, a white van pulled up in front of me. A man perhaps in his twenties, opened the door exposing his erect penis. I blinked in astonishment and froze. Eventually some commotion happened, the door slammed closed and the van sped away. There was something terrifying and wondrous about seeing such a thing. I didn't know how to comprehend it.

My sister Pearl was eighteen years old at that time and came home from college for a visit during her Christmas vacation in 1968. My parents had her stay in the other twin bed in my room. She told me many years later about her distressing experience of seeing me. There was her younger sister, skin on bones and in appalling emotional pain, not sleeping and pacing around like a caged animal. She recalled how I had confided in her about what was happening with Dr. Carter and asked for her help to get away from him. Pearl said, "Talk to Mom and Dad."

"I can't talk to them." I said. It was hard for Pearl to conceptualize the different relationship I had with my parents. To her, my father was a hero, a noble, trustworthy man. She had a completely different experience with him and my mother than I had. Pearl kept the secret I told her, later saying it tore her apart to witness my demise accompanied by my parents' rage. She couldn't surrender her own attachment to who they were as her parents in order to speak up on my behalf. I was drowning without help.

It was decades later when she told me that what she witnessed happening to me created a crisis in her own mind that gradually formed a wedge in her relationship with our parents.

Pearl described her horror at seeing and reading the images and words of pain I painted onto the walls of my bedroom that winter. I can no longer remember what I wrote or drew. I only know that it contained the psychic emotional vomit of what I was experiencing then. My mother painted over those walls after I went to Elgin in the spring of 1969.

LEAVING

There was a day that winter after Pearl returned to college when I packed up some of my clothes into my small round white patent leather bag from modeling school and zipped it closed. I hid the bag and managed to get it to school. That day I did not come home after school. Jane's mother said I could stay at their house because she felt sorry for me and believed my parents were crazy. When my parents called and said they were coming over, I had to leave. Different kids' families from school let me stay at their houses. I was able to find a place to stay for three days. One mother of a boy from school told me she would be willing to adopt me and let me stay there as long as I wanted. I considered that possibility and wondered how to make it happen.

The sharp, masculine, hawk-faced department head of counseling at Center Lake High School called the home I was staying in and said she wanted to come over and talk with me. I thought about running away again, but she convinced me to stay there and speak to her. When she arrived she asked me, "Has your father hit you?"

I looked into Miss Wright's eyes to determine her sincerity. "Yes," I answered. She appeared to come to a conclusion quickly, without further conversation.

"Get in the car," Miss Wright spoke with fierce determination, hinting at protection. She drove me to school and called my parents to come in for a meeting. This began more meetings in which I was discussed but not included.

Over time my parents had several conferences with the counselors. Carter attended the conferences and afterwards continued to pressure me with his twist on things. How was he able to talk with my parents and gain their trust while cornering me alone in his office? He took advantage of my vulnerability and their gullibility. He told me the nature of the meetings with my parents and the serious trouble I was in. Then he told me he wanted to take me out for my fourteenth birthday to celebrate my becoming a woman. He assured me he would be a gentleman and take me to a wonderful place where I would be treated like a grown up. I was confused and afraid yet agreed to go. I managed to find a way to slip out that night.

Carter took me to a restaurant in Chicago. A woman in a shimmering, close-fitting gown greeted us as we walked in the door. She seated us at a small round table with a white linen tablecloth on it. There were flowers on the table and a live orchestra playing. People sat at other tables around us. They were all fashionably dressed adults. My previous experience eating out was only occasionally at fast food restaurants with my family.

Carter ordered two martinis for us. The woman in the gown smiled at me as though I was eighteen years old and brought clear oddly shaped glasses with long stems and a skewered green olive in each one. Carter taught me how to drink the martini and when to eat the olive. It was my first time drinking publicly and being treated like an adult. I found it intoxicating.

Afterwards Carter took my hand and brought me to a puppet show. He changed from treating me like an adult to handling me like a young child. He began acting as though he was my father. In just moments, I went from feeling eighteen to a ten year old. It was confusing. I did not like the puppet show and wanted to leave. It was scaring me. I was beginning to feel closed up and dizzy in the dark theater.

Carter told me he had to get something at his office. I didn't want to go. He told me he had some wine upstairs. I became interested in the wine but told him I didn't want to have sex with him. He said he wouldn't, but of course he tried.

Upstairs in his Chicago office he poured me a glass of wine and told me about Greek sexual positions. After explaining cunnilingus and fellatio, he tried to get my dress up to demonstrate. I felt disoriented and frozen with no response. It was as though a black cloud encased me. At one point, his ugly little penis came close to my mouth, startling me. He didn't force it in. When he drove me back to the suburbs, he gave me a colorfully wrapped present. In the little box was a pendant. It was a golden tear-shaped wire wrap that held a green jade ball hanging from a chain. On my fourteenth birthday, he offered me a golden cage. While in a daze, I took his gift though I never put it on.

Not long after that, I ran away from home again and was picked up by the police. I was taken down to the village police station where Sergeant Hastings of the police force asked me a lot of questions. He asked me about my parents and if I was drinking and taking drugs. He took me back to my parents' house. After the second time of being brought in for running away from home, Sergeant

Hastings told me that if I was caught a third time, I would be sent away to a detention center for girls. My picture was taken and kept at the police station.

At night I waited until 1:00 or 2:00 a.m. to get up, quietly leave, and walk through the wintery dark streets on my way to Jane's house. She would leave the side door of her family house unlocked for me. After silently slipping through the door, I ascended the stairs to her room where I slid myself into bed with her. At about 6 a.m. I snuck back to my parents' house and into my bedroom before my father's alarm would ring.

A highway separated my part of town from where Jane lived. There was no other way to her house except to cross that highway and risk being seen. There was a curfew in force; young people were not allowed out after 10:00 p.m. I already had curfew violations on my record.

Sergeant Hastings saw me crossing the highway one night and turned on his red and blue lights. He followed me slowly down the street until I finally stopped. He signaled for me to get into his squad car. I sat in the back of his car as he drove me to the police station again, but it wasn't the station. It was an empty model home.

He took me into the model home and told me he was going to give me a chance and not take me to the station or tell my parents. He talked with me for a long time making it sound like he was doing me a favor. Dressed in his dark blue uniform and hat, he sat with me on a sofa. I looked at the gun in the holster on his belt. I couldn't take my eyes off his gun for long before I found myself staring at it again.

His hands reached toward my shirt and began to lift it up. He told me he wasn't going to hurt me. I wouldn't have to go to a detention center if I let him take some pictures. This began a terrible cat and mouse game that occurred over many nights. I would look both ways, trying different times of night, or going farther down the road before crossing the highway, yet his police car would continuously appear.

Many times, while I sat next to him in the passenger seat of his police car, Sergeant Hastings would tell me personal details about his difficult life with his crippled wife. I don't know if what he told me was true or not. He took me back to the model home or sometimes he had me lie in the back of his squad car in some rural spot and pulled down my underpants and took pictures of me. When he was satisfied, he would let me go.

After his sexual dissection of my adolescent body with his camera, Sergeant Hastings dropped me off at my darkened family house. I would go in the side door I had escaped from and wait. Sometimes I would dash over to Jane's house in time to spend an hour before going back to my house. Everyday life grew worse and worse. When I could, I drank alcohol or took drugs before going to school trying to ease the pain.

I pleaded with Jane to run away with me and go to England where we could live free and love each other. She thought that was funny. "Where are we going to get the money to do that?" she countered. I decided to write Carter a note and slipped it in through the slightly rolled down driver's window of his VW bug in the school parking lot. I'd been avoiding him as much as possible while at school. I was skipping classes more often.

I asked Carter in the note to give me $200 so I could leave the area (I hoped with Jane). I think it was $200. I had no idea about the expenses of travel and cost of living at that time. I wrote in the note that if he didn't help me leave, I would tell the school about what he had done. Nothing happened. I waited.

One afternoon my parents came in through the garage side door, glaring at me with cloudy intense eyes. My father's face distorted into a grimace as he began shouting at me, "You filthy woman!"

I watched his mouth contort to form each word distinctly and then hurl them into my face. His right knee bent back and then his lower leg and foot flew toward me as I quickly turned to run. He proceeded to kick me in my rear-end as hard as he could, while I fled from him. "Filthy, filthy woman!" he repeated as he chased me and kicked me all around the house until I escaped up to my room and locked the door.

No one asked me what had happened from my perspective. I already knew no one would listen or care. My credibility was zero. Although incensed by the treatment I received by my authority figures, unfortunately the child within me also wondered if I was innately flawed and deserved to be treated badly.

I was expelled from high school. Carter told the school and my parents that I seduced him and that we had a consensual relationship. When asked, my parents decided not to press charges. They didn't want the shameful situation publicized. Carter moved to Florida and got another job in a school there. Later, Sergeant Hastings told me that Dr. Carter was known to have had sexual relations with a number of other young girls. I wondered, but did not ask, about the other girls or how Hastings knew about Carter. Everything around me was collapsing.

My parents took me to a psychiatrist at a private suburban mental institution with a children's unit. At first my parents disappeared into a room as they often had before at other places, while I waited. Then I was told to go into a large office. My parents left. A male doctor in a finely tailored grey suit sat behind a desk. He had dark brown hair and a neatly groomed beard and moustache. He didn't look up from his papers as he told me, "Sit down." I waited while he continued reading. When he looked up, he began asking me extremely direct questions. "Do you masturbate? He probed. "Why do you think you are a lesbian? Have you had sexual relations with a girl? What did you do? Tell me about your dreams. Are they sexual?"

This psychiatrist had a dastardly look in his eyes, prying ever more deeply into my sex life and wanting more and more details. His cold eyes looked at my breasts as though they showed through my blouse. He was creepy. This man was in a position of power, and he knew it. It was clear that I was nothing but a young girl in a sexualized body that he could take apart and utilize as he wished. I sensed the predator in him and felt like a little plucked chicken trapped in a cage with a wolf. This doctor who flashed cruelty seemed capable of even greater harm than Carter. I wanted to get out of there and hoped my parents would not admit me to that hospital.

My parents decided they could not afford the fee for the private suburban hospital. My father's insurance would only cover a partial amount. I was relieved to never see that doctor again.

Early spring began to melt the last of the snow, revealing naked earth and deadened grass. Jane asked me to come over. It was late afternoon. I managed to get away from my house. I was excited that I would have time with her, but when I got there she was talking on the phone and ignoring me. I waited on the couch for her to finish. Shortly after she hung up, two older guys came over. I was disappointed at the interruption and looked down at the floor. Eventually I looked back at Jane. She was being friendly with them. She looked over at me and smiled. "I want you to do me a favor and go with Red and Jones."

"Why?" I asked. "I thought you and I were going to have some time together."

"They are friends who like to party and are going to give us some drugs. Just get the pills and come back. Then you and I can have some fun together." I didn't want pills I wanted to be with Jane during the day, not only at night, but I did as she asked. Reluctantly I agreed. I had never said "no" to her.

Shortly after taking off in the car with the two men, police lights came on behind us. I sat in the back seat of the car with Jones while Red got out and spoke to the policeman. The officer searched the trunk of the car after we all got out and waited on the sidewalk. I was nervous about what the police might find. He didn't find what he was looking for and let us go. I did not recognize then how unlucky that was for me. The two men in the car with me laughed as we drove away.

I didn't even know who these men were. I was uncomfortable. I went because Jane asked me to. I sat in the back seat watching through the side window as the buildings got closer together and higher. Night came. Somewhere in Chicago we stopped in front of a red brick apartment building. I wanted to go back to Jane. I hoped getting the pills wouldn't take too long.

Upstairs, someone offered me a glass of wine. I drank it. There must have been something in it. Shortly after, I was extremely dizzy. Everything became distorted. My vision blurred. I was sucked into a black void, fighting to pull myself out. My body became paralyzed. I struggled to stay conscious yet could not speak.

Time evaporated. Eventually I roused from my deadened body on a bed, aware of a man on top of me and then another man. I was vaguely conscious of my head being at the corner of a bed hanging off. Light came in from somewhere but could not penetrate the grey of that room. I was trying to get my clothes pushed down over my body. I felt sick. I couldn't get up. Vomit flew out of my mouth. Where was I? How could I get out of there? I wanted to go back to Jane. Finally, movement and sound returned enough to my drugged body to say, "Take me back to Jane's house!"

In the car, I felt suffocated. I couldn't get air. A third man was strangling me with his hands and mouth on my neck, sucking the life out of the shell of my body. Their car pulled up in front of Jane's house. Two men carried me out and dropped my body onto the lawn. One of them rang the doorbell, then quickly jumped back into the car with the other two and drove off. Jane came out and found me lying on the lawn.

Jane managed to get my body into the house and helped me get upstairs into a bathtub. She ran warm water. Her eyes had tears in them. I sat in the warm, swirling bathtub water, staring ahead. When she left, I got up and opened the medicine cabinet and found a package of razor blades. When Jane returned the water was red. Blood was running out of my left wrist. "Please don't do that," she asked, wrapping my wrist in a paper towel and then applying bandages. The phone rang. It was my parents. They were on their way over to get me. When I got out of the tub I could see black and purple bruises reflected in the mirror from my collarbone up to my chin.

My parents arrived and took me back in their car to our house. Years later, I learned that the police told my father the identity of twenty-year-old Red. He had just been let out of jail for using a specific type of drug to sexually violate women without their ability to defend themselves. Although asked, my father never pressed charges. He was ashamed of what had happened and blamed me. My heart grew numb from silent agony.

The next day I lay in bed for a long time in a semi-aware twilight. The house became silent. Everyone was gone. I crept out of my room and into my parents' bedroom. I found my father's rifle in his closet. Locating a box of bullets, I went back into my room and locked the door. I took some pills that were downers. I inserted bullets into the long chamber along the barrel. When I closed it and reached for the trigger, I noticed that there was a lock on it. It was made of plastic and metal. I was still groggy from the night before and began to lose my balance as I started down the stairs. Grabbing hold of the banister, I struggled to keep myself upright while moving my body down. Opening the door to the garage, I began searching around until I found a pair of pliers and a screwdriver. Pulling myself back up the stairs, I went into my bedroom and locked my door again.

I wrestled with the lock on my father's 22-caliber rifle, forcing the end of the screwdriver into it, twisting and pulling until pieces began to crack off. I closed one eye to try to see through my blurring vision as I continued. The drug dose I had ingested was taking effect. Eventually I managed to break the lock off the trigger. I lay down in my bed with the rifle muzzle under my chin. I positioned my head in such a way to allow the bullet to go into my brain. Placing my thumb through the trigger guard and onto the metal trigger, I prepared to pull it back.

My parents found me lying under the covers of my bed, passed out with my father's loaded rifle next to me. They pulled me out of bed and took me to a doctor's office nearby. It was night. The doctor spoke only a few words to me and closed the door. He left me alone in an examining room, while talking about me with my parents in a different room. I rummaged through the cabinets and the refrigerator, taking all the drugs I could find. My vision was blurred so I couldn't see what was written on the labels. When my parents came out they took me home. I slept.

The next day my parents told me they were sending me to live with my Aunt Minnie in Long Island, New York. I wanted to go to Jane's house one last time.

The night before I left, I didn't sleep. I crept out of the house after midnight attempting to meet with Jane. That night Sergeant Hastings apprehended me again while I was crossing the highway. While in his squad car I told him my parents were sending me away to New York. He seemed to be sad about my leaving. "Why are they sending you there?"

"I tried to kill myself."

"How?" he asked.

"With a rifle," I told him.

He laughed and said, "You wouldn't have the guts to kill yourself or even know how to use a gun." He was wrong. I didn't want to live in this world anymore. Not with the way I had learned the world could be.

I was tired of adults telling me about myself and discounting what I felt and said. I was not an idiot who did know how to use a gun or end my life when it had become impossible. My pain was as real as the lead in the bullet I longed to release me from my agony.

I'd known how to use a gun since childhood. On land in Pennsylvania where my great-grandparents once farmed, my great great-grandfather and his son built a house that still stands today. I spent my summers on this farm with my family and relatives when I was growing up. In the summertime when we visited, I could out-shoot even the older farm boys, knocking the cans off the rocks and shooting dead center into the paper targets tacked onto trees. Without much experience, I discovered I had a natural born ability with guns.

Hastings taunted me. He even unsnapped his pistol from his holster and acted as though he was going to hand it to me. I grabbed his gun. A look shot from my eyes into his. He pulled his gun out of my hand and quickly snapped it back into his holster. He was convinced. Hastings kept me in his squad car talking for hours that night. He looked like he might cry about my leaving him. He asked me a lot of questions and then wanted to kiss me good-bye. I felt sorry for him for a moment, but then the deadened feeling returned. I just sat there with him, wondering how I was going to get out of there to see Jane again. He dropped me off at my parents' house at dawn.

I begged and begged my parents to stop at Jane's house and let me say good-bye before we went to the airport. I felt I had to see her again. My mother eventually surrendered to my constant appeals, and my father pulled the car over in front of Jane's house.

Jane was waiting for me when I rushed in. She gave me a tender kiss and put her favorite soft blue sweater into my arms. Looking into her eyes at that moment, I believed she loved me as much as I loved her. As Jane held me tightly in her arms and cried, I felt as though she would never let me go. I could feel her heart was breaking. We promised each other we would be together again.

MINNIE

It was mid-March 1969 when I flew to New York City to live with my Aunt Minnie. She was my father's sister, ten years younger than him. My grandmother used to say I looked like Minnie when I was a child. When I arrived at the airport in New York City, my aunt was waiting for me. She smiled when she saw me and greeted me with a big hug. Minnie drove us to the home she lived in with her husband and her three sons. I was shown to a small room that would be mine.

My days with Minnie might have been fun if I had any capacity left for that. She took me out shopping for new clothes. I was able to walk barefoot everywhere. We went on long walks on Long Island beach and talked. The doctor I had seen shortly before leaving Illinois had prescribed Librium as a sedative for me. Minnie doled out a pill once a day. She admitted that she too had been prescribed Valium for depression.

I shared with Minnie my desire for her to be my mother, and she said she wished she could be. Minnie even talked to her husband and my parents, who said they were willing to let her adopt me. I wanted to stay there. I played with my young male cousins, sometimes playfully wrestling with them on the living room floor. My wrist stayed wrapped and covered to hide the fresh wounds that cried open when we roughhoused. Those little red mouths seemed to release for an instant the pressure of my agonizing despair.

I liked Minnie. We talked about many things going on in the world and at church. Minnie later told me I had influenced her to become more interested in women's value and rights at that time. My love for Jane was not a problem for Minnie. She listened to me and had much to share about her own life. She was wise and funny. We laughed together. I wanted to stay with her, but it was too late. I was already lost. An essential part of me had come apart and could not be retrieved. Not then.

By the time I got to New York I did not believe that my mother loved me. Her swings between emotional extremes or absence of emotional care had not imbued me with any confidence in her.

Years later, I found two letters written by my mother at that time. I can hear my mother's love and pain in the words she wrote in her letter to Minnie after I arrived. She encouraged Minnie to put me into a hospital saying I needed professional physical and mental help. She put into parentheses that I might even be pregnant or have V.D. My mother did not recount the incident that could have caused those occurrences. She confided in my aunt saying she didn't believe anything had ever made her and my father feel so miserable as I had over the last several months. My mother confessed to Minnie saying, "We feel that we have failed her completely as parents and yet are helpless to know what to do about it. We do love her and want to help her so much, but it sometimes seems so hopeless. Thank you so much for everything. Please let us hear from you soon."

My mother also wrote a letter to me saying "We miss you." Although she recounted that my younger brother was relieved to not be inflicted by my loud rock and roll music at night. "You know it is very difficult for people to help you unless you yourself want to be helped." She went on to suggest that my aunt and uncle might be able to get me into a good hospital. " I was hoping for a letter to let us know if you forgot to take anything else besides your duck. I will send the duck today or tomorrow. Be good. Love, Mom."

I look back at the child I was at that time and wonder what happened. Why had so many destructive events converged so quickly and thoroughly on my innocent life? My mother was telling me to let others help me, but I had too many experiences of why that wasn't in my best interest. My mother didn't know and couldn't understand that the people who were supposedly helping me were hurting me, including her and my father. Although my mother encouraged my aunt to take me to a doctor, I never did receive any medical attention for the violence that happened to me other than being sent to a different environment and given a sedative.

During that time of so much violation, it was Jane who touched me with love and compassion in her childlike way. She listened and cared even while she was going through her own chaos of immaturity. She was the only one I trusted to tell what I was thinking and feeling, but that trust had limits. I didn't tell her about my pain or about the sexual violations and violence happening during the time of our tryst. Even though she had contributed to it, I never blamed her. I was caught amidst my own confusion and shame.

My mother's intermittent affection encouraging my trust was fraught with danger. Many times, I experienced a betrayal after trusting my mother. I could be dazzled for a moment at the promise of her really being there for me and possibly understanding my struggle, only to be disappointed and frightened by repercussions from my father after she told on me in a disparaging way.

As an adult, I feel compassion for my mother's suffering then. She was forty-four years old, striving to do something in the face of so much harm happening to her newly adolescent daughter. She still thought I was the problem that needed to be fixed. My mother told my aunt that she and my father loved me, and I'm sure her letter to me implied it, but as a young teen, nothing she said to me could get in anymore. By the time I reached New York I had locked the door of my heart. I didn't trust my parents or other adults, with the exception of Minnie.

My childhood initiation into womanhood continued in New York City in the spring of 1969. One evening I sat down on a couch with my Aunt Minnie and told her that I had cut myself. I had slit a much deeper wound into my left wrist that night. We talked about what I was feeling. Minnie let me tell her about my pain and how I couldn't manage it anymore. I didn't know how to let it out. I wanted to die. She heard some of my story. I felt as though a desperate agony was swallowing me from inside. I was disappearing more and more every day. She listened compassionately and suggested it might be a good idea to put me in a hospital so I could begin to recover from my pain and so I would not harm myself. Then I could return to live with her. Minnie treated me with respect. She took me to Meadowbrook Hospital in Long Island, New York. I was admitted to their psychiatric unit. I came in at night after all the patients were already in bed.

On the hospital ward everything was stark and bright, with fluorescent lights reflecting off white walls, floor tile, and the nurses' uniforms. I was taken to a room with four beds and placed close to the door in a hospital bed with the railings lowered. Someone was crying loudly down the hall. I heard a woman's voice asking over and over for someone to come. "Please help me," she kept saying.

After listening to the woman crying for some time, I got up and went into a dark room where the voice was coming from. There was a woman in the shadows writhing in a bed. She saw me and stopped crying. She asked me to help her get up. She said she needed to go to the bathroom. I untied her wrists and her ankles from the restraining bands. It was difficult to untie her in the dark. I helped steady her as she pulled her legs around and set her feet on the cold tile. I walked with her into the bathroom and stayed outside of the door until she said she was done.

I helped her get back into bed where she took both of my hands into hers and looked into my eyes, pulling me close and giving me a kiss on my cheek. "You are my angel. Thank you," she said.

Soon a nurse came running in and began yelling at both of us. "Why did you untie her?" the nurse demanded of me.

"She was crying and needed to go to the bathroom." I told her.

"This woman is dangerous. She could have killed you!" the nurse scolded me. "Go back to your room. Get into your bed and stay there." I turned and exited the room while the nurse bent over to tie the woman down again. Right then, I knew the nurse was the one who was insane—not the woman she was tying down.

At fourteen years old, I was the youngest patient in the psychiatric ward in the hospital where Minnie had taken me. The next youngest was a fifteen-year-old girl who had flipped out on LSD. She didn't say much. An attractive woman with long thin brown hair had a bed across from mine. Deidre was twenty-one years old and addicted to heroin. She was detoxing and being treated with methadone. She explained what it was like for her. I listened to her story. Quietly as I lay on my bed, I scratched out my own story through poetry with a pen onto a small pad of paper. Sometimes I wrote while sitting on a bench in the hall. Writing helped me feel better. One afternoon a gym shoe came flying across from the other side of the hall where women sat in a row of chairs set against the wall. The shoe hit me in my neck. It startled me. I looked up to see an older woman with heavy-lidded eyes scowling. She yelled at me, "No children allowed in here. Get out!"

In the New York hospital, I was forced to take daily adult doses of 200 milligrams of Thorazine liquid from a small paper cup. My eyelids were weighted, my vision blurred, and my tongue became thick. I couldn't speak clearly. I struggled to see and to hold my head up enough to write. I closed one eye and squinted. After about three days, my body began to adjust to the drug and I functioned a little better. Women gathered in the day room at the end of the hall. That is where food was brought in for our meals.

I often sat next to a girl in her twenties who had dull eyes and didn't speak. I noticed she had yellow tartar-coated teeth. She sat silently for hours with her head hanging. I spoke to her every day. I'd tell her about whatever came into my mind as she sat there, maybe listening. I asked her questions, but she did not answer. Sometimes she seemed to acknowledge my presence as her head pulled back and her eyes re-focused. I felt safe around her. She seemed gentle and good. One of the other women in her twenties was a motorcycle momma who sat down next to me once to tell me about her wild adventures. She seemed rough on the outside but was kind to me. There were a lot of older ladies on the unit who would have nothing to do with me.

One day there was an encounter group therapy session. It happened in the day room, where two staff people, a man and a woman, came in and started yelling at people incarcerated there. They used an aggressive method to confront specific patients until they responded in a way the therapists thought they should. I watched this going on with great discomfort from the furthest place I could find to sit in that room.

Eventually the male therapist targeted me. "Why are you in here?" He yelled across the room at me. "Why did you cut your wrist?" What I noticed in previous exchanges was that there was no respect for women held there. Their lives were ridiculed and their pain minimized. Something was activated within me, and I automatically stood up when he shot his question at me and was positioning himself to knock down my response. His arrogant entitlement incensed me.

In a clear loud voice, I said, "I'm here for loving a woman, and I don't want to live in a world that doesn't allow me to love!"

The proud man was suddenly taken aback and paused for a moment, thinking. The silent girl I had been talking to every day was sitting close to his right side at a table. She raised her head and stood up out of her chair saying, "Leave her alone!" Nobody there had ever heard this woman talk before. It seemed like some kind of miracle. The therapy session ended abruptly.

I walked over and thanked the quiet girl for speaking up in my defense. She began talking more often with me after that incident. We had several long conversations. I listened to her stories and responded. She just needed someone to care in order to show up in her own life again.

At night, I comforted myself by holding my stuffed yellow duck that my mother had sent from Illinois. I wasn't allowed my own clothes or shoes in that hospital, but because I was so young they let me have my soft duck to cling to. One night they brought a woman in and tied her to a bed outside our room in the hall. She cried incessantly pleading constantly in a language I didn't understand but was told was Spanish. The nurses let her sleep untied after a few days, but she was still kept near the nurses' office in the hall, away from the other patients.

This woman with dark, curly, shoulder-length hair kept taking my duck. I tried to get it back from her. I went out and asked the nurse to help me. The nurse would wrestle the duck out of the woman's arms as she sobbed and cried long after it was taken away. I waited and then took my reclaimed duck into bed and curled myself up around it to sleep. After each successive theft, the duck began to feel less and less like it was mine. Each time the woman stole my duck I would go and try to retrieve it again with the same sad drama taking place. I asked the nurse if she knew what the woman was saying. The nurse told me she was crying for her children.

The next time the woman in the hall stole my duck, I told the nurse to let her keep it. The nurse spoke to her in Spanish. I could tell that the woman was extremely grateful. She said many words all strung together that I could not understand, but I saw in her eyes how happy she was.

My duck transformed in the care of that young mother. Using an ink pen, she wrote the names of each of her children onto its soft fuzzy body. She became quieter and more peaceful as she held onto the soft yellow stuffed animal. Her husband came to visit on a weekend and looked quizzically at the duck. She spoke to him and pointed at me. He smiled.

It seemed like I might get out of that hospital and go back to live with my aunt. They let me make a phone call, and, of course, my first call was to Jane. Our conversation had a potent effect on me that plummeted my emotions into an abyss. Something Jane said or maybe just the impact of hearing her voice after everything that had happened ricocheted around in my mind and tore deeply into my heart.

After my call to Jane, I suddenly found myself running to an edge inside of me and slipping off. Crouched in a corner of a room, I cradled myself with my own arms around my head while I cried. The staff didn't know how rare it was for me to cry at all or how important it was for me to get in touch with my feelings connected to what was happening in my life. It seemed that because of this behavior, someone in authority decided to transfer me to Elgin State

Hospital instead of releasing me back to my aunt. My parents had not been able to get me into the overcrowded Illinois state hospital when they had tried before, but Elgin accepted me when transferred from another mental hospital out of state. My parents were relieved to have found a possible solution.

My father flew to New York to return with me to Illinois, so they did not have to hire a security person to escort me from one hospital to another. At the time, my father told me he was taking me to a girls' school. Maybe he thought that lie would keep me from trying to run away. I was discharged from the New York City hospital after one week and flown to where the door was waiting to open into the separate world that was Elgin.

SHABBAT

Coming up for air after swimming in the steady flow of memories, I ponder how it was that I managed to rise up from such a destructive flood and transform myself and my life.

Is it possible that experiences in our lives cluster and create forms much the way droplets of water configure into clouds and are carried by the wind? Could it be that even our most destructive moments and their devastating results are part of some greater alignment and synchronicity?

This memoir has been cascading out of me since the Seder at Passover thirty days ago. As I write, the jaws of a giant machine have torn the road apart outside my building. Black asphalt has been ripped into pieces, dropped into open-backed trucks, and hauled away. Large ancient oak trees were chopped down in moments. Sidewalks were pulled apart and lifted up. Men with shovels reworked old ground. Gravel and new earth were brought in. A steamroller flattened the layers.

This house has been shaking and trembling as I remember what happened so long ago. Sometimes the noise and disruption interrupt my writing and I have to leave. Today they began to pave a new road. Can my path become new? As I dig up and release the past while assembling some meaning to it through these lines of black on white, will my new path of liberation come?

I recently attended the Shabbat morning service at the local synagogue with a Jewish friend who wanted to attend after a long time of non-involvement. I felt perfectly at home going with her. Although I was not raised in the Jewish religion, its influence has coincided with my life path. I grew up in a Jewish Italian neighborhood in New Jersey. At twelve years old, I read several moving memoirs written by Holocaust survivors. At fifteen years old, I read the complete history of the Jews and taught myself the Hebrew alphabet. I learned how to write with it. I purchased a large old wall clock with Hebrew letters instead of numbers that I use to this day. Jewish people have continually come into my life at significant times and are my dear friends.

All my life I have connected to a consistent spiritual thread running through many religious traditions I have been exposed to. Each experience contributes to who I am and how I live. I was happy for another opportunity to learn from the Jewish faith.

On that Shabbat, the rabbi launched into an extended discussion with the nine of us about the Jewish holidays and the traditional, mystical meanings they carry. He spoke about the first thirty-three days after Passover being a grieving time. The rabbi said a mystical transformation could occur during those days that would allow our deepest potentials to be liberated. We could then be free to accomplish our mission in life. A celebration of the new fruits occurs on the fiftieth day after Passover at Shavuot. It opens up a new time, the eighth day after the seven days of creation.

Then the rabbi apologized for having gone on about these details for so long with visitors in attendance. I was glad he had. It resonated with meaning for me and gave me hope for my own internal liberation. How have these past and present experiences connected together so perfectly at this particular time in my life? Synchronicities of internal and external events meld together producing a change in my consciousness and my life as a whole.

I see now how middle age shares similarities with adolescence, menopause with menarche. Here I am at the same doorway, but I am crossing through from a different direction. For women, this timing is marked by the blood tides of our menses flowing in and later ebbing out. Certain themes are experienced in adolescence that circle back around again during mid-life. Like a snake biting its own tail, the end and the beginning of a cycle overlap.

When I sense a familiar theme emerging, I trace back to where it began. A doorway of transformation opens when a cycle ends and a new one begins. The seeds that are planted grow into the next cycle of living, replicating their encoding. There is a space created during the changing eras of our lives, providing an opportunity to reconfigure the original code from earlier imprints. The promise of what might be possible is worth every effort to consciously sort and choose which seeds will be planted into the next cycle.

Even though it feels chaotic, choice and change are more readily available on these thresholds when the time of ending the old and beginning the new is separated by a profound *between time*. In the medicine wheel, this is the direction of the north, a place of wisdom and stillness.

A significant seed was planted within me when I hung onto the maple tree during a storm as a child. I was conscious of making an agreement about the direction of my life. I felt held by a spiritual presence that connected through the tree to the elements of the storm and to my time on earth. My spirit was willing. I felt joined with a larger pattern my life might flow through, a destiny I was on some level, choosing to say yes to. Saying yes with my soul's knowing of my life purpose was not translatable to my child-mind. I could not comprehend the magnitude of what I was agreeing to. At that time I imagined that I might be orphaned like a character in a Charles Dickens' novel. I thought I might be forced to become a pickpocket in order to survive. I knew on some level that a different and difficult road lay ahead of me. I was intrigued and willing to go, accepting the calling I intrinsically felt was mine.

At ten years old I began keeping a diary of my thoughts, feelings, and experiences, attempting to record and literally create a map of my journey in life. I did not play it safe while in the maple tree as the storm opened its fury. I went out on a limb to the furthest reach until I could experience something completely real beyond all that existed on the surface. My soul remembered my calling and enacted it in reference to and in preparation for what was to come.

Although in adolescence it seemed that I was in a maze with dead ends and darkness, my soul had agreed to a labyrinth, not a maze. There is a difference. If I could just keep going, I knew I would get through. It is true that my life has been laced by loss, and yet, I have also been extremely blessed and guided.

My dear friend Lonnie called the other day and began telling me how many people all over the world love and respect me. She said, "People entrust their lives and souls to your care. Do you realize how precious you are?" I listened as Lonnie's words rolled around in my head and neared falling into the hole that instantly negates compliments. But this time I heard her. I let it in.

"Oh Lonnie. You just said what I needed to hear and I let it into my heart. Thank you. I love you." Lonnie reminded me that I have become the catalyst of change for others that I needed in my early life. I work in the battlefield of suffering, fueled by a transcendent joy, coming from being willing to consistently listen to the voice of spirit guiding my path. I experience more harmony when I surrender to this presence, greater than myself.

As I reach back into the war zone of my adolescent self from midlife, I say yes again. Yes to my calling and yes to my teenager. I touch my hand to my heart and tell her, "You have survived and you will survive." Yet, paradoxically as I write these stories, I also see how a part of me died and did not survive. My life and self were eclipsed by something more formidable than my adolescent self could overcome or understand.

Death exists in life, side by side. In death with the surrender of self comes the possibility of transformation, something different than survival. This is my hope and why I am here taking all the courage I have to go back to this place when the door closed and my younger self could not get out. As an elder, I have become the tree; and although chaotic, this recent midlife storm of change has all the elements of creation that allow new life to spring forth.

You, my child, were not afraid of the storm while hanging onto that tree, believing in something Divine loving you. You kept a record of the journey. As an older woman, I must pass through my fear. How can I ever be completely whole if I disown or silence you, if I pretend you don't exist or try to edit, and mask your story? What is my worldly persona and accepted identity worth if I too cast you out? Together we tell the story as it emerges, trusting a symbolic map will become discernable from it. I follow the thread that held you back then, while weaving your experiences into the tapestry of my transforming life in the present.

As I write, what was once separated is reconnected in a circle. Nothing is ever really lost, only changed. What was hidden in shadow returns to light. This crucible of fire I enter holds an original wound that is not mine alone. I can understand how my life is an echo of a greater human wound that has been bleeding for thousands of years. What happened to my younger self carries the imprints of collective trauma.

Perhaps my soul chose such human experience so I could also embody a pathway out of repetitive suffering. If I am able to awaken and experience liberation in this woman body, surely, I can transmit that awakening to a larger realm of being. This becomes my offering, a ceremony from my heart.

Where are my deep resilient roots as I hold this inner child's unfolding story within me? They are right here. Right now. This is the moment when suffering becomes grace.

MIDLIFE PRAYER

We are all the ages we have ever lived.

Life spirals over decades from birth until seven times seven.

In midlife, we begin to spiral back, energetically re-experiencing and reviewing all we have lived until we arrive to zero, where birth and death are one.

May we embrace all of who we are with love as we spiral around the center of our miraculous being.

SUMMER

What occurred before I arrived at Elgin in early 1969 became locked inside me when I was locked away in the institution. I did not talk about it. My new situation in the hospital required all my attention. I was treading water to stay afloat while waiting for deliverance. As the days wore on, spring gradually became summer.

A big dark green bus arrived to take the children's units at Elgin State Hospital to Camp Big Timber in the town of Elgin. We piled into the bus and found our seats. Ann and I stayed close to each other. As usual, Ann seemed to be the expert on everything. She knew how long we would be there and what the camp was like. The whole experience was so foreign to me that it returns in patches like worn out movie film footage with images hardly discernable.

There were other wards at camp with us. I had a chance to get to know the girls on the Halloran ward better. They had their own social order over there. One group of older girls seemed to have more privileges and to receive special attention from others. Linda and Marilyn were part of that group.

I was immediately attracted to Marilyn. She had medium length wavy dark brown hair and golden brown eyes. Her stature was one of grace and strength, with a maturity that was unusual in that place. We looked at each other as though we both recognized something about the other but didn't say much at that time. We stayed involved in activities with the other kids we knew better, only occasionally glancing at one another.

I was getting to know a younger girl named Cindy from Halloran. She was quiet but hung around and stayed close to the group I was with. The boys were doing their best to interact with the girls but were watched closely by their adult male aides. Our aides sat at picnic tables, smoking and relaxing with each other.

John Johnson was a small, thin boy with black hair and dark soulful eyes. He came over to talk with Ann. They knew each other fairly well after having been in Elgin for more than a year. John was interested in the occult and gave

Ann information while I listened. He showed us two elaborate drawings of pyramids with symbols on them. He gave one drawing to Ann and one to me. John told us how to meditate on the picture, "Just look at it, then close your eyes and let images come." I folded up his drawing and placed it into my purse. Later, on the ward down by the OT room, I unfolded his drawing and stared deeply at it, letting my mind and eyes change focus. I saw a pyramid appear with a winged being above it. I sketched what I saw on a piece of paper. I began teaching myself how to meditate using the shape of the pyramid as a focal point. Eventually I found a peaceful state of silent stillness within me that I could go to regardless of what chaos was occurring in the daily life of the hospital. I didn't need a picture to focus on after discovering that inner space.

John tried teaching Ann and me about the practice of Satan worship, but I wasn't interested. Even though I felt God had abandoned me, I did not believe Satan was a solution. I let John know how I felt in a note I passed to him one morning. He continued to offer hand-drawn pictures to me. We developed a friendship.

Camp counselors helped organize activities. At lunchtime, they placed sandwiches on the picnic tables for us to eat. As everyone began sitting down, Ann jumped up, pointed and yelled, "Look!" Down a hill in the lake stood Sue up to her knees in water. She had the biggest smile on her open lips as her teeth were biting into a living, moving fish. Sue had managed to catch that fish out of the water with her hands and was eating it just like that, raw. An aide went down and stood by the edge of the water, trying to coax Sue out, but not quite sure how to get the fish away from her and not get bit.

There was something terrible and wonderful about Sue standing there so happily biting into that wriggling sparkling fish. In that moment, Sue seemed more alive than any of us as we sat in the shadow of the woods. In contrast to Sue, we were not really present with the natural world around us and unable to recognize our connection with it. Sue continued her private rapture with the water, the fish and the sun. The aide decided to let Sue eat the fish rather than risk a struggle.

"That's her lunch." The aide called back to us. Everyone laughed at Sue and talked about how disgusting her act was. I was silently fascinated. When dusk came, we piled into the hospital bus that drove us back to the institution each day from our summer outing.

Back on the ward at B-1-North the summer dragged on. The ward was terribly hot, since only a few windows could be cracked open at the bottom of the sill. Girls languished during the day and many lay on the cool linoleum floor to acquire some relief. Of course, we had all learned to pull ourselves up if the big metal door started to open. We could not be caught lying on the floor. Puri didn't care, but if any one of the other staff in authority saw us, we would be in trouble.

I spent a lot of time in the back alcove. I lay on the floor with my legs bent at the hip, leaning against the wall. It was cooler and quieter back there. Staring for hours at my own legs on the wall with my back against the floor, I began to wonder if I could reorganize my thoughts enough to slip through gravity's hold. After a while of sitting like that, the wall became the floor and the floor became the wall.

I became convinced that I could stand up and walk across the floor and touch the other wall that was actually the ceiling, if only I could believe it completely. Living inside this optical illusion kept me preoccupied for hours and days. I was training myself and my mind to perceive things differently than they appeared or what was accepted as real. I wondered if changing my beliefs could make other things in my unmanageable reality different. Perhaps I could become aligned with a more harmonious reality if I could shift the way my thoughts perceived my experiences.

I retained my sense of wonder about everything being composed of tiny invisible atoms that could be part of a body, a wall, or an atom bomb. If I could train my mind, I might move through the wall and out to the other side. I speculated that if I redirected the molecules of my own body to move in a certain way, they could pass through without disrupting the molecules of what obstructed me from freedom.

Another favorite pastime was picking at the peeling paint and plaster in the back alcove. When my fascination with perceptual shifts vanished, I'd sit up and begin a fanciful picking party on the wall. Heavy layers of two-toned pale puke-colored paint wrinkled and separated over a wide stretch of the wall. I pulled at it. If I carefully lifted an edge and ran my finger underneath as I drew it away, long pieces would slowly fall off. Enormous satisfaction came from separating this paint from the wall. I left the fragments on the floor as though they had come off by themselves. One of us swept and mopped the remnants away every morning after breakfast. Eventually a big piece of plaster fell off making it easier for the paint and other pieces of plaster around it to crumble. Girls noticed when we lined up by the big metal door waiting to go to the dining hall. They picked at it too. The aides yelled at them to stop or they'd be put on restriction. I enjoyed every moment I spent silently picking at the paint, helping the wall fall apart.

One hot afternoon I was lying with my legs resting on the wall on either side of a gaping hole. I was imagining the wall being the floor again. Doris suddenly appeared next to me. Generally I didn't have much to do with Doris if I could avoid her. Without saying a word, her hand quickly began reaching into my shorts and wiggling around in my underwear. Then she began pushing her heavy rounded body onto mine. Before I could fully register what was happening, I could feel the nail on her finger scratch me as it jammed sideways into my vagina. I was confused and afraid, but I stayed still and silent. I didn't want her to get angry because she was bigger than me and could be violent. After Doris grew disinterested and left, I got up. After that, I stopped hanging out in the back alcove alone.

Heddy, the masculine looking young girl who hung around Tracie and Doris, showed me her clitoris. Tracie told me Heddy had shown them and suggested I ask her for a look. One night after showers, Heddy pulled her nightgown up and leaned back on her bed in the big dorm. She wore skirts or dresses without underwear because of an injury that did not get better. I looked between her legs. Tracie said Heddy had a penis. It wasn't a penis. It was an enlargement of her clitoris as a result of her injury. Doris and Tracie gave her some kind of special honor because of this abnormality that had become her badge on the ward. I felt bad for Heddy showing me her private parts like she was a circus act. My curiosity overrode my concerns as I bent down to bed level to get a better look. "Wow, that's really something," I said as I moved closer to examine her big swollen organ sticking out between her small labia. Her clitoris had enlarged to about two inches long and nearly an inch wide. It was dark red. Tracie had wanted Heddy to stick it into her vagina, but it hurt Heddy too much to have it touched at all.

Heddy disappeared one day. We didn't see her again. I heard about her at dinner in the cafeteria. All of a sudden Tracie took her food tray and turned it over on top of Doris's head. The food was bad, but I didn't understand at first what was happening. Other girls walked up to Doris and threw their food at her. She sat there silently, offering no resistance to being hit. Still confused, I remembered that I'd seen black bugs in contrast with the cheese and noodles on our plates, but I wasn't about to throw it at Doris. I wasn't going to eat it either. Most of the time the girls would eat just about anything, especially those who didn't have money or access to the commissary. But it really wasn't about the food. It was about Heddy.

"That's for hurting Heddy," Tracie shouted at Doris. The aides just watched and didn't move. The whole cafeteria turned its attention to Doris sitting there with food dripping from her hair. She looked like she was starting to cry. I hadn't ever seen Doris cry or act so defenseless. Why would Tracie turn on her friend like that? Nothing was unusual in this place, but this seemed out of character.

Ann leaned over and told me that Heddy had gone to the hospital on the grounds to have an operation. Heddy's surgery involved a complete hysterectomy and clitorectomy. Tracie shouted close up into Doris' face, "Heddy will never be able to have children because of you!" Doris just sat there, still, with her spine especially straight against the back of her chair. She didn't say a word.

We didn't know why such a radical operation was performed on Heddy that day. Was it because of the damage done when Doris threw Heddy onto the metal arm of a chair? Ann said something about different doctors coming to examine Heddy to try and figure out what to do. She had an unusual injury. Their decision and action was irreversible. I felt sorry for Heddy. I wished I could talk to her and find out how she was and what had happened to her. But something about Heddy really scared me, so I rarely spoke with her, even when I might have.

Sexual violence seemed to have many ways of coming into a girl's life. What happened to Heddy was frightening. The whole situation changed me in some way. I didn't want to know that a girl could be taken apart by her friend, and the doctors who were supposedly there to help her. There was no one to trust in a situation like hers or in my own life. I didn't want to think about Heddy. No one mentioned her again. I redirected my thinking to romance. Romantic fantasy served as a powerful antidote for my fear and emotional pain.

Tracie called me to her bed almost every night. She expected me to sneak over and give her my attention. The aides ignored this activity. We kept it out of view whenever possible.

I was becoming more interested in Marilyn at Halloran. There was something about her that pulled at my attention. Tracie was friends with her. Marilyn had a depth and presence I wanted to understand. I tried to get to know her, but the opportunity to do so would have to wait. Marilyn was discharged that summer and left the hospital.

I had less contact with Jane. I continued to call and write her letters. I felt I would love her unceasingly and believed that she loved me too, but Jane had made a decision to be with a man. After I had given her a diamond ring and asked her to marry me, her boyfriend gave her a larger diamond ring. Tim was older than Jane and lived in Chicago. Jane spent most of her time with him and mentioned him each time I called her. I couldn't compete with Tim, but I continued to love Jane. She welcomed my attention and seemed to treasure any contact I made with her. Some part of me accepted that I would always get mixed messages from Jane. I received all the love she was able to give me while unsuccessfully attempting to deflect the feeling of not being quite good enough for her to completely love me. I once asked her if she would be with me if I had an operation to become a man. She thought that might work. After she said that, I became uncharacteristically angry with her, got up, and left. Even with Jane I knew I just wanted to be loved for who I was.

On B-1-North, Tracie introduced me to music by Laura Nyro. I asked my parents to buy me the album of her first songs produced in 1968. Tracie let me use her little portable black plastic record player. I lay the wide vinyl record with a central hole onto the spindle sticking up from the smaller flat round turntable. Moving the black plastic arm with its sharp stylus, I carefully let it rest into the first groove on the edge of the disk. The black spiral track atop the circular plate turned round and round, pulling the needle toward its center as it played the songs over and over through the little speaker into my hungry ears. Memorizing the words, I felt I understood their deeper, symbolic meaning. I was moved by the song, *And When I Die.*

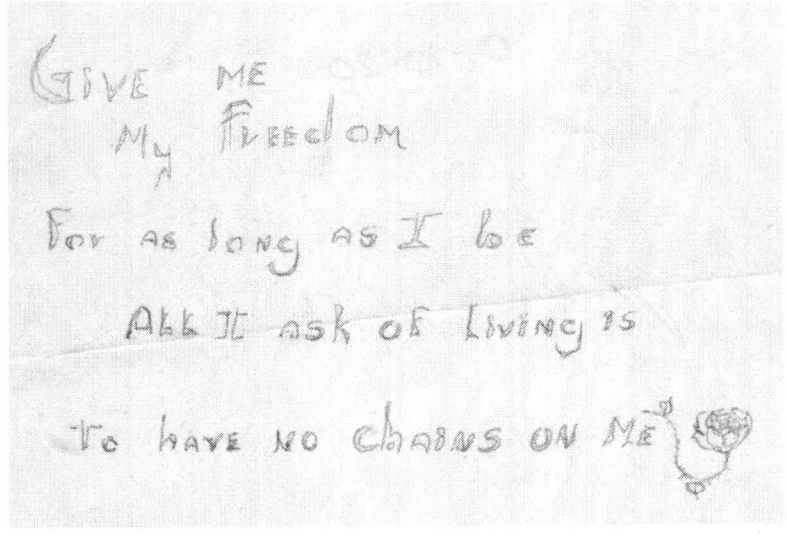

Drawing © 1969 by J. M. Seis

Laura Nyro's voice reached in and became part of my very breath, which made my miserable existence in Elgin more tolerable. I believed that she could understand my pain, my love, and longing. Laura's second album came out shortly after I acquired the first one. *Eli and the Thirteenth Confession* was even more validating to my poetic lover's soul that was aching in the ravages of a romance-driven young life. The song *Timer* became my daily anthem, while seductively symbolic *Emmie* brought images of forbidden love into radiant light. The lyrics transformed a cameo necklace my mother gave me into a symbol of strong, beautiful woman-oriented love.

In the dull summer of 1969, Laura Nyro became a source of life for me in the deadness of Elgin. One afternoon, I heard her voice singing from the TV across the hall from the big alcove. Walking closer, I stood in a trance watching her slow-moving body in sensual rhythm as her fingers danced gracefully across the keys of a grand piano. I had never seen such powerful sensual expression from a woman before. I felt as though she was making love to me through her songs. With every movement of her hands on the keyboard, my heart rose and expanded. She created a space for me, a tangible opening, allowing me to be. Laura swayed almost imperceptibly. Her dark black hair flowed elegantly over her white shoulders arising from her long black dress.

Roses opened their deep velvet petals as they stretched seductively from the vase perched on her piano. I could almost smell their sweet fragrance. The black and white TV screen metamorphosed into living color surrounding me. Laura's presence melted away the frozen grip of Elgin State Hospital. She sang me back together with the warmth of her exotic affection. Her lyrics gave validity and acceptability to the love I felt inside me. Nothing could have been more powerful in that moment.

Through her music, Laura gave me permission to love and be loved as a woman with a woman. Public broadcasting aired her performance live. Tracie knew about it and spoke to the aide who turned it on. My forlorn distressed self died and was reborn in those thirty minutes. Suddenly I had an anchor in the storm, a mentor through song. She was a real person who might understand me. Her music helped me understand myself. I began to realize it was okay to be a sexy, powerful, creative woman in the world.

In mid-summer of 1969 when I was eventually given permission to go on my first home visit, I began painting a portrait of Laura Nyro on a canvas-covered board. I hadn't used oil paints for a while. I pulled the board and paint out and mixed the colors to an exact hue. I studied Laura's face and body on the cover of her record album, trying to create a likeness of her image. My patience grew thin. It wasn't good enough. I tried harder and then put it away. After a while, I took it out and decided to paint her with no clothes on. Her breasts rose out of my imagination from the bottom of the canvas board. I hung the completed painting on the wall of my room in my parents' house. Laura's dark eyes followed me around my room. She seemed to be looking back. My brush strokes came together into an unconsciously projected image of Laura Nyro that had a dash of Puri and a hint of my mother and myself mixed in.

Laura's music helped me thread my way through a maze of loss and challenge. Ten months after I was admitted to Elgin State Hospital, I begged my parents to let me go to Laura Nyro's concert. It was unheard of to send a state mental institution patient to a pop music concert, but my persistence and persuasion, Puri's efforts, and my parents' eventual willingness, allowed this incredible feat to occur.

It might have seemed out of character, yet on a home visit, Saturday February 21st, 1970, my mother and father escorted me to the Civic Opera House in Chicago and attended the concert with me. I saw how hip and liberated the people in the audience were and felt ashamed for just a moment at being there with my uptight, conservative parents. Yet at the same time, I was grateful they were willing to make the experience possible. I felt happy to be a part of the creative loving spirit, even alongside my bewildered mother and disinterested father. The concert was like a religious experience that expanded me into a larger self, filled with love. It rekindled my exuberant soul-filled passion for life and helped me begin to see a world outside of Elgin.

I wrote letters to Laura Nyro, but I never got anything back from her. Every day I hoped she would write to me and maybe she did. Any letters addressed to me that were sent to Elgin State Hospital were intercepted and read by the nurse, Wertheim, and perhaps by Reynolds. They were either approved of and given to me or not. Any letters from Jane or friends on the outside were held and not given to me. Notes that I exchanged with Marilyn and other girls at Halloran could be discovered and forcibly taken away or found and removed from my hiding places. I had to be cunning and vigilant to maintain communications and express any of my deeper feelings.

I secretly mailed and exchanged letters and notes, but if anyone responded I could get in trouble. I was able to pass notes to some of the girls at Halloran when they walked by in the cafeteria. Other girls taught me how a piece of paper could be folded into a small triangle that fit into my palm. As the girls from Halloran walked by to put their trays into the opening in the wall near where our tables were situated, our hands would move quickly to pass whatever we held for the other. Most often these exchanges took place without the aides noticing or perhaps sometimes they just didn't care.

I told Tracie about my relationship with Jane. Tracie told me she wasn't interested in girls except for when she was locked up. She preferred boys on the outside. Even so, Tracie explained a lot about being a lesbian to me. She used the word "gay." I'd never heard that word used in that way before. I liked it better than the word lesbian that sounded more like some kind of scaly desert creature. I hadn't heard about Lesbos or Sappho yet, but I imagined myself "gay," as I carefully repeated the word out loud.

Tracie had friends in New York City who told her about a conflict with the police that took place the week before in June at a bar called Stonewall. I paid special attention to what she was saying. Tracie told me that gay people were fighting back against police attempting to arrest them. They fought for their right to be who they were and to love who they wanted to. This was exciting news. It gave me hope the way Laura Nyro's music did. It made me realize there was a possibility for me to be who I was in the world when I got out of Elgin. From that point on, I knew there were people out there like me. They were doing powerful things. I marveled at how those messages made it to me through all the barriers between Elgin State Hospital and the outside world. I was meant to hear of these warriors of love saying there was nothing wrong with us being who we are. I wanted and needed to find these people fighting for our right and freedom to love ourselves and one another.

I longed to go back to New York City. I contemplated running away from Elgin to join up with a gay group on the outside fighting for our rights. I desperately wanted to get out of the locked hospital ward I was being held in and be a part of that other more exciting world. I thought about how it might be possible for me to run away. I'd seen other girls run and some of them actually made it and didn't come back. Stacey ran away from summer school and her parents took her home.

Jane tried to see me at the hospital that summer. She came out with a boy and a girl from high school. I knew she was coming because I had called her from the pay phone. I could hardly contain myself. We had it all set up so that she would be there when I went on commissary pass, but contacting Jane had a dual effect on me. At first the call lifted my spirits to an extreme high. Later my mood plummeted into a most desperate depression. Suddenly I slammed my fist into my dorm room wall and bruised it badly the evening before she was to arrive. I thought it might be broken. My behavior became erratic. I lost my commissary privilege and fell deeper into pain within myself for having sabotaged our long-awaited rendezvous. I couldn't control my emotions that became devastating waves crashing inside me. I cut myself and hid the wounds.

Jane arrived at the hospital at our appointed time and waited. I saw her in the hall later when we walked through Center Building toward the dining hall. There she was. It meant everything to me that she would come all that way to see me. She was hanging out in a shadowed archway that led to other wards. We spotted each other, and she ran toward me to embrace. It was a slow motion moment with Jane running in my direction as I walked in the line of girls. The aide saw what was about to take place and began moving quickly to prevent contact and sever the encounter. Jane and I grabbed each other despite the aide's efforts and hugged each other tightly. As the aide pushed her away, I saw tears falling from the corners of her green eyes onto her high radiant cheeks. I was pulled to the front of the line of girls who were all suspended in rapt attention by what was taking place.

Down the hall we marched away from Jane who was standing there looking more helpless than I had ever seen her. I was struck by the love and sorrow she demonstrated. The risk she had taken to see me meant a lot. I got into trouble for that contact, but I didn't care. I sank into a fog that I could not get out of. It didn't matter what they said or did to me. Jane loved me. I could see and feel that it was real. Later when I had my session, Puri told me she had spoken with Jane in the hall and had invited her to come talk in her office. I was fascinated by the idea of Puri and Jane speaking to each other, yet found it hard to believe it had actually occurred. We were separated from each other for only a few months, but so much had occurred during that time.

Jane had become iconic to me, belonging to the separated era before I'd gone to New York City. I hadn't seen her for a couple of months that felt like years. Every night since I'd last seen her, I slept with the sweater she gave me. Somehow I managed to keep it out of the laundry and from being stolen. My parents must have brought it on an early visit. It still carried her scent during the first month at Elgin. Gradually the fragrance of her soft skin had worn away under the weight of more intrusive chemicals ambient there. I kept her sweater under my pillow, yet here was the real physical Jane from my previous existence. Seeing her brought the focus of my original romantic awakening into the world of Elgin, a world that had blurred and nearly extinguished my previous life. Jane and Puri together was a bizarre combination I couldn't fathom, even though Puri was telling me it was true. Had she really spoken with Jane? What did they say to each other? Had Jane actually come on our ward and into Puri's office? It felt like fiction, untenable realities.

Puri told me that she thought Jane had some pretty serious emotional problems and was completely unstable. She said she thought Jane needed hospitalization more than I did. What? In my mind Jane was perfect. I couldn't hear what Puri was telling me. As soon as she finished speaking those words, Puri returned to being an adult I did not trust or believe anymore. It was easier for me to turn against Puri than to see Jane in need of hospitalization. How could Jane or anyone else benefit from being where I was anyway? Puri must be crazy, I decided, just like the other adults telling me strange things and trying to control my life.

Tracie and Doris disappeared from the ward. The word was that they were discharged. I wasn't sure what they had done or what the procedure was to be released like that. One day they were there, and the next day they were gone. There was rarely much if any explanation for things that happened at the hospital. Tracie left me her small portable plastic record player and a higher status on the ward in her absence. New girls poured in. Those of us who had been there longer became the elders of the pack.

When I was first allowed to go on a home visit, it was not as exciting to me as the privilege seemed to other girls who did not have a home to visit. Ann was one of these girls since her mother was mentally ill and deemed unfit to be a caretaker for her two children.

Ann told me about the last foster home she was in, where the man in the couple came into her bedroom at night and began touching her. She relayed her experience to her social worker and was sent back to Elgin to be kept until they could find another foster home for her.

I could tell that Ann was more excited about my home visit than I was. She reminded me that I could do a lot of great things on the outside, like eating better food than we had in there. I would be able to take a bath and use a toilet in private. I could watch television in color.

My parents were as nervous as I was about my coming home for the weekend. They could hardly look at me when I got into the car. I felt like a stranger with them. We drove back to the suburbs and to the house that had once seemed so big when we moved there in 1967. Now the yellow split level home with white trim sitting at the end of a cul-de-sac seemed tiny and artificial.

Stepping into the house, I blinked and squinted my eyes. All color suddenly appeared terribly bright. Curtains on windows gave the impression of being foreign. I went up to my room at the top of the stairs. My mother had repainted the walls in my room and rearranged the furniture. It looked like a dollhouse room, all prettied up. It was for my mother's fantasy daughter, not me. There was almost nothing of me left in it. I pulled open the white louvered closet doors that ran along a track. They folded in half on either side of the opening, revealing bags and boxes from my previous life. I pulled down one white plastic bag and looked inside. A large stuffed monkey was all curled up in there. A flash of my childhood love of monkeys returned for just a moment as I gazed in at it and then pulled the ends of the bag closed and stuck it back onto the shelf above my hanging clothes. I began looking through my clothes and picking out what I wanted to take back with me. I laid the clothes on one of the twin beds in the room.

That was the high point of the weekend. Everything went downhill from there. My younger brother and sister said hello but acted afraid of me. My youngest brother who was just four years old was preoccupied playing in his room. Hurt and anger flew around that house like a hurricane everyone tried to ignore. I locked myself in the bathroom and took out a razor blade and began cutting words into my abdomen, P_A_I_N carved to the right of my pubic hair, J_A_N_E, to the left. A deep cut over where my ovary might be as a slice of anger toward being born female in a crazy, unfair world. Then at the closest possible level before my newly grown pubic hair the letters bled, F_R_E_E_D_O_M. Sharp lines continued to become words in blood that dripped out of a bottomless agony expressed from my left forearm, R_E_M_E_M_B_E_R.

I felt the pull to run over to Jane's house in the night but was disoriented by being in my old reality again. I didn't go. I cut myself instead, hungering for a love I could not find with my family or Jane. It had morphed into bottomless obsession and internalized rage. I still longed to be with Jane, yet was also filled with pain at the thought of seeing her again. Elements of what happened before I went to Elgin felt electrifying even though I did not think about actual incidents. I could feel their resonance on my return. My mother's paint could not obscure the violent emotional imprints on the cave wall of my devastated entry into adolescence.

My parents took me to church on Sunday. People looked at me with curiosity and disdain. I felt terribly out of place and suddenly couldn't wait to get back to Elgin. On the way, I asked to stop at a grocery store. My mother took me in while my father waited in the car. As I walked through the aisles, my mother seemed willing to buy each item I picked out and put into the cart. Pringles potato chips, cheese in an aerosol can, Ritz crackers, cookies, lots of cookies, candies, canned fish. Ann liked sardines. I picked out food I thought the other girls would like.

When my parents parked their car in the back of B-1-North and brought me to the door on the porch, my mother reached up and rang the bell. As I heard it ring, I felt anxious to get back inside and away from that whole situation. When the door opened, all the familiar sounds came echoing out. Magee, an older tall, thin aide welcomed me in. Almost every girl on the ward was crowded around the door to see me return. I carried in my sack with clothes and the bag of food. I said goodbye and gave a perfunctory hug to my mother and father, then gratefully heard the door of separation close and lock behind me. I had come home to a different family, or had I? Perhaps this was the moment of my becoming institutionalized after finding ways to survive and adapt to being inside.

I told Magee I had food to share with the girls. She opened up the room to the left of the aide's station, revealing a small kitchen. This was the first time I noticed that we had something vaguely similar to a home hidden behind a locked door on our ward. Putting that room to use helped to develop a warmer more hospitable facet to life on B-1-North.

I took the food out of the brown paper bag and put some away into the refrigerator. I placed packages on a shelf. Magee went into the aide's station to make a note with my name on it to place with the food. I made a plate of cheese and crackers, cookies, and candies, bringing it out with cans of soda. Most of the girls sat in the big alcove as I spread all the food onto the pink wooden table. Everyone was happy. It felt like a celebration to have me return with that cornucopia of food. We all sat together eating and talking. I asked what had happened while I was gone. There was perpetual news of incidents as well as comings and goings in Elgin. Amidst the chattering and high-spirited exchange, someone said, "Cindy is coming to our ward for a week." I could hardly believe what I had just heard. Cindy and I had been passing notes back and forth since summer camp. The fact that she was coming to live with us meant that we could be together!

It was rare to have any girl the staff thought I might be attracted to on B-1-North. Even new girls were whisked away just as we were getting to know each other. I had been placed in a small dorm with two beds in it to keep me away from the other girls who might be potential lovers. At first they placed me in the small dorm with Sue. I protested vehemently against this because Sue was within a foot of my bed. I wouldn't have any time to escape her biting attacks. I would be the only target in that small room and might never get a moment of rest. Appealing to the aides was useless, so I spoke with Puri. Sue was moved to the far dorm on the other side of the unit. Instead a tall, light brown-skinned, blue-eyed girl named Bertie was chosen to be my roommate. Apparently, their theory was that I wouldn't be romantically interested in a black girl.

The small dorm was a big step up. It was a special room because it was more private. It had a dresser with four drawers that sat against a wall by the side of the door. The little dorm room was across from the bathroom and had heat. The other dorms were not heated in the winter. I discovered that the misfortune of my being segregated had benefits.

When I first moved in, I noticed there were names carved on the wall by the foot of my bed. I looked closely and recognized Marilyn's name. Other girls I'd known of or heard about had stayed in that room too and left their mark. The wall was an archive of the lives of girls who had been where I was now. Using a safety pin and then a ballpoint pen, I scratched and then inked my name into the plaster on the wall alongside theirs.

PRESSURE

Visitors came into the institution. Dr. Vico brought in groups of men wearing suits and ties and women in proper dresses with hems that fell appropriately one inch below their knees. These groups of adults would come through the big metal door in the small back alcove and walk down the hall into the big alcove. Then they would huddle together in a closed, tight bubble looking out at us. We knew from the fear and horror that flashed in their eyes what we must look like to them.

The aides reminded us to behave ourselves and sit or stand when visitors arrived. There were some girls who sat rocking, mumbling, crying or yelling anyway because that was how it was there. It wasn't quiet, except for a few hours in the night.

Those of us who were angered and humiliated by being put on exhibition would sometimes act out on purpose. It was not uncommon for one or more of us to start making sounds and motions like we were monkeys in a zoo. Once Jeri came out of the bathroom with a string of tampons tied like a necklace around her neck and quietly snuck up behind the visiting group. As one woman began to turn around, Jeri jumped into the air and yelled, "Boo!" The visiting woman practically fainted. The rest of the visitors gasped and huddled closer together. It wasn't so funny when Jeri was tied down to a bed and given a shot of Thorazine. We thought she was brave and that her stunt was hilarious. We told the story over and over afterwards. It was worth punishment to mock the visitors. We felt light-hearted and empowered when we did. It was much better than being the miserable lost wretches we saw reflected in their fear-filled, pitying eyes.

The church ladies came once a month and sat down to visit with us. They brought us cookies. When there were holidays such as Christmas, they brought presents. None of us wanted to hear them talk about God, but we tolerated them because they treated us like human beings.

I had been fake-swallowing my medication every morning. We had to open our mouths and let the aides roll a pill in from a short, white pleated paper cup and then were given a cup of water to swallow it. Afterwards they checked under our pink tongues lifted in opened mouths to make sure we had actually swallowed the pill. Those pills made me so sleepy I couldn't even sit up in a chair during the day. I lay on the floor in the small back alcove along with Ann and another girl, unable to do anything until an aide would come back and yell at us to get up and get in line for lunch. After about a week of a miserably drugged struggle to function, I figured out how to hide the pill in the back of my mouth on the side of my tongue where it met my cheek. It was concealed perfectly so I could open my mouth and lift my tongue for the aide to examine. Over time I collected a stash of pills to overdose on.

The day I chose to take them turned out to be an unusual day. After I took the handful of pills in the morning, two aides gathered the more functioning girls together for an outing to town. I went with a group of girls and two aides to a movie theater on the outside. The movie was *Flowers for Algernon.*

I fought with the drug that was taking me under while I sat in the dark with Ann next to me watching the movie about a young "retarded" boy. Quietly I slumped down in my seat unconscious at one point. Ann shook me awake when it was time to go. I pushed myself to move my body and go with the group back to the hospital. After that, I began to throw the pills away, down the toilet.

Bertie continued to be my roommate. I considered it an odd choice to be assigned to a room with a girl considered homicidal when I was suicidal. Bertie was attractive and smart. She seemed fascinated by me and loved my clothes. We were about the same height and body type, so I let her wear some of them. She told me about her life. Her parents had separated and divorced. She and her brother watched her father come in one afternoon and murder their mother in the kitchen with a knife. Bertie lied, so I wasn't sure how much of what she told me was true. An aide later verified this part of her story. She lived with her grandmother until she began acting out violently toward other children at school. Bertie was light-skinned. Her mother had been white. She once got on her knees and begged me to be her friend even though she was black. That bothered me, and I wanted to make her get up and quit acting like that. I felt uncomfortable when she behaved that way. I told her I was her friend and didn't care what color she was.

Something was happening on the ward. Things were changing. There was constant drama and chaos going on. More girls were admitted than there was room for during the late summer. New girls were sleeping in beds brought in and put into the hall. There was a larger population of black girls on the ward that stayed for a longer time than usual. The aides were irritable with all the extra work to do. They couldn't keep track of everything that happened on the ward, yet they were responsible for it. Sometimes they would go into their office and close the door. We all got nervous and excited when that happened. It felt like a moment of freedom. At the same time, we knew they might come out and spring some new rules or a more difficult reality on us.

The girls in the far dorm sometimes stayed in their room during the day. A severely "retarded" girl was in a crib. Several of the other girls had epilepsy. One of them went into seizure on a sizzling afternoon, and both aides ran into the dorm to tie her down. Instead of helping as we often did, Ann looked at me with a glint of mischief in her eyes. Jeri ran over and without saying a word closed the door, trapping the only aides on the ward inside. The three of us sat down together with our backs pressed against the door and our feet firmly on the floor. Other girls noticed and came over to watch. We all began laughing about how funny it was to play this joke on the aides by turning the tables on them.

Pretty soon pressure came from the other side of the door. We pushed back. They pushed harder. Other girls came in closer and put their hands on the door and leaned their bodies against it. Seven or eight of us became one body of resistance locking the aides in that room with our joined effort, feeling powerful and connected to each other. These exhilarating feelings of power were fleeting. A litany of threats barraged the door from the other side, wedging into our fears and lodging within the part of us that was trained into submission. Ann and I looked at each other, then together we yelled, "Run!" The girls holding the door with their hands above us all took off running down the hall. They stopped after a while and turned around to gaze back innocently as the aides' burst of power forced the door all the way open. Jeri flew off sideways, spinning around on the floor behind the open door before jumping up. The aides knocked Ann and me off our feet as we tried to stand up and run. We fell face down as the aides tumbled on top of us, angry as hornets. Their eyes reflected the kind of fear all of us understood but were not used to seeing in them.

No amount of explaining could get us out of the trouble we were in. Wilson and Harris swore at us and grabbed us up off the floor fast as lightning. We were both taken to beds that they barked at other patients to push out into the hall. We were stung by shots of Thorazine and tied down to be an example to the other girls. They didn't say a word about their involvement. Neither did we. There was a brief time on the ward when silent solidarity spread among the girls who experienced being the ones to imprison the adults instead of the other way around. Later the aides calmed down and appeared to see us in a more favorable light again. Soon it was as though it had never happened. Ann and I returned to our dominant roles on the ward.

Then Ann went away. After a few weeks, she came back. She was excited when she left that she might have a new home and be discharged. I'm not sure what happened. Normally Ann and I told each other everything, but when Ann came back she didn't talk to me.

Over the preceding months, there were many times Ann and I discussed how to die in great detail. We both shared our accumulated experiences of trying and what we had learned from others. Ann always seemed to know more than I did about everything. "You can't die from cutting your wrists," she told me. "That's a myth. You have to cut up higher to get the artery, here," she pointed by pressing her finger into the white flesh of her forearm. "You'd have to practically cut all the way through your wrist to die, and it would take too long to bleed to death that way."

She told me that one of the adult patients on a ward above ours had jumped out of a window trying to kill himself. "He wasn't high enough," she said. "You have to jump from a level higher than three floors and grab your ankles so that when you hit the ground your neck breaks." These macabre conversations could go on for hours and brought both of us a sense of comfort and power. When we talked about suicide, we each felt understood by the other. Voicing our thoughts and feelings released pressure that helped us to not actually do it. We both needed to know that if life got bad enough, we could get out through death.

On a particularly sweltering summer evening, Ann screamed and smashed her arm through the window in the bathroom. It was a thick window with wire running through it. Her right hand and forearm had deep gashes and began bleeding profusely. She was taken off the ward to get stitches. When she was brought back, she was tied down in a bed with restraints in the hall. I could tell the way the aides tied her that they didn't really want to.

Ann had a close relationship of respect with most of the aides. They appeared to know something about what had happened to her while she was away. It was strange to see Ann being tied down like that. She appeared broken. It made me feel like crying. I hung around her bed, but she wasn't talking to me. She acted like she felt humiliated.

"Can you read to me from the bible?" Ann finally spoke. I was surprised by her request but went to my dorm and brought out a bible that Cindy had given to me with her love declared inside a front page. I was allowed to keep that bible. Cindy's message could be held there without suspicion.

Ann knew exactly the passage she wanted me to read. I began reading aloud to her, "...though I walk through the valley of the shadow of death, I will fear no evil..." Psalm 23

Ann was sitting in the main alcove a few days later. She was subdued and quiet. She didn't tell me why she threw her arm through that window or what happened when she went away. I didn't ask. Maybe she told Puri in her session.

Ann and I both stood quietly watching TV one morning. An aide had turned it on and was standing there alongside us. Other girls immediately gravitated toward the talking box of black and white pictures. We all hovered there in a cluster, suspended, not sure why we were looking at it. Normally the TV was not turned on until after dinner. Then a newscaster spoke. Apollo 11 was counting down to send some men to the moon. We watched the plume of combusted fuel pour out as the rocket flew high into the sky. A few days later we watched the TV again as Neil Armstrong stepped onto the grey powdery surface of the moon that Edwin Aldrin described as "magnificent desolation."

CHOICES

I knew nothing about being a victim, even though by this point in my young life I had experienced what could be considered victimization many times. In my own mind, I painted another story about myself. It was a rich narrative about choosing freedom and experiencing inevitable adventure. I was determined that love could eventually change anything and everything. I wanted a life like I saw in the movies, where I could overturn any obstacle and discover opportunity.

What did I really know about living in the world in the summer of 1969 at fourteen years old? Love and freedom was my credo, and it only strengthened when I became weighed down and more tangled in the bondage of seemingly endless complications. I was a poet, an artist, and a lover seeking my beloved in the disarray of shifting times and hidden societal landmines. I would not give up. I had to be free to live the truth of my love. I wanted to feel the fullness of life, to be outside in the park under the trees in the green grass on a summer day, not locked up in that stifling hot, airless mental hospital ward. I wanted choices.

RUNAWAY

Jeri ran away and then Bernice. We heard from the aides that they were apprehended. When they returned to the ward, they were tied down in the hall for a week and given shots of Thorazine for punishment. They each lay there in a bed as an example to the rest of us. I would stand by their beds and talk with them until yelled at by an aide. Jeri told me how great it had been to be on the outside again. Her smile was so bright despite her current lack of mobility. She talked about the fields she had run through and how she had hitched a ride to the town she was from to be with her friends.

Jeri had a beautiful voice. She played guitar and sang Bob Dylan's music as well as other folk songs. Jeri also wrote her own songs. The poetry of her music reflected her dreams, her anger, and her love of life. She wrote one song about living in Elgin. The girls would gather around when the aides gave Jeri her guitar and let her play. She was expressive and generally said exactly what was on her mind. When Jeri cried openly to be let up from the restraint bed, no one responded. She struggled and swore at the aides and the staff when they walked by. An angry cloud engulfed Jeri when they finally let her out of that bed. The whole ward felt like a pressure cooker with the lid about to blow off. It was hot since there was no air-conditioning. One solitary fan stood in the hallway, noisily pushing heat along the trapped corridor.

I decided to run away. I planned to go to Chicago and meet Jane there. I felt like I was a spring ready to fly out after being squeezed down too tight. I don't know exactly what I was thinking. I just decided to run one day. Jeri told me how to walk along the hospital grounds to an area where there were no security guards and then to cross over the fence. The highway was down that way, and I could get a ride to Chicago. I took a sweater, my commissary money, and make-up in my purse. I asked if any other girls wanted to go. At first no one did, but then Bernice said she would go with me. Bernice was the girl who ran away with Jeri and knew her way to Chicago. She lived on the South Side before coming to Elgin.

I figured out a time and a way to slip off and not be noticed by the aides for at least an hour. It would give us a running start. I walked along the buildings to an area I'd never been to before on the hospital grounds. I kept going the way Jeri told me to. I found a way out where there wasn't even a fence, just a road. It suddenly seemed so easy to walk out of there and into the world.

Bernice appeared on the road beside me a little later. She had come a different way. We slid down through some gravel from a viaduct and walked along the highway beneath it, getting farther away from the hospital grounds. "Which direction is Chicago?" I asked. Bernice pulled me across the highway and stuck her thumb out. She didn't say much but stayed close to me. Before long, a middle-aged white man with thin, greasy black hair picked us up in his dark green Chevy sedan. He was delighted to drive us to Chicago.

Off we went on a perfectly beautiful summer day, two runaway girls from a mental institution, one black, one white. The man driving the car began asking us all kinds of questions while he drove. I was looking out the window. I felt nervous and excited to be outside.

The older man took Bernice and me to his apartment. He was becoming more jumpy. He offered us both glasses of wine. We took them and drank. We sat on a couch with a window behind us. He gave us pornographic magazines to look at. I had not seen pictures like that before. Bernice pointed at one picture of a naked man and laughed. Flipping quickly through the pages, I stopped when I saw a picture of two women together. One of them had a fake penis strapped on her to stick into the other woman. I didn't understand why a woman would want to wear a penis. I hated penises. I didn't like how the women's eyes looked, but I turned the page, curious to see what else happened. Then I put the magazine down and went to the bathroom.

When I came back out, the nervous skinny old man was trying to seduce Bernice. He looked at me and made a feeble suggestion that we both have sex with him. Bernice picked up a wooden based candleholder from the corner table and threatened to knock the man's head off if he touched us. She told him to give us some money. The little man got scared and took out his wallet. His shaking hand held out a twenty-dollar bill. "More!" Bernice demanded.

"That's all I've got," he said turning his billfold inside out. "Please don't hurt me," he pleaded.

"Yo should be ashamed of yo sef hittin on us with your sorry old white ass," Bernice told him as she turned her back on him. We left his apartment. I looked back to see him sitting down cowering on his couch as she shut the door behind us. Bernice put the money he gave her into a small back pocket in her jeans. We hitchhiked to a park downtown next to Lake Michigan.

I could hardly believe we actually made it to Chicago. Bernice had known the way to get there and how to handle the man in the apartment. She was streetwise. I didn't know how I would have ever found my way to Chicago without her. At that moment, I felt grateful that she had decided to run away with me. I had gained the respect of the girls on the ward. Bernice showed that she was protective of me. Finally feeling somewhat safe, I let myself relax under a tree on a grassy hill in the park, the effect of the wine was making me sleepy. I could hear the sounds of people all around us. There were hippies with long hair dressed in cool colorful clothes, playing guitars and beating on bongo drums. Families and couples walked by. Finally I felt like I was part of life again.

I thought about what Tracie said before she left the hospital. She reminded me that there was a music festival happening in upstate New York. I couldn't remember when she said it was, but she was planning to go. My old boyfriend, Sam, had talked about the festival before I went into Elgin. Maybe I could connect with him and see if he was driving out there. If Jane wanted to go, we could go together. I longed for the joy and freedom of an outdoor music festival with an abundance of creative expression and love. I began feeling hopeful. There must be so many interesting people out there to meet. More possibilities seemed to open up as my mind drifted off. New York was the place I romanticized. It was where I wanted to live when I turned eighteen. What was the name of that festival? Where was it? Then I remembered Tracie said, "Woodstock." I wanted to try and get there. Then I would go live in New York City where I could be gay and free.

I must have momentarily drifted off while daydreaming under the tree. When I woke up, Bernice was sitting in the grass nearby talking with a man sitting across from her. I sat up but didn't have much to say. Feeling strangely disoriented, I remembered that I wanted to get to a telephone so I could call Jane and let her know where I was. We had discussed various ideas about finding a way to get together before I ran away. Jane might be able to pick me up. She sometimes stayed in Chicago with her boyfriend Tim. Maybe I could stay there with her. I'd met Tim. He didn't seem to mind Jane's undefined relationship with me. Maybe he didn't know how intimate it was, at least some of the time.

Bernice turned toward me and told me that this man was a friend of hers. He was going to let me use his phone and give us some food. I wasn't sure. He smiled and said he lived nearby. I looked around the park and thought about staying. Bernice continued to smile at the man talking to me in a friendly tone of voice. He and Bernice kept laughing. Everything appeared to be fine. Bernice assured me again that he was going to help us. It was okay. It seemed that she was telling the truth, so I got up and we walked into the city, out of the green.

We must have walked for at least a half hour. It was quite a few blocks away from the park when we finally arrived at a group of high rises with a chain link fence around them. Another man came up and spoke with Bernice and the friendly man from the park. He seemed like he was a friend too and rode up on the elevator with us. We got out and went into an apartment. I wanted to use the phone, but the new man said the phone didn't work there. He suggested that we could go to a different apartment and try using that phone. I told him I would wait for my friend before going anywhere and sat down on the couch. I turned my head around looking for Bernice. The new man sat down next to me. Bernice and the friendly man had disappeared somewhere further into the apartment. I was beginning to feel uncomfortable. The new man continued acting friendly with me, but I wasn't interested in what he was talking about. I could see his dark brown eyes looking at me as I looked away and out the sliding glass door.

Impatiently the new man grabbed me and dragged me into a bedroom. I struggled against him. "Let me go!" I cried, "Bernice, where are you?" The man's big rough hands started to pull my shorts down. I held them up, struggling with him. "No, I don't want to. Stop!" Then he hit my face with his open hand and said in a loud serious voice, with all friendliness gone, "Ya can make dis hard or easy; it's up ta ya." His eyes were a burning fury, a wasteland of deadly anger exposed. I knew he was stronger than I was as his arm cocked backward preparing to punch me. He wanted to get my shorts off. I froze. I couldn't figure out what to do. My body seemed to drain of vitality and become cardboard thin. He wrestled my underwear down, twisting my legs as he picked me up and threw me onto a bed. My head flew backwards. I noticed a window partially covered by a tattered dull cloth. Through a portion of the uncovered glass, I could see bricks from the face of another building next to the one I was in. Where was I? How could I get out? Where was Bernice? "Bernice!" His rough hand covered my mouth.

It suddenly seemed to become dark in the room where I lay. I could hardly see anything. A black oily cloud overtook my senses as my body separated into parts. The man pulled out his thick black-veined phallus from the opened zipper of his pants. I said something about the scabbed-over cuts on my abdomen with the words in dried blood facing toward him. I threw out a distraction uselessly to make him notice I was already wounded, so he shouldn't hurt me anymore. He didn't care. All that concerned him was jamming his overwhelming reality into my small, injured girl body. Grunting then breathing hard, faster he pounded his penis over and over into the small vagina that was no longer my own. I was trying to survive and get through it somehow. I could hardly think because my brain turned to white paste squeezing out of my head and disappearing. I brought my awareness back enough to think about how I could get out of there. He groaned and pulled himself out of me, rolling over on the bed. I didn't move.

I hurt. I felt torn open. I tried to get up but he held me down. It was quiet and still for a moment. Then I heard sounds. The man got up and went out of the room, fastening his pants as he left. I jumped toward my underwear and shorts, grabbing them off the floor, and pulled open the door to run out. I saw another man talking with the man who had just left the room. They both looked at me and then the first man quickly grabbed me, telling me to keep my mouth shut. His hand came over my mouth as I raised my voice anyway and told him to let me go. He did not let me go. "Where's my friend?" "Bernice!" I cried out. He grabbed hold of my arms, twisting them while walking me backwards, and roughly pushed me down on the bed. He left the room and closed the door behind him. The room grew darker. I heard more sounds, voices. I was only aware of one side of the room. The other side seemed to drop off into complete darkness in a kind of void or non-existence. There was only the left side of the room, the window, the dresser, and the door. That door opened and a new man came in.

This man didn't say anything I could understand; he mumbled while opening his pants and then came toward me. Pushing me down on the bed, he ripped into my vagina with his enlarged penis, pushing it back and forth until he was finished with me. There were more voices outside the door. Another man came in as the last one left. More of my brain squeezed out of my head. I fought to maintain enough consciousness to accommodate some possible strategy of escape. Another man came in, did what he wanted with me and left. I jumped up and tried to pull open the door, but it was being held on the other side.

A young man with a smaller stature came in and spoke to me. He portrayed a friendly face and smiled while meeting my eyes with his, asking how I was. It seemed totally absurd that he was trying to have a normal conversation with me. I felt like a caged animal. Fiery terror coursed through my veins. The small man tried to soothe me. Some part of my mind registered this. I looked at him.

"Help me get out of here." I pleaded.

"Cain't, he said.

"I need to go to the bathroom."

"They won let ya. They gonna use you as a decoy. You come from da suburbs, don't ya?" He asked. He went on to explain how they wanted me to go out to the suburbs and ring the doorbell at houses out there. Once the people inside opened the door the men would surprise them and push their way in so they could steal. He was trying to convince me to join their gang and do this willingly with them.

I listened and then repeated to him, "I need to go to the bathroom. Those men are hurting me. I need to get out of here. Please help me."

"Ya cain't leave." He went out and closed the door.

Another man came into the room. I was as still as a dead person. He left and another man came in. Sharp hoes dug into forbidden soil they believed held opportunity and access to a world they were denied. A part of me died over and over on that bed. After a while there was no me, just a body of female flesh being pounded by what seemed a sea of male bodies, penis after penis parading into that room.

The little man with a smile popped in between them to continue his bafflingly friendly conversation. Each time I begged him to let me go to the bathroom. I said I was going to wet the bed. That seemed to get his attention. He opened the door and held onto my arms from behind, not letting me go.

As I glanced back at the men gathered in the living room, he pushed me down the hall toward the bathroom. I noticed another door closed on my right. Something in me burst through the husk of my deadened body. I pulled my arm away from the little man and grabbed hold of the doorknob twisting it. I pushed the door open and saw Bernice in a darkened room on a bed with a man on top of her having sex. She seemed to be enjoying it. I yelled out to her, "Bernice! Don't you know what they're doing to me out here?"

The little man behind me pulled the doorknob out of my hand as he closed the door. I saw Bernice slowly turn her head out of her sex-glazed stupor and meet my eyes with a look of surprise. He pulled the door shut as he pushed me hastily into the bathroom.

"Ya shun't ave done that. You could git yourself hurt like that. Ya don't want ta git da brotha's mad at ya."

I was already hurt. I went into the bathroom and tried to shut the door. He wouldn't let me. Finally, he let the door be partly open while I tried to urinate into the toilet. My body was sand. I hurt from pressure in my bladder but could not seem to coordinate the function of urination. Eventually hot fluid burned through emptiness beneath me. I was taken back to the room and pushed into it. The door closed.

While I was in the hall, I'd noticed more men coming into the apartment through the door from the balcony, filling up the living room. The door opened. Another faceless dark-skinned man came into the bedroom, pulled his penis out of his pants, and shoved it into my vagina. The darkness of that room became a poisonous dust suffocating me.

The little man came in and again attempted to calm me down by saying that I would be allowed out soon. I pleaded with him to help get me out of there. Finally he said he would. Then he left and another man came in.

Each time the little man came, I would rise up out of the darkness and reach out for the shred of light he seemed to offer. "It's okay," he said. "Thay's jus one mo." The next man came in, and I disappeared somewhere outside of my body. Maybe this was the last one. I dangled precariously on a fragile hope of being let out so I could run away from there. Where was the rescuer, the hero who comes in the nick of time and sweeps the young girl out of the forbidding danger, returning her to a safe castle of dreams? I had fallen out of the movie. There was no rescuer for me, only terror and pain shattering any dream I might have.

After the man pulled himself off of what had become a lifeless girl's body, the little man came in. I got up. I thought he was going to help me get out of there, but instead he began to undo his pants, unbuckling a belt and zipping down his fly. "But I thought you were going to help me," I stammered as he pushed me back onto the bed.

"I have ta do dis," he muttered, his face no longer friendly. "We all gotta do it." His voice tumbled acidic words down onto my wounded flesh and psyche, "The brotha's want me to."

Frantic, I pleaded with him. "You could tell them that you did it and not hurt me." He looked at me and said, "But I've neva had a white girl before." With that, he pushed me back down on the bed and took out something I had not seen before. There appeared the most horrific phallic structure. It stuck out of his small hips like a sea monster. It was at least a foot long with a small tip that became wider and wider as it finally attached to his narrow torso. It looked to be four inches wide at the base, not even human. It was so ugly and frightening moving independently like a demon as he stood on his knees over me. I recoiled from him with my head all the way at the top of the bed bent against the headboard. As he pulled at my lower body forcing his gigantic organ into me, I cracked out of myself completely. All hope was lost.

Suddenly, I was up in the corner of the ceiling above the window looking down at a young girl in a wretched bed with a small man on top of her who had an unnaturally large penis that was pushing her womb into her stomach.

All at once, the searing pain ceased in that girl body and a subtle calm blew in as though from the window. I felt something loving enfold my unphysical self, hovering in the air. Some unexplainable divine presence brought my attention to the girl lying as though dead on that bed. Flung out of my physical self, I was seeing the luminescence of a human being in a strange juxtaposition of realities. An indescribable message was imparted, "The Goddess is being defiled." At the same time my essential self was being radiantly held and connected to everything.

In that moment, I was one with the dead while also realizing I was more than that brutalized adolescent girl. From that calm, still crack between the worlds, I saw all the babies, all the children, all the women, all the earth that had gone through something similar. I was no longer one girl with one identity in time. Who I was, until that moment, burst into a violently turning orb of life and death born out of generations of human suffering. That girl-child severed from her source and cast onto the cruel cross of creation's collision with itself, seemingly without recourse, was also plunged into an ineffable mystery that unraveled everything as it seemed to be.

The sound of a woman's voice sliced through the wall. Men's rumblings grew louder. Waves of noise from crashing and moving around suddenly came into the dark room through the closed door. The little man jumped up and pulled on his pants, quickly exiting the room while leaving the door ajar. Instinct jolted into my body while my consciousness was still reconstituting.

I jumped up in a flash, grabbed my shorts and underwear while running out of the room. My mind had repetitively rehearsed this scene and when the opportunity arrived, my body began acting quickly. I jumped into my clothes and began running. I saw a female figure standing in the kitchen. In the blur of my peripheral vision, I noticed her brown, rounded face with dark foreboding eyes and thick lips that began shouting, "What are you nigga's doin in here?" Her eyes caught mine for a second and widened, her mouth dropped open, soundless.

Instinctively sliding my feet into my sandals, I ran for the sliding glass door and down the metal fire escape stairs as fast as I could. I kept running and running on the sidewalk away, away, away. Then behind me, Bernice came running after me shouting, "Wait!"

"No," I said as I kept running until my lungs felt ready to collapse.

Bernice shouted towards me, "I didn't know what they was doin to ya."

Slowing my pace, I turned toward her as she ran alongside me. I looked into her coal black eyes that held a hint of brown sincerity. I was angry with her and exclaimed, "I left my purse there!"

"Come on back wit me, we'll git it." Bernice offered.

"No!" I repeated loudly, and kept walking away as fast as I could.

Bernice turned and ran back to the high-rise to retrieve my purse. Afterwards she told me she demanded the men give back the money that they stole from my purse. As she handed it to me, I could tell she thought that might make things better between us. She had caught up with me blocks away in a commercial area that had a hotdog stand. I went into the bathroom and put my hands into the cool, clear water running from a faucet, splashing some of it onto my face. I looked into the mirror at a reflection not sure what I was looking at anymore, trying to remember. Bernice came in and said she had ordered me a hotdog. I went out and looked at the dog in a bun in a red plastic basket and pushed it away. It looked like a penis. Bernice ate both of the hotdogs while I called Jane from a payphone. I waited.

Soon Jane arrived in a car driven by her father, not Tim. I went into the bathroom with Jane while her father waited. I started to cry, unable to explain anything. Jane held me and pressed her lips into my temple gently. As we walked out toward the car, she told me the police were looking for me and had contacted her parents. Bernice sat in the front seat with Jane's father, who drove her to her family's apartment on the South Side of Chicago. After she got out of the car, he talked about what a dangerous housing project it was. Then he drove us back up north to the suburbs.

I sat with Jane in the back seat of her father's car. Just being with her as her arms circled around me helped me exist in that moment. I rested my head on her shoulder. Only my head felt present. Everything else below it was absent, stolen. Over an hour passed before we arrived at my parents' house. I said goodbye to Jane as I turned from the car and walked into the little yellow house with white trim and drapes in the picture window. My parents shut the door with my girl body inside. They told me the police had come looking for me. The hospital called, checking to find out if I'd been found. My parents returned me to the institution the next morning.

Many years later, I learned that the hospital never told my parents about what had happened to me. (From my father's diaries). When I saw my medical records from that time, the dates of being treated with medication for my injuries didn't match the time period. There was no mention of my running away in my records. It was as though it never happened.

All the girls were standing around the porch door as they brought me in. No one was smiling. Bernice had been brought back the night before and was tied down in a bed out in the hall near the Ping-Pong table. She'd already been given a shot of Thorazine. The aides on the ward had me come sit in the aide's station. They shut the door behind me. Harris gave me my medication. I swallowed it.

The two aides in their simple pastel shifts with big pockets were talking back and forth to each other and then to me. I looked into Wilson's wide flat dark brown face, broad nose, and bright brown eyes, her hair in an Afro style. She smiled for a moment, exposing her right front tooth encased in a gold cap with white showing through a five-pointed star cut into it. Wilson was heavier and shorter than Harris, who stood a little taller than me and was slender with chin-length straight brown hair. Normally the two of them would joke with cutting humor and sarcasm toward the girls, but they were both dead serious as they turned toward me at that moment. "You could have been killed out there," Wilson said, scolding me. "Cabrini Green is a war zone. You don't know how lucky you are!"

I didn't feel lucky, and there was nothing green about the place I had been. I sat there silently looking up at them, knowing that there was a war out there that was much bigger and more devastating than anyone was talking about. Bernice had already been interrogated and must have confessed to what happened in Chicago. Harris told me I would lose my commissary pass for two weeks and pushed the door open to let me out. "You aren't going to tie me down and give me a shot?" I asked.

"No," Harris said. "You've been punished enough already."

"Punished?" I thought as I walked out of the aide's station and toward my little dorm room. Although it was unusual during the day, she opened the dorm door for me to enter. Is that what happened to me? I wondered as I made my way to my bed and sat down immersed in a cloud of emptiness.

After that day, I didn't see Bernice again. I heard that they shipped her off to the girls' detention center. I wondered if she was being punished for what happened to me.

PROMISE

After my return to Elgin, the emotional pain inside me was so great it nearly engulfed everything else. My physical pain was intense. I tried to forget that I had a lower half of my body. I resided in my head, but barely so. I didn't eat. I don't remember talking much with anyone, even Ann. I stayed quiet and kept to myself, doing all the usual routines of hospital life. Finally, one day the pain became so excruciating I couldn't block it out anymore. I found it especially difficult in the bathroom. There I would clench my fists, tears rolling involuntarily out of my eyes as my skin perspired. I forced back screaming. I withstood the pain for as long as I could until either I said something or someone else did. I was sent to "gyne."

Gyne was a terrible place where none of us ever wanted to go. It seemed more like a torture chamber from the Middle Ages than a doctor's office. At first all I had to do was urinate into a cup, but then they wanted to examine me. They drew blood. I left my body and came back to it later. I have no memory at all of the gynecological exam then or any other time at Elgin. It was much too frightening for me to be present for.

Days went by. The aide on the ward told me I had "Trick," a venereal disease they were going to give me a pill for. The pill was delivered in a white paper cup. I swallowed it with water and soon dropped down into an abominable-drugged illness, disoriented, nauseous, and dizzy. I couldn't walk. Ugly hallucinations darted in and around my bleeding awareness. I lay on the floor and then slowly moved to my bed when they opened the door that evening. Bits of me slipped away like splinters flying into the hall, straining down through the little black holes in the silver metal basin of the water fountain and between the tiles on the floor, crowding into other pieces of broken girls, lying restlessly there.

My session with Puri came. I sat in her office listlessly. She started talking about what was happening on the ward and about my home visits. They would be suspended. She said that I would be going back to school soon. I told her that I was feeling pain about what happened when I ran away. Usually Puri tried very patiently to coax me to express my frozen silenced feelings, but this time she interrupted me, quickly dismissing what happened as my own fault. I had brought the misfortune on myself and needed to change my behavior and follow the rules to prevent it from happening again. I didn't mention anything about my experience running away after that session. It all went underground. I flipped a switch inside my heart to make my brain forget anything had happened. Forget it! Instead I turned my attention to the activities and constant drama of the girls on our ward.

I quickly developed an infatuation with a new girl. Experiencing another romance was a relief. This girl captured all my attention, distracting me from other more painful thoughts and feelings. Ann and I resumed our talks about suicide and stayed current with all the happenings of life on the inside. We discussed who had just been admitted and what was going on at Halloran. Cindy wrote me love notes, and I wrote back to her. I sketched little drawings of flowers and sunshine next to poems I wrote for her. I suggested times when I thought I would be on commissary pass. We exchanged our notes in the dining hall every day. Our attempts to coordinate a meeting time at the commissary fell through.

The new girl I was infatuated with shunned me in some slight way. My fantasy crumbled as I internally collapsed into the reality of my true agony. Early one evening I felt the pressure building inside me. I sat rigidly in one of the metal-armed vinyl backed chairs, half aware of the blaring TV in front of me. Why shouldn't I lash out at others? I could learn to fight, be mean and tough, I pondered. As I sat there, I sank deeper and deeper into the chair and into my own malaise.

I heard a voice over my left shoulder and without even looking, spun around with my right fist forming an upper cut, landing right under a young girl's chin. Her head flew back as her eyes filled with shock, then fear and tears. I looked into her young face as I jumped up reaching out to her. "I'm sorry!" I cried out. I was sincerely regretful. "I didn't know what I was doing." I told her. I really didn't want to hurt her. She was one of the younger girls who looked up to me. I made a decision that day that I would not lash out at another person in anger again. I didn't want to be like that. I didn't like the person I had become in that moment. It wasn't me. The feeling of hitting someone was worse than how I'd been feeling before I struck her. Following my unexpected aggression, the young girl drank up my affectionate attention toward her. I let her have my esteemed seat in front of the TV and wandered back to my dorm.

Sometimes Ann and I would talk late into the night. I would sneak back to her dorm, the smallest of three connected dorms down the hall toward the big metal door. We could pretty much predict the timing of the night aide coming through with a flashlight. The oldest aide on our ward was Magee. She worked most nights. Magee had the most experience of any of the aides on our ward. She was tall, thin, and wrinkled. She had short wavy graying hair and laughed easily. Magee was tough. The girls knew there was no messing with her. She didn't waste her energy on manipulations, appeals, or attempts to outsmart her. Magee had worked at the institution since she was a young woman. She told us stories about the way it used to be there.

Sometimes in the evening Magee would sit back in one of those uncomfortable vinyl-covered metal chairs in the big alcove and light up one of her unfiltered Camel cigarettes. She'd pull a long drag off one end with her lips closed tight together and then exhale, slowly rolling smoke elegantly out of her lungs into the open air.

"In the old days when girls acted out, we used to tie them up in sheets and dunk em into tubs of ice cold water," she told us. "There weren't no drugs back then. We used water and electricity to shock the patients out of their emotions and settle em down."

Long ago, a younger Magee had entered the catacombs, walking through the tunnels that ran underneath the buildings. She told us that she had seen chains with cuffs hanging down from the walls. There were cages that humans had once been held captive in. I thought about those vacuous tunnels running underneath us. I was curious to explore them and see firsthand what was there. I knew there must be many stories that would never be told of the people who lived in the institution. Maybe I could discern the essence of those stories if I went down and witnessed the places they had been.

Magee told us that there were hundreds of bodies buried in the hospital cemetery and neighboring graveyards. They were the people who died in Elgin State Hospital and were never claimed by their families either for lack of money or disgrace. Who were they, I wondered? What happened to them? I wanted to know their stories.

Magee lit another cigarette and pulled in a long drag as more girls sat around the table in the big alcove to hear her tell us what she remembered. She said that before we were there, B-1-North had been used for unwed mothers. Underage pregnant girls would come in and give birth to their babies, out of sight from society. After they were born, their babies were given up for adoption, often forcibly. "Could they get out then?" asked one of the girls.

"Sometimes," Magee said with a flash of something unspoken running through her eyes. We looked at Magee quizzically.

"What happened to them?" Jeri demanded.

"Some of them girls are still here," Magee finally blurted out. She nodded with her head up toward the ceiling. "A couple of them are up on the ward above us." I wondered which of the old ladies we sometimes saw sitting out on the porch might have lost their babies and their minds.

Soon it was time for lights out. We all went to our dorms and got into bed. I stayed awake thinking about what Magee had told us. Waiting until stillness, I eventually crept out of my dorm and darted down the hall into the little dorm. This was a common occurrence. I would huddle between beds, sitting on the floor to quietly talk with Ann late into the night. If I heard the sound of an aide, I would duck under Ann's bed. I didn't want Magee to catch me in Ann's room. It was against the rules for me to be out of my bed at night, except to go to the bathroom. I knew if I was found in Ann's dorm, my punishment would not be as severe as when they found me in one of the other dorms. The aides did not take kindly to my romantic attempts in the dark.

If discovered, I would be put on restriction, and whoever the girl was, and no matter what had actually been happening, that girl would soon be sent away somewhere else. The other girls were usually sent to Halloran. I stayed on B-1-North because it was the most restricted, locked down ward. They thought they could control me there. I had learned to move with lightning speed and absolute silence. If I even heard a tiny sound, I'd be back in my dorm instantly. Sometimes I would stuff my bed to look like I was in it and then hide under a bed in another dorm when the flashlights scanned over to count heads. It all worked out fine unless someone told on me.

My emotions stayed hidden most of the time. I was stoic yet unceasingly romantic. I loved sharing my affection with Cindy and with Jane or other girls I attempted to get to know. I thought I could love almost any girl and see the best in her. Romantic attractions were the only outlet for my emotions, while hidden anger and pain built up pressure inside me. I ignored and denied those uncomfortable feelings as long as possible, but eventually they would break the surface. Then I would look for some way to change or hide them. Often unmanageable pain caused me to lose hope that love could ever make a difference. Agony awakened from its love-drugged sleep. I needed to stop the pain. I could not allow myself to feel the true nature of my sorrows or the desperate situation of my life. Soon after I ran away, death beckoned as a shadowy lover.

Since I rarely slept, I was familiar with the cycles of flashlights shining into dorms at night. It would be about an hour before the first head count when the aide called lights out and then about two hours before the next bed check. I made a plan one night. Magee called out for all the girls to get into bed. The lights were turned off. I was already in bed. I lay there with a brand new thin steel razor blade poised between my fingers. That forbidden object had been taped under a drawer in a dresser in my dorm. I heard Magee trying to get a couple of girls out of the big alcove and into the beds of their assigned dorm. I waited until I heard Bertie's breathing change, signaling that she was asleep in her bed next to mine. When Magee made her rounds and shone her flashlight over our beds, I stayed completely still. Then she went down the hall to the other dorms. After that she went back into the aide's station. The lower half of that door creaked when it opened or closed. The smell of fresh cigarette smoke was vaguely present in the air. There was a little black and white TV with a telescoping aluminum antenna in there. I could hear it being turned on.

I made a tent with my knees to hold the sheet up above me. Then I moved my right arm with the razor blade held in my right hand to a position over my left forearm. Ann and I had talked about methods of suicide often. I'd rehearsed the movement. Now was the time. But, I thought, maybe I should make a vertical practice cut along my forearm, before I did the long horizontal one, so I could figure out how deep the razor would cut. Holding tightly to the slip of steel between my fingers, I moved it a little lower down from the inside of my elbow, feeling the sharp edge touch my skin. It was completely dark under the covers. I couldn't see. My hand tensed, holding the blade as my right arm moved in one swift motion down toward my hand. I didn't feel anything. I wondered if I had cut myself at all. Then I felt warm liquid beneath my left arm. My knees dropped down as I realized that the blade must be sharp enough to cut a fatal wound. But I didn't move. I stayed still and quiet. I had two hours. I knew that I could cut a deeper wound into my arm and still bleed to death before anyone found me, but my arm was bleeding. Maybe it was enough. My right arm felt heavy. I was not ready to make another incision. I decided to rest.

I couldn't tell what condition I was in and didn't want to get up and go out into the hall to look. I lay there still, quietly drifting off, my body porous in the night's embrace.

Then I heard a woman's voice call out, "Get up!" I opened my eyes, and for a moment I thought I saw a tall shadowy woman with long dark hair standing between the foot of my bed and the door. The voice sounded familiar. I strained to see who it was. Nothing was visible. I drifted off again into a sucking void siphoning off my life force. "Get up!" A woman's voice spoke even louder. I opened my eyes and looked around. Bertie was still asleep in the bed next to me. Everything was still. I drifted off. Again, this time so loud it sounded like someone was shouting right into my ear, "GET UP!" Automatically I pulled both sheets around my body, dragging them with me as I got up out of the bed. Walking flat-footed and stiff like a zombie who had just been ordered by its maker to move, I stumbled out into the hall and stood there for a moment blinking in the subdued light.

Pulling the sheets more closely around me, I shuffled over and stood in front of the aide's station. There Magee sat behind the big wooden desk with her cigarette dangling between her fingers, while watching the little TV set off to the side. She turned her head slowly toward me while her right eyebrow descended lower toward her green eye. "Magee," I started. "I did something."

"Wha'd ya do?" she asked me, beginning to stand up from the desk.

"I cut myself," I answered. I hadn't seen my arm yet.

Magee came around from the back of the desk and opened the lower half door and told me to come in and show her. I opened up my cloak of sheets and let my left arm come into the light. A long gaping wound in the flesh of my forearm hung open. Blood was spurting out rhythmically from the crevice.

Magee and I both stared at the red fountain shooting out of my arm as the blood-soaked sheets formed a crimson and white gown framing my rigid body. At that moment, Magee looked as though she might pass out. I stood still and felt a wave of dizziness and nausea hit me. Finally, Magee grabbed a towel from the counter under the cabinet and applied pressure to my wound. She sat me down in a chair in the office by the door. Grabbing my right hand and placing it on top of the towel on my left arm, she ordered me, "Hold that down hard!" Hurriedly she opened the locked cabinet and began pushing things around, looking for something.

Turning toward the desk, Magee reached over and picked up the big heavy black phone receiver and dialed the round plate with holes over the numbers on the telephone base. She called over to Halloran ward. I heard her ask one of the aides to come over and help her. "Bring a tourniquet," she said, "and call a doctor!" After hanging up the phone receiver onto the base with a bang, Magee walked over to me. She continued to put pressure on my arm as we waited for the other aide to arrive with a tourniquet. More blood seeped down onto the sheet.

After a period of time an aide I wasn't familiar with arrived on our ward. As she came through the big metal door, girls began to stir from their sleep. When the aide from Halloran got to the office, Magee told her to come in and close the door behind her. "Lock it," she stated flatly. "Did you find a doctor?"

"No," the aide said. "All the doctors have gone home for the night."

The other aide took my arm and pulled a rubber tube around it and tied it. Magee was back on the phone trying to reach a doctor. Finally, Magee spoke with someone and hung up the phone. "He's on his way," she said and came back over to where I was sitting. We waited for what seemed like an hour. The girls were milling around outside the door. We could hear them talking and trying to figure out what was going on. "Hey, Jan's not out here." I heard one of them say. "What are you doing to Jan in there?" Ann and Jeri's voices shouted through the closed door. I heard the doorknob turn while the lock held it in place. Someone's fist banged on the door.

Magee yelled back threats. "Go to your dorms and git into your beds, or ya'll be put on restriction!"

Eventually a doctor arrived. The aides opened the door to the office and a pudgy, dark-haired, balding man entered. He was angry. "I had to get up out of bed and come in for this?" He looked at me with cold eyes. "Show me what she did." Magee pulled away the towel she was holding on top of the wound. The doctor examined it. I looked and then looked away. I could see the inside of my arm. There was a layer of fat exposed over muscle with veins and an artery severed.

I could hear the girl's voices on the ward getting louder. "What are you doing to Jan in there?" They continued to yell out.

We heard loud banging and crashing as girls began throwing chairs against the door. They turned over the table in the alcove. A riot broke out on the ward, with screaming and yelling and every piece of furniture thrown against the walls and the door. The doctor told the aides to get some things out of the cabinet. He looked at what they offered him and said, "That's all you have?" He began swearing. The Halloran aide opened the office door out into the wide eyes of all the girls who suddenly stopped what they were doing and stared at us. The doctor led the way as the two women brought me out of the aide's station into the room next to it.

I wanted to scream at the girls to stop looking at me. I felt humiliated as their eyes followed me into the room being unlocked by Magee's key. The door opened and the doctor went in, then Magee took me inside and closed the door. The other aide stayed out in the hall directing the girls to clean up the mess they'd made and go back to bed before she left the ward to return to Halloran. I was told to lie down on an examining table in the small room next to the aides' station.

"Give me your arm," the doctor demanded and then began pouring cold liquid over my wounded arm, wiping around the cut with a cloth. I thought I smelled rubbing alcohol.

"Look at me," Magee ordered firmly. I turned my head toward her on my right. She took my hand into both of her hands and held it tightly. "Just look into my eyes," she said as she locked her eyes with mine. "Don't think about anything else right now."

"What a no good, crazy girl, wasting my time like this!" The doctor continued to swear and complain. I don't know if he gave me a shot or not. I could feel the piercing of the needle and the line of thread being pulled through my skin over and over again. He only sewed together the top layer of skin to close the wound in my left arm. I later learned that in an ideal situation I should have had the inside of the wound closed up first, then the surface.

That wound didn't heal properly, coming apart in the weeks that followed the removal of the stitches. It refused to hide its red open-mouthed scar. An infusion of blood might have helped my body's long effort to replace the amount of blood and vitality lost that evening. At that point, in my young life, I didn't know I had value or was worth saving.

None of the danger and pain mattered to me as I stared into Magee's strong, unwavering eyes holding mine. I was seeing her seeing me in my pain, and that made it less. It didn't matter anymore what the doctor was saying or doing to my body or what effect it might have. Magee was seeing me. She was lifting me up with her eyes. I felt the touch of deep caring reach from inside her heart into mine. That tender-strong connection with an adult woman began to awaken my grieving heart. One drop of real compassion was all the medicine I needed in order to begin recovering from a wound my arm was screaming about, a wound much deeper than flesh. Magee's eyes had locked onto a part of me worth redeeming. It felt as though something inside me might be good.

After the doctor left, Magee walked me out of the side office. She helped steady me, holding my right arm and hand. We carefully walked back to my dorm room. The aide from Halloran must have cleaned up the bloodied sheet and remade my bed. Before Magee let me go to my bed, she stood in the doorframe and looked at me quietly, pausing. "You must promise me you will never do this again. Promise me," she said firmly.

I looked into her piecing green eyes and responded, "I promise." I kept my promise to Magee.

PILGRIMAGE

Three months have passed since I began unraveling this story locked inside me. Writing about what happened to me when I ran away from Elgin shook me to my core. I cried with my whole body after listening to the child within me tell her story in such detail. After having completed menopause years earlier, it was a shock to find I was bleeding as though I had suddenly regained my menses. The power of my body to tell the truth was breathtaking. I needed to set down that early violent experience but wasn't sure how. Some part of me knew I had to transform the energies I had inadvertently become bonded to. It was hard for me to realize that I was still carrying a great burden, not aware that it wasn't mine.

I needed a break. For many years I have been teaching classes and workshops on spiritual healing, rooted in our relationship with the earth. My life is deeply involved in healing practices passed down from the people of the earth. During this time I shifted my awareness out of the past back to my present responsibilities.

I took a group of my students, along with a friend who is a medicine woman from Chile, and two of her students, to sacred sites in Peru and Bolivia. It is an annual pilgrimage I carefully plan each year, preparing a journey to engage in ceremonies of personal and shared intention. Local medicine men and women offer their powerful connection to the earth and spirit. Each year is uniquely potent and perfect for those who feel inspired to come. Seeds of healing and awakening that are planted on our journey continue to gestate, sprout, and bear fruit long after the initial experience.

Before dawn on our second day at Machu Picchu, José led us, as he has each year, to a crystal cave overlooking an Apu called Putukusi. Apu is a Quechua word for mountain spirit. Quechua is the spoken language of the original people of Peru. Putukusi is a smaller mountain facing Machu Picchu across from the zigzag road of constant buses carrying tourists up and down the mountain. At a certain time of day, I've noticed the play of light and shadow reveals a hummingbird image along one whole side of the mountain. "Look there," José pointed out. "You see the river at the bottom of Putukusi?"

"Yes, I see."

"That river runs all the way around the mountain. Putukusi is a feminine Apu because she is encircled by water. Come over here to this rock outcropping." José walked over and straddled the natural curvature of the giant boulder reaching over the edge and pointing toward Putukusi. He sat there a while in silence, and then got up. "Now you." I climbed up onto the back of the ancient altar. I put my arms around the narrowing neck of the stone as it jutted out in front of me over the edge of the mountain, hiking up my legs around either side of the wide girth beneath me. I leaned down, holding tight. "Close your eyes. Let go." José whispered. I did and felt as though my whole body was flying.

José quietly went over to set up the cave area with colorful textiles and sacred objects used for ceremonies. Keeping my eyes closed, I held onto the stone and felt myself flying into majestic inner space, while feeling connected to everything on earth. I sensed the ancestors' support and encouragement surrounding me. As solar rays reached up over families of vertical mountain peaks crowning the new day, a rush washed through my whole body from crown to root. Undulations accompanied a brilliance of inner joy. It was as though the entire earth had expanded into me, allowing all the physical, sexual, and emotional violence that had occurred to my younger body to change form. In an instant, I felt suffering melt away. Old stuck, heavy energies flowed out. The sacred earth reclaimed what was never mine, while returning me to what I could never lose–my infinite self.

My eyes snapped open. I stared into the heart of Putukusi that seemed to have a lavender tinge to her greenery. I had not taken any plant medicines to achieve this state. Something incredible had taken place. It was a free gift.

A week later my group and I journeyed south to Bolivia where we stopped at the exquisite Basilica of Our Lady of Copacabana. We were taken inside to see the altar of the Virgen de la Candelaria. There was a curtain drawn over the glass enclosure central to the ornate golden altar covering the expansive wall. This manifestation of the Divine Feminine as a Great Mother Archetype stands facing the congregants during mass. Our guide led us out, around and up a stairway to a small, simple chapel behind the large one. As I walked into that quiet room, I saw the Virgen de la Candelaria, facing the direction of Lake Titicaca, as is the tradition since her image was first created by Francisco Tito Yupanqui, a descendent of an Incan ruler. The Marian image of the Blessed Mother first arrived in Copacabana on February 2nd, 1583. There she stood dressed in a golden white gown, holding a basket and baton in her right hand and a happy Jesus doll-child in her left.

Our guide went away and left us to our own experiences. Soon after being with the golden enshrined Virgin, we wandered back to the ground level outside the basilica. I had heard about the Dark Madonna of Copacabana and began searching for her shrine. While walking around to the back of the building, a small group of us came upon a blind beggar woman seated on the ground in front of a narrow open doorway. Something in me knew that this old woman was also an aspect of the Dark Madonna sitting on the threshold of her altar. Before entering, we knelt down and offered her gifts that we brought with us, including some paper money. The old woman gratefully accepted our offerings mumbling prayers in Aymara, her native language. We moved towards the shadowy entrance behind her.

Immediately I sensed a shift as I stepped into the cool darkness of that narrow cement hallway leading toward an enclosed, lighted glass shrine. As we walked toward the plain wooden plank tables where dozens of small white candles were burning, I noticed prayers and the names of loved ones written all over the walls. When we reached the tables, I saw that many of the candles had burned down into solid rivers of comingled wax. My friends and I each took time for our prayers and lit the candles we brought. After this, I stood for quite a while in front of the altar of the Dark Madonna.

This Dark Mother at street level was different from the Mother of Light, far above where humans live. In the place of worship above us, our eyes had to look up to grasp a glimpse of the Virgen de la Candelaria in her high altar. Conversely, the Dark Madonna was hidden away in the bowels of the same building. She stood at eye level with dark wavy hair, dark skin, and fierce eyes. Her gown was red and gold. She held up a sharp sword in her right hand. Her left arm was missing. Instead a baby Jesus-doll emerged sideways from her armpit area, out of the folds of her gown. This was the more accessible Madonna people came to with their prayers and offerings, asking for healing and help. She stands facing the people, as an untamed, compassionate mother on the edge of Lake Titicaca, a place known as the birthplace of humanity in Incan lore.

The symbolism of these very different shrines portrays the dichotomy of a once whole Goddess, a Great Mother, reflected now in women's lives and in our relationship with our bodies and the earth. She is split as I am as a woman.

The Dark Mother had a sword. Swords often denote cutting the false from the true. She was missing her left arm. In this way, she typifies how dismemberment can happen to women. My own scarred left arm expresses the wounding of and healing from the war I went through as a young girl. Incest, sexual abuse and violence on any level can cut parts of the whole authentic self away, leaving phantoms of self that are perpetually haunting the greater self. These ghosts are trying to tell their truths and come home.

The light and the dark as separate mother archetypes express an important universal principle about our underlying beliefs. The virgin and the whore, the good and the bad are telling their stories through the shadow of our unconscious. This duality shows up in how we express the divine and denigrated feminine in our relationship with ourselves, others and our concept of deity. These figments of our collective ghosts can divide or unify us. Consciously accepting our light and dark can begin a process of integration and wholeness.

When I entered adolescence, I was radiant with the fire of puberty's powerful, creative mysteries. Religious influences and the lack of crucial information made me ill-equipped to handle the challenges I faced. I was too innocent to understand the significance of the sword of sexual conquest being thrust into my budding womanhood, plundering treasures I had not yet learned to value or protect. I could not know then how it split me into light and dark parts, causing them to operate independently of each other while inhabiting the same house of self. In the midst of such dualism, good and evil warred within me trying to gain prominence.

My experiences at Elgin plunged me into aspects of humanity hidden in darkness, where the gap between being valued and being expendable became glaring. The sacred site of the light and the dark Madonna's in Bolivia made possible a change in my awareness, joining opposites within my beliefs and in my concept of myself. I remembered what I always knew deep within me.

Later we stayed on the Island of the Sun, after visiting the ancient temple of Witacocha. We hiked down the vertical mountain on its crisscross paths toward the water where our boat was waiting. Several of us walked along the shore and around boulders where we created a safe and sacred way to offer ourselves in ceremony into the holy grail of the highest, largest body of water on earth. I consciously shed all my earthly presentations, my roles held symbolically by my clothing. Then stepping carefully and consciously, I completely immersed myself naked into the sparkling cold waters of Lake Titicaca. In her watery embrace, I felt myself sun-kissed and blessed by the pristine waters. I experienced purification and rebirth as a woman willing to embrace both my dark and light. The split between my inner selves was bathed and illuminated into awakening harmony.

We had a full itinerary of many experiences that culminated at Tiwanaku, the most ancient sacred site currently known in the Americas near the southernmost point of Lake Titicaca. Our ceremony with a Bolivian Aymara medicine man at the closure of our journey gave us each a sense of our value amidst the turmoil and wonder of life. Our prayers joined with all those who had prayed on their pilgrimage in this place since ancient times. Pilgrims came from all over the world for hundreds and now thousands of years. We contributed our experiences to the shift of yet another click in the wheel of humanities spiritual and emotional evolution.

My once lost and ignored inner teenager felt held by a greater presence of love when I returned to North America. That part of myself, separated and exiled, began sensing an unfamiliar yet necessary wholeness.

MOVING

After I arrived in the Midwest from Bolivia, I moved to Florida. Now I live in the Southeastern United States near the Atlantic Ocean. It geographically fits with my writing the south direction in the medicine wheel of this Ceremonial Memoir™. Since my symbolic rebirth in the waters of Lake Titicaca, I moved my home next to the ocean connected to my birthplace. The ocean's water and subtropical warmth support my continuing journey of listening and giving voice to what has remained hidden and silent in the dark of my unconscious.

I allowed a chain of memory fragments to fight to the surface of my consciousness before I left on pilgrimage. Doing so reorganized a system of energy that had kept me perpetually leaving and returning to the Midwest. Many years of coming and going enacted a compulsive search for something lost. My unconscious self paradoxically needed to run away from the site of trauma, as well as return and reclaim what belonged to me. Reorganizing my history allowed me to hold my experiences differently in my body. As I write my stories, these separated parts lost in the Midwest, are in a process of reconnection. I can come and go more freely, more consciously now. I have a choice to act, rather than being in an unconscious reaction to what I had not fully digested.

On the way to Florida, I stopped to visit my friend, John Johnson, who still lives in the town of Elgin. We are the same age. When John was twelve years old, the court admitted him to Kane County Youth Home. He was sent there with his father's approval, for refusing to attend school.

John's mother heard voices. She liked to go into places where she could hear her own echo. John remembers his mother standing in corners of the house, where she raged and screamed at the voices she heard. She was admitted and discharged several times from Elgin State Hospital.

John entered the world of Elgin State Hospital in 1968 when he was thirteen years old. Being the only child in his disturbed family, it seemed destined to happen. After John's mother was released, she committed her husband to Elgin State Hospital during one of his drunken episodes. Eventually John's father, an alcoholic and a wealthy treasurer of a cookie company, died in restraints on an adult ward while John was in the children's unit of the hospital.

His mother used the fortune her husband left for her own needs and provided nothing for John. He remained in the hospital until he turned eighteen years old in 1972. When the state decided he was legally an adult, he was discharged to a small apartment with another man from the hospital. The social worker on his ward helped him to get Social Security benefits through his deceased father. Later a woman from the clothing room at Elgin became friendly with him, and he moved in with her. She helped him manage his new life in an unfamiliar world and became his cover and shield from it. He is the only person I still know from that time in my life. I am the only person John speaks with besides Linda who continues to help him in Elgin.

I often send John a birthday card each year with a gift. I was surprised when I called and he told me he was celebrating forty years of excellence. "What do you mean?" I asked him.

"I've had a fairly quiet life since getting out of Elgin State Hospital. I haven't had to hear all that screaming or be around psychological terrorism."

I listened to John in his calm demeanor and pondered what he had said. While I assumed he was living a difficult and limited life, he was quite happy and satisfied with it. My assumptions as to the quality of his life was refuted in seconds as I realized he was much more peaceful with his life than I was with all the opportunities and benefits of mine. Who can judge?

John has maintained a love for me since we were teenagers. He found me by calling my relatives to get my address some years after we were both discharged. After that he continued to write to me regularly. Eventually he began calling me once a month from a payphone in the town of Elgin. This pattern of contact eventually changed to twice a month on the new and full moon cycles.

As a sensitive poet and artist, John creates a perfect life for himself out of intense solitude. He lives in a studio apartment filled with his collection of recorded sci-fi TV shows, movies, Egyptian art and hieroglyphics. He has studied ancient Egyptian culture and has become proficient at interpreting and recreating the images and words onto metal file boxes he buys at garage sales. John has given me one of his painted boxes sent in a cardboard box each year filled with meticulously wrapped small treasures and an accompanying descriptive list of everything he gathered for me over the year.

I haven't visited John in person very often. However, when I was there, he showed me how everything he values in his home has my name and address written on it. John is a kind and gentle soul. He lives in an isolated world designed to secure his great need for safety from other people. John learned early in life humans could be dangerous. Perhaps the flame burning in his heart that he directs toward me has given him more direction and meaning. There were times I wondered about his devotion, but over the years I have come to appreciate his authenticity and sincerity. We share a history that is hard for others to comprehend. That alone is a bond that can connect us through time and any differences.

While I was visiting John, he gave me copies of the drawings he made of the hospital wards he was on during his four-and-a-half year stay at Elgin State Hospital. He also gave me a copy of a note I wrote to him.

After visiting John, I drove to what is now called Elgin Mental Health Center. It was hard to recognize the area I had once lived in. The Center and Annex buildings had been torn down. Weeds and grass were growing through cracked sidewalks, breaking apart the asphalt driveway and parking areas, some of which had nearly disappeared.

I took pictures of the field of grass and weeds in which a large mound of desolate looking dirt rose up where Center Building once stood. As I did, I noticed a security car with two guards slowing down behind me. I got back into the car and drove toward the exit on the grounds and stopped. I took a photo of the sign at the entryway. Then, instead of driving out, I drove farther into the hospital grounds where I found some buildings. I discovered the Burr ward. It had not been torn down. I pulled the car into a parking space in front of it and stopped to stare. While taking a picture of the building through the windshield, I noticed the security car slowly pull up beside me.

There were two young male guards in the car. I opened my window as the one in the passenger seat began to question me about being there and taking pictures. He demanded that I give him my camera. I said, "No. I'm not going to give you my camera." I was respectful but determined.

He softened a bit. "Show me your pictures. I need to check your photos to be sure there are no patients in them."

"Okay." I said. There aren't any people in the photos except for me."

I took my camera over to the security car and pushed the button so my camera screen lit up to let him see each of the images I had taken. I explained them as they came into view. "That's where the Center Building was, and the Annex and the steam heating plant with its tall smoke stacks behind it."

"How do you know so much about the history of the hospital?" The young guard asked me.

I was still for a moment, looking into his eyes, judging his capacity to be receptive to what I might share. I struggled momentarily to verbalize what I had kept silent about for so long. Finally I made an internal decision and broke my silence. "I was a patient here when I was a child." Then I explained that I was on my way south, moving out of the Midwest, and decided somewhat spontaneously to stop there and look at the place that had such an impact on my life. Tears began forming in the corners of my eyes as I continued describing to him what I had seen on the Burr ward in the spring of 1969. I told him that it is hard to carry the experiences and not be affected by them. I was trying to make peace with what happened there. He seemed to understand and became more respectful.

The inquisitive guard saw that there were no pictures of other people and told me I could get prior permission if I wanted to come back and take more photographs. He let me know that they would escort me. I thanked him and left. I was shaking inside as I drove away out of the hospital grounds and, at the same time, felt a resilient strength growing within me.

While driving out of Elgin State Hospital, now the Mental Health Center, I reflected on having found something on the grounds. In the weedy parking lot in front of what was once Center Building where I was housed as a child, I found a small, smooth, dark red stone that I slipped into my pocket. It is not unusual for me to find and keep a special stone from places that have significance for me, but there was something else. I got into the car and while backing up noticed a striking view of the two tall smoke stacks through some bright yellow goldenrod. I stopped again and got out of the car to take a picture.

The security guards drove around and rolled slowly past me, looking intently at what I was doing. Just as I was turning to get back into the car, I looked down and saw what appeared to be two hollow eyes looking up at me. A skull-like presence appeared to be coming from the ground with a most haunted look. Without pausing I bent down and with one smooth movement of my right arm, my hand scooped up the rough hard presence in mere seconds and placed it onto the floor of the backseat of the car. I then shut the door. When I later examined the object, it turned out to be an old brick worn down in a rounded way as to appear human-like. It felt as though it held a presence in the Center Building wall for over one-hundred years, bearing witness to what happened there, but having no mouth to speak. "Let my mouth speak," I said aloud. "Let my words tell a story for those who have no voice, for those who have been forgotten. I have returned and I remember."

SEX

It is difficult to talk about my experiences in Elgin without including the influences that molded me. I was raised in an ultra-religious household that attempted to protect innocence and cultivate a certain standard and style of living aligned with LDS (Mormon) church doctrine. This set of beliefs had a prescribed and expected outcome. Gender roles were specifically defined. Modesty was observed by everyone in my family. I was not allowed to sleep over at the house of any friend who was not of our same religion. Growing up in a Jewish and Catholic Italian neighborhood in New Jersey did not provide many options.

We attended church several times a week. We also had a "Family Home Evening" night once in a while when we would read from the bible and then all kneel down around the sofa to pray. That was one of the only times we were physically close as a family. We all pressed together in order to fit into the opening of the couch. Often I would bump my younger brothers hip with my hip, which would cause his hip to bump my father's. It was a chain reaction I couldn't resist. I knew he wouldn't get into any trouble for that disruption of enforced reverence. I had fun with this prank. If I was in the middle of the couch, I could swing my hips both ways, bumping my sisters who would then bump my mother as well. Often laughter would erupt between my siblings until my father would tell us to be quiet and fold our arms into prayer posture.

Sex was never mentioned, although babies kept showing up. During my childhood, hugging, kissing, or hearing the words, "I love you," was unknown. Physical affection was rarely shown, with some notable exceptions. On summer vacations when my father would drive us away to some far-off destination or to the ancestral family farm in Pennsylvania, I would sometimes notice my parents holding hands as they walked along in a natural setting. There amidst the chaos and flurry of so many lives jumbled together and trying to flow along a religiously ordered pathway, there were moments where real tenderness was shown.

I knew my parents had known each other since they were twelve and were sweethearts by fifteen years old. As far as we know they had only been sexually intimate with each other. They struggled with anger and hurt feelings throughout their relationship, but stayed together and found a way to continue to love each other. Their mothers were best friends. My parents were each the oldest child in their family and the favorite of the opposite gendered parent. They were good children and did as they were told by their parents and church, with the exception of my father's father.

My paternal grandfather was the only family member who was not a member of our religion. He was quite an unusual and interesting man, who frequently drank alcohol, studied astrology and became a Rosicrucian. He was a vegetarian and practiced yoga. I remember picking up one of my grandfathers many books and reading Abbie Hoffman's *Revolution for the Hell of it,* and *Steal This Book.* My grandmother often seemed to despise her husband. She adored and protected my father from his father.

Seventeen years younger than my father, my aunt Celeste told me that she never saw her parents sleep in the same bedroom. She assumed that my father slept with his mother as a boy until just before Minnie was born, and then baby Minnie slept with her mother. I don't know how long my father, as a child, may have slept with his mother, but he was in some ways emotionally fused with her all his life. After Celeste was born, Minnie slept in her father's bed from seven years old until she was eleven. Aunt Celeste slept with her mother until her older sister Minnie got married when she was finally allowed to have her own room.

My father's father was a quiet man who enjoyed listening to the opera. Without fail, there were cats around who trusted only him and were rarely seen by anyone else. He stood on the edge of the extended family, somewhat as a mystery yet with a strong influence in both recognized and unrecognizable ways.

I asked my mother how babies were born and she told me that a man has sperm and a woman has an egg. The sperm and the egg come together to make a baby. I didn't understand how they came together. I think I was ten years old when my mother told me this story about the egg that hatches into a baby. I had seen my mother nursing the babies when they came home from the hospital, so I'd made the association of her having a baby inside and then outside of her body. She told me about these things while I was in the bathtub.

For some reason my mother bathed me until I was ten. She would talk to me during that time. I didn't know that it was unusual until I said something about it to my girlfriend who lived next door. She exclaimed about what a baby I was to still have my mother bathing me at that age. I asked my mother to not bathe me anymore after that.

I sucked my thumb until I was ten. It was how I soothed myself to sleep. My cousin Tina caught me sucking my thumb one night when we were sleeping over at our grandparents' house. I stopped this behavior by tightly holding my right forearm between my knees when trying to fall asleep. I stayed with my maternal grandparents quite often where I enjoyed the company of my cousins.

I tried to understand and adjust to the world of adults but could not navigate the path. Sex was hiding under a thin guise. In my young years, I became tangled in the brush and tripped on shadowy roots that protruded from the dark earth, the secrets of my ancestors.

My mother rubbed *Vaseline* on my vulva when I was four-years-old. I was in a bed next to a crib with my baby brother in it across from my parents' bedroom in New Jersey.

My brother was two-years-old then. I am not sure why I had so much pain in my private parts during that time. At night, the pain caused me to cry until my mother came in and applied thick, viscous gel to the private little folds of skin-bundling upset nerves. Red, raw, and on fire, illicit dark seedlings split off from daylight and grew tangled into what I was not to know or remember for many years.

Unspoken, unnoticed, and yet poorly hidden, an early unknown influence surfaced again and again in various forms of what I would later uncover as my grandfather's covert sexual encounters when I was very small. It would be quite some time until I began to put fragments together in the puzzle of my early sexual shattering and its resultant confusion. Although generally hidden and minimized by others when evidence surfaced, those buried fragments have had lasting effects. I've learned that childhood sexual violation disrupts the natural development of a sound sexual self and can create exaggerated reenactments and confusion about healthy personal boundaries.

I don't know much about the sexual experiences of my siblings or if any of them encountered what I did. We don't talk about sex. We don't talk much at all. I do know that soon after we moved from New Jersey my oldest sister came home for the summer from BYU college in Utah and suddenly had to marry a co-worker. He was a Catholic man and neither his family nor my parents seemed too happy about it. It was the first major tremor in our fractured family after we moved to Illinois. My own difficulties tangled by sexual influences came soon after when I turned thirteen.

In the summer of 1969, after I had run away from Elgin and come back to B-1-North, I realized I was not going to get to the festival in Woodstock, New York or live a gay life in New York City. I was not going to rejoin my friends from high school. Jane had her own life and a boyfriend. My parents and siblings were going on with their lives and seemed relieved that I was not there disrupting the household anymore. I had only Elgin, so it became my home.

I was the resident lesbian at B-1-North. The other girls had a strict dress code to follow, but I was allowed to wear pants that had a zipper in the front. I was also given permission to wear a man's shirt and collar with a tie. It was actually a ludicrous privilege because I was feminine at that time and was attracted to feminine girls, but I played the game. My mother purchased a bright pink men's shirt that I picked out while on a weekend home visit. The shirt had tiny dark green lines running vertically through the pink. I didn't know how to tie a tie so I got a long tie that could be clipped onto the collar. On certain "lesbian days," I would ask the clothing attendant for this pink pinstriped shirt and tie, wearing it with trousers to the widening eyes of the aides and the girls on the ward. They were cognizant enough to recognize the textured innuendo.

My romantic interest, Cindy, appeared on B-1 North one day from Halloran ward. I could hardly believe it. She was processed in at the aide's station but eventually came out onto the ward. She and I immediately sat together at the table in the big alcove and began talking. We had been passing notes declaring our love to each other for months, but now we could actually sit and talk with each other. One of the aides gave me a sideways glance as she told me sternly, "Behave yourself!"

Cindy was there for only a short time, but we made the most of every moment we could. The back alcove became our love nest where we would lie together on the floor with our bodies entwined. Sometimes talking, often kissing and gazing into each other's eyes, we found the long hours on the ward between meals had suddenly become too short. Cindy told me about how her mother had put her into the institution when she was twelve years old because she became pregnant by her stepfather. Her mother was angry and blamed her for taking her man, and so she got rid of Cindy. Cindy lost the baby.

No one came to visit Cindy. She had a boyfriend but decided she liked me better and gave him up. I was happy about that. A couple of the black girls on

161

the ward often strolled by as Cindy and I lay together off to the side of the locked clothing room door on the cool pale-speckled linoleum tiles. Our heads were toward the wall with our torsos stacked. I was facing down on top of her stretched out softly beneath me. Our legs intersected, sprawling out toward the center of the small alcove.

I discovered a most wonderful sensation between my legs when I began moving my hips up and down over her hips. Tanya, a short bow-legged, sixteen-year-old, ebony-black girl, called it "grinding." "I saw you grinding on Cindy with your booty bumping air," she teased me.

"Grinding, what's that?" I asked.

"Tha's what you doing over there with your nasty self, humping on her." Tanya laughed loudly.

"Oh, I like grinding," I said smiling and made sure to continue this grinding procedure with Cindy at every opportunity possible. Tanya persisted in spying as she sat near the back alcove. She also became our warning signal, telling us when an adult was coming our way.

It was hot on the ward. The heat and humidity seemed to collect inside the walls and squeeze the air out of the rooms with languid intensity. Windows were sealed except for three authorized windows on either side of the hallway and in the large alcove. Those three windows opened to allow rare inches of air to come in or out. The beige bricks of the Center Building became radiant oven stones, slowly releasing the blazing sun they had absorbed throughout the day. Shower time became more popular as the only relief available.

I was completely comfortable in a sweaty embrace with Cindy. One early evening when all the girls funneled down toward the open shower room door seeking relief from the heat, Cindy and I slipped into the newly opened dorms. We slid onto Cindy's bed in the middle dorm near the open doorway to the big dorm. No one was there. We lay down on the cool white sheets. I pulled her panties off and raised her blouse, carefully unlatching the back of her bra to allow my hands to caress her full warm breasts. My lips opened to exhale warm breath and then inhaled, kissing each of her nipples slowly.

Being in a bed with Cindy was a luxury. I was lavishing in our intimacy and flowing with the growing tide of intensity building in my body. As I kissed her belly it was so easy to slide my hands down and touch inside her vagina, twirling my fingers into her wetness. I longed to kiss every part of her, to take her in and experience her fully. My lips touched her vulva, my tongue extended. I could smell the sweetness of her fluids rising into my passion for her. There was no time or space between us, only ecstasy in our combined affection.

Cindy's body shuddered and moved up into my mouth, while at the same time the peripheral vision in my left eye caught sight of something foreign and different from the soft rapture we were sharing. No. Then, a little clearer came the recognition of an angular presence in the dorm doorway near the hall. I didn't want to look but turned my head slightly while not interrupting our tender deep enfolding.

While Cindy quietly gasped and her body gently receded back from my embrace, the figure to my left continued to stand more erect with a penetrating presence. I turned my head slowly to my left and let my focus rest on that backlit being in the door. It was Harris, the younger white aide who had made fun of me recently in the main alcove.

Some weeks earlier, I had taken an aerosol can of feminine hygiene spray and was goofing around with it, spraying it into the air and then starting to put the nozzle into my mouth. Harris stopped me, disgusted and amused. She made a comment about me not really being a lesbian and said that I wouldn't know what to do if I had the chance. I'd heard that before.

This time Harris stood in the doorway open-mouthed. Her eyes were boring holes into me. I jumped off Cindy and prepared myself for what I expected would be a miserable punishment, but there was no reprisal. In fact, Harris walked out of that dorm and never said a word. She went back to the aide's station and from that day on, treated me with more respect than she ever had before. I really did not understand the world adults lived in at all.

HIGH SCHOOL

Cindy was taken back to Halloran. It was hard to be separated after sharing such closeness. We continued exchanging love notes passed in the dining hall. I romanticized our affections and held them close in my heart as a way of surviving day after day in Elgin. I developed plans and attempted to carry them out in order to see Cindy more often.

School started. Puri told me I was to meet with the school counselor at Harkley High School my first day. This was a different school than the one I had attended in the summer. It was a newer, larger school in a better part of town. Cindy was on the bus going to school too but was headed to the middle school. John and Ann were also going there.

I lost my bearings on that first day when the chalk green school bus marked Department of Mental Health, Elgin, Illinois, arrived at the new high school. After running away from the hospital, I was secretly terrified to go back into the outside world. Parts of my consciousness scattered like dust in a sudden wind. I wasn't in my body anymore when I stepped over the rotted hole in the wooden floor and down the sagging steps of the miserable old school bus parked in front of the high school door. I left the bus all by myself, leaving my lover and friends inside. The faces of bright, clean, young students flashed what appeared to me as abnormally naïve eyes in my direction as they watched me exit a hellish world that finally felt safe and enter a forbidding opportunity. Cindy and the others watched me leave, casting a shadowy trail into the enormous building with its clean sparkling colors of middle class suburbia.

Immediately I became lost in a sea of human beings that resembled my age and stature but had nothing else in common with me. Eventually I found the guidance office and an adult person. I cannot remember clearly if it was a woman or a man who gave me directions. Too much new information and stimulus confounded me as I ended up wandering hopelessly on different floors of the school, passing endless doors, unable to determine which one to enter. I missed my first class. "That was a serious offense." I was told when I returned to the hospital.

"I got lost," I told Puri.

"The school reported you as an escaped mental patient," Puri scolded me. I explained to her what happened. Eventually after wandering around lost, I had gone outside to sit in the grass and write a poem. Poetry calmed me and helped me center myself. When I returned to the school, a fretful looking counselor found me and took me to my next class.

After seeing me leave the Elgin State Hospital school bus in full view of other students at the high school, the other patients who were taken to the middle school made a quick and conscious decision to demand that the bus driver drop them a block away from the school door. They did this so other students would not associate them with a bus branded with the Department of Mental Health along its side. That decision spared them stigma and allowed them a better chance of blending in.

It was too late for me. My identity was immediately stapled to being a patient of a mental institution. I wore it defiantly as I continued to attend that school. Eventually as the weather turned cold and icy, I appreciated being let off in front of the high school door. I developed two friends in that school. Both of them were social outcasts. One was a white boy, who had an obese body and a great sense of humor along with a love for art and movies. The other was a thin, olive-toned girl who dressed as creatively as a movie star living in poverty. We sat together at lunch and visited during study hall. I was grateful for their friendship in the outside world.

ELI

The fall and winter of 1969 marked a golden time during my stay at Elgin. I attended high school in the day and returned to the hospital in the afternoon. After discovering a Burger King across the street from the high school, I began purchasing burgers and fries to bring back to the institution to share with other patients who never got out. With the constant turnover of girls coming in and going out of B-1-North, I became an old-timer who had accumulated status and privilege. I used my abilities and advantage to make the ward a more peaceful place. I no longer needed bodyguards watching out for me. Most of the girls respected me and did what I asked. The harming of younger and more vulnerable patients ended abruptly as the girls began to watch out for each other and let me know when some harm was done.

One Sunday evening when I returned from a home visit, I noticed that Julie looked funny. Julie was the girl who'd been in Elgin since she was two-years-old and couldn't speak except in monotonous rhythmic sounds or screams. She sat rocking most of the time, making singsong sounds. Julie had no eyebrows. She looked strangely naked without those thick, long, chestnut-brown lines of hair perched above her lonesome eyes.

I could count on Darcie, a short, young, freckled light-skinned black girl, to tell me who did what to whom. Unfortunately, Darcie also tattled on me to the aides for a variety of things such as when I would sneak out of my dorm in the night or rendezvous with a lover during my commissary pass. Then I would become angry with her.

"Jeri smeared Nair on Julie last night as a joke." After I heard Darcie speak, I understood what happened to Julie. Nair was a widely used depilatory cream. I turned and went over to speak with Jeri. Ann joined me. Ann and I both announced to Jeri that no one was ever to take advantage of Julie again.

"Okay. I'm really sorry you guys. I didn't mean no harm," Jeri offered and then explained to us that she was feeling bored and restless while she was using the cream on her own legs and decided to try it on Julie. She was curious to see if it would work on eyebrows. Julie seemed to enjoy receiving the attention. Jeri continued to explain how the liquid drug Melleril the aides made her drink out of a cup every day, made her feel angry and confused and caused her breasts to fill up with milk. She showed us in the shower later how she could squirt whitish fluid from her nipples. Ann and I laughed. I could hardly believe it. Her breasts took on a whole new quality that seemed to defy her age and her childish nature. She later got into trouble for squirting her breast at an aide in the office. She had run up naked to the open half door after showering and squirted her bodily fluid at the bewildered aide and then ran away laughing.

Laughter was sunlight. Even with all the suffering and chaos perpetually erupting on the ward, the girls wanted to play and be children. During this time, I began opening up more of my ability to shift my perceptions. I could see people as animals. I focused my awareness as I looked at a girl for a minute or two. Soon the image of an animal would appear and become part of her face and body. Then I burst out telling her what that animal was. The girls liked that. One after the other came over to ask me what animal they were. Even the aides came up and asked me what their animal was. One aide we all liked stood still in front of me once while I looked at her face and then beyond her face until it disappeared. She developed yellow fur and big brown eyes. "Cocker spaniel!" I shouted out to all those standing near, hearing their happy laughter in response. Everyone seemed to feel better when we played the animal game. I could see animals connected to everyone, even the extremely ill, non-functioning girls.

There was one girl named Gretchen who frightened me. I hated to look at her. She was anorexic, refusing to eat, and skinny as a scarecrow. Her head was a bone skull with translucent white skin tightly stretched over shallow cheekbones and tight across her long, curved protruding nose. She had stringy thin wisps of yellow hair sticking up from the top of her head.

Gretchen was forced to go to the medical hospital for a while, where they pumped food into her stomach. When she came back to the ward, she grabbed the top of a metal chair from the back and began rocking her bony body back and forth, screaming. A different sounding scream would come out with each in-breath and change back with the out-breath, over and over for hours and days. It was maddening. We had all kinds of strange girls on the ward, but this one really bothered me. I was better able to tolerate her when I saw her animal. She became a rooster crowing over and over for a dawn that never came.

During the warm days of fall, the aides would occasionally take some of us out to the playground on the hospital grounds near our ward. There was a tree growing near the swings, a teeter-totter, and a spinning disk that was like a small, barren merry-go-round. I preferred to climb up into the large oak tree rooted beside the playground and sit there in its branches. Mostly the aides let me do as I wished by that time. I felt more alive and awake when I was sitting in the tree.

That old oak, rooted in the playground, became a presence of nurture for me. I would climb around in it or sometimes be completely still. I began to see how things in the world looked and felt different from when I was on the ground with everyone else. I watched as ants climbed along the rugged bark on paths they seemed to know, marveling at their perfect bodies and invisible connection with each other. None of the people around the hospital ever seemed to notice the ants. I hadn't either until they came and reminded me. There was a world with other living things in it beyond the omnipresence of Elgin.

Once on a walk within a line of girls, I found a young pigeon at the other end of Center Building south of our ward. It was lodged between some bushes and a brick stairway leading to a locked door. Slowly reaching down, I gently picked it up. Magee gave me a sideways look as I tucked the grey and white-feathered bird into my shirt and carried it back to the ward. She didn't prevent me from bringing it into my room across from the bathroom. That was my lesbian-quarantine-room. I shared the room with Bertie who occasionally tried to harm me by placing broken glass or razor blades in between my sheets. Once she attempted to seduce me romantically. Another time she touched my body in an intimate way when I was tied down and half knocked out on Thorazine. None of her efforts resulted in what she seemed to be trying to achieve. She also stole half my clothes and yet we remained friends. I didn't hold her strange behaviors against her.

Together, Bertie and I provided shelter for the little pigeon in a cardboard box near the door in a corner of our room. I gave it water and fed it bits of meat, bread, and cereal carried back from the dining hall. After a week or so, Magee led me outside with the bird that had learned to trust me. Gently, I held my feathered friend in my hands, then swung my arms up into the air, opening my fingers to watch the jubilant winged one fly away. I felt myself breathe in deeply as I watched it disappear into the sky. How I too longed for flight with my restless wings pinned behind me.

I turned fifteen years old at the end of November in 1969. We were told that pictures were being made at school, and I needed to bring in some money and a permission slip signed by my parents or guardian. The form gave permission for my photo to be taken and used in the school yearbook. I don't remember who signed my slip, the hospital or my parents. In most ways the hospital had become my parent. The day arrived, and I wore my best dress to school. Lights flashed as others looked on while waiting in line for their turn in the school auditorium.

It was fall and winter's cold was beginning to blow in. After a home visit one weekend, I carried in a little metal cage along with the groceries I brought back to share with the other girls. Inside that cage was a black and white mouse. Somehow I obtained permission to get it. I named the mouse Eli after the song by Laura Nyro, *Eli's Coming*. The cage with Eli sat on top of the dresser I shared with Bertie. Bertie was immediately fascinated by Eli. All the girls were, except the ones who couldn't see out of their own heads.

Eli became the B-1-North mouse that amused all who saw him. He was especially tame and let me hold him for hours. I would talk to him and teach him tricks. When I sat watching TV in the evenings with the other girls, Eli would sit with me on my lap or circumambulate when my legs were resting on the TV table. He walked around and down one leg and across the table and up the other leg back to my waist or my shoulders and continued down again.

Eli had silky black fur with a perfect white ring around his tail. The ward seemed to come alive and even felt a bit like a home with Eli there. I fed Eli and kept water in his cage. On weekends when I was away on a home visit, Bertie would feed and water Eli. Sometimes she forgot and Eli seemed especially happy when I returned.

At school I was learning to make jewelry in art class. At first, the middle-aged male art teacher taught us how to make a mold from a piece of wax we'd carved. He burned out the wax from its white hardened matrix in a kiln to later fill with silver. After I carved a little pig out of hard green wax, I used the lost wax process to cast it. I learned how to use a torch to solder silver links into a chain. Then I attached the chain to the pig's body and set a round turquoise cabochon into the center of it. Art was my favorite class. Next to that, I was extremely fond of creative writing in my English class.

I did not like algebra, but the teacher was patient with me. I continued to show up to his class even though I did not understand what he was talking about with all those numbers. There was no one to help me with my homework back at the hospital. The aides looked at the problems as if they were written in

Chinese, and all the other kids who were going to school were in grades beneath mine. When it came time for the test in algebra class, I took the paper and sat quietly at my desk watching as all the other students busily wrote answers onto their exam. I decided to write a poem onto the test paper with my most sincere intention.

The algebra teacher looked down at my paper, then up at me with quizzical eyes, after I placed my oddly finished test on his desk. He didn't say anything. The discomfort I noticed in his gaze reflected that he knew I was a state mental patient. I could see that he partially pitied me. At the same time, he revealed a moderate level of respect and I, in turn, carried myself with a kind of self-contained dignity. He passed me in his class with a D grade. That's all I needed to get by in my sophomore year.

The temperature was cold on the ward. There was no heat in the three main dorms. These dorms were closed in the daytime and separated by locked doors from the paltry distant radiators that attempted to warm that elongated, chopped-up space.

"My make-up is frozen!" Jeri cried out one morning as she angrily threw the hardened container down onto the floor. She pressed herself between other girls all struggling to get near the four bathroom sinks and use the mirror, before we were funneled out to the dining hall.

Magee came in and asked, "What's the problem in here?"

"We don't have any fucking heat is the problem!" Jeri yelled out. "We're freezing in that icebox dorm with only one blanket. Look at my make-up." Jeri picked up the frozen tube. "It's hard as a rock. I can't even get anything out." Jeri continued shouting into the mirror looking back at Magee's reflection, as she stood unperturbed near the door.

"Nothing I can do about that," Magee said as she turned to leave. Soon she called toward us as we squirmed and shuffled around each other on the cold gray cement floor. "Hurry up and get in line. We've got to go to the dining hall, right now!"

As I was leaving, I passed Sue squatting over a toilet. Sue, the biter, had her own toilet. It was only because she didn't use toilet paper. After she defecated in the morning, she reached her hands down through her thin thighs into the soiled water and splashed it up on herself as though to clean herself off. No one was going to mess with Sue. It wasn't worth the risk and wouldn't make any difference. Her domination of one toilet caused the other three toilets to be in greater demand.

We waited in line until everyone was there. I started talking with Ann about the day, trying to figure out how I was going to get my history homework done before it was due that afternoon at school. Harris arrived with big, round, "retarded" Paula and pulled her to the head of the line. Jingling keys rang out, and the tall narrow metal door opened, allowing us to pass through the maze of halls and doorways. We knew our way instinctively. The drill was embedded into every part of our bodies.

In the dining hall I grabbed a tray, sliding the blue plastic sled down the runway toward the finish line where it would crash into a sad bowl of sickening oatmeal. I wasn't thinking about food. My mind focused inside myself as I squeezed my body between the rails of the counter and the wall to my left, with other girls in front and behind me. I could hear the sound of voices echoing through the hall, mixed with clicks and clacks of metal utensils on plastic.

I rarely slept and didn't like coffee, but I was looking forward to the thick black liquid at the end of the line. It tasted more like rusty nails soaked in tar, but it helped me wake up enough to get myself on the bus and go to school. Looking down for a moment, I noticed something in front of me change. It wasn't a girl's back anymore. It was a front and a face with two bright, sparkling, brown eyes blinking into my face. A trap door opened and a human hand with tiger claws flashed out fast, ripping down my nose, top lip and then tearing out the soft pink skin of my lower lip. Sue laughed merrily as she attempted to grab me with her other hand while her mouth was opening wider. My instincts lifted my body backwards quickly as she began lurching forward. How had I not noticed that it was Sue in front of me? I should have left more space. The line of girls behind me groaned as I fell backwards and began knocking into them like dominos. Harris grabbed Sue's neck and arm as she was about to pounce on me. I was standing on someone's feet behind me, scrambling to keep my balance. Sue was taken away and tied to a chair. My lip bled and swelled up in my mouth.

When I arrived at school, I felt embarrassed by my swollen, discolored lower lip with three bloody nail lines running over my nose and down my face. My English teacher examined me from the front of the room. I looked down into my books as I sat at a small desk in the back. She told us we were going to do a creative writing exercise and to think about our experiences that morning and write them down. I took the time she gave us to write about my encounter with Sue that morning. When I looked up, the English teacher was smiling at me from her desk. I smiled back at her, stretching my swollen lip thin, then continued writing. That teacher showed me that she valued me as a person. She noticed my writing, penning compliments and encouragement into the margins. I liked going to her class, but soon it was time for vacation.

Christmas came and I was taken back to the suburbs to stay at my parents' house for a longer period of time. I was dismal and lonely without my friends. I didn't feel comfortable in the house with my parents, two brothers and sister anymore. It all seemed foreign and artificial to me. My next older sister came back from college for her Christmas vacation. Pearl managed to find time to play with each of the younger children. She had a knack for noticing and appreciating what the younger siblings did or said. Pearl made sure that each of the children had some fun by making cookies or going out sledding with them. I didn't want to participate in the family activities.

My completely foreign world was momentarily spliced into the lives of my family. We had so little in common. A thick cloud surrounded me. I stayed a couple of steps removed, often isolating myself in my room. There were moments when I softened and felt a touch of the holiday spirit connect me with my siblings. I watched them open their presents. I played with my little brother on the rug with his new truck and then joined my younger sister assembling a jigsaw puzzle.

My parents and I struggled to avoid conflict. Silent tension eventually broke when I refused to attend church. Angry arguments ensued, resulting in hurt feelings. A fragile nonchalance became my best defense amidst an awkward hostile environment. Oddly, I was glad to get back to the hospital again.

When I finally walked in through the back door, the welcome I'd grown accustomed to was lacking. The church people who visited once a month had come and brought presents, but no one was cheery. I brought back lots of food and presents for the girls, laying them down on the table in the big alcove. Out of the unusual silence, Darcie spoke up first. "Eli's dead" she said in a monotone voice.

"What?" I ran to my dorm and looked into the cage that was still. How could this be? No Eli. I looked at Bertie who was silent, and then another girl told me that Bertie had been given permission to get a mouse while I was gone. Her mouse chewed out of its cage. It disappeared and then reappeared. The aides put it in with Eli. Bertie forgot to feed them.

"The new mouse ate Eli," Darcie blurted out looking for a reaction from me. I could hardly bear hearing her words. "Bertie's mouse ate Eli," she said again loudly, still waiting for me to respond. I wanted to cry, but I stood still.

"What happened to the other mouse?" I finally asked. "Bertie flushed it down the toilet after it ate Eli," Darcie offered with pride, as though she had given the prize-winning answer. I went to my dorm room and took Eli's cage out into the hall and shut my door. No one stopped me. We weren't allowed to shut doors, but I shut it. I disappeared inside myself and did not talk about it again. The thought of Eli starving and then being attacked and eaten by another mouse was too much for me.

"My little mouse, my Eli." I'd let him down by leaving him there all alone without my care. I didn't protect him. That was an intolerable end to my beloved companion. I could not bear to think about him and his terrible fate.

It wasn't until 2009, forty years later during the writing of this memoir, that I finally cried about my little friend Eli. Unexpectedly, tears and feelings returned. It happened while riding on a hydrofoil crossing Lake Titicaca, as all the others slumped in their seats sleeping. What had been cut off and shut down in order to survive became reconnected to the miracle of love that entered my young, imprisoned life as a mouse. Reuniting with my pain allowed me to remember my joy. Thank you, my sweet little Eli, my light in the dark.

WEDDING

Bertie got a job at Burger King near the high school I attended. It was another experiment by the administrators to try training a teenage mental hospital patient to hold a job. Before that, the only work opportunity for patients was at a factory on hospital grounds, where the institution employed them to assemble plastic bubble pipes. Mostly adult patients performed those mindless repetitive functions and made pennies for their labor.

I don't know why Bertie wasn't sent to school like the others were. Bertie was black. The kids who went to school were white. Maybe that had something to do with it. Bertie made the best of it. She learned how to flip burgers and take orders for food. She came home from work with french fries and hamburgers along with lots of stories that made us laugh and choke in disgust. She told us how one guy at work took a booger out of his nose and put it on the meat patty and covered it with lettuce, tomato and a bun. He spit into the soft drink and closed the lid on top of it. Bertie and the cook snickered when the server handed the packaged burger and drink to a nicely dressed white man. After a while that man came back in. The cook and Bertie got scared that maybe they were going to be found out and in trouble, but the guy said the burger was so good he wanted another one. The girls were grossed out and laughed hysterically at Bertie's story. We demanded that she bring us good burgers and not tainted ones. She assured us she would.

Tanya didn't go to school or work. She sat by herself most days at the end of the hall. Bertie told me she had been a prostitute on the streets of Chicago. "She's been shot," Bertie told me. "Ask her to tell you about it and show you her scar."

After dinner one evening, I sat in the back hall in a chair and started talking with Tanya. She seemed open to my conversation, so I pulled my chair closer to be directly across from her.

Tanya's coal black hair glistened with oil and was combed straight to form a tight bun on top of her head. Her angular body was compact, tight and muscular. Her physical structure had a chiseled look to it. She was shorter than I was and walked with bowed legs, her wide feet pressed into low-heeled shoes. She wore a brightly colored tight skirt and blouse. I asked her if she'd been shot and she said, "Yeah girl, right here." She pulled up her skirt and revealed a round indented scar about a half-inch in diameter on her upper left thigh. I stared at it, imagining what that moment must have been like for her. "Cross fire," she said. "Gangs. Fools don't know who they shooting at. Got me. Messed me up for a long time. Couldn't work." I listened with rapt attention.

I asked Tanya about her life as a prostitute. She told me stories about getting into cars and being with a lot of different men. Many of them were white men, "Right outa youz suburbs," she said. I asked her how many men she had sex with. "Hundreds" she told me.

Looking into her eyes and then down at the floor, I raised my eyes again to look into hers and asked, "Have you ever seen a man that had a really big penis?"

"Of course I have, girl. I seen every shape, size, and color of dick you could imagine."

"No," I said, "a penis that is about this wide." I made my hands into a circle, my thumbs and forefingers touching. "Like this at the bottom and long like about this long, getting narrower toward the end." I motioned with my hands to demonstrate the length and size.

More subdued Tanya said "Yeah. I knew a guy like that. Could do a lot of damage to a girl. Thay cain't pay me enough to mess with those dicks. Did that happen to you?" she asked, looking me straight in my eyes, her small black pupils widening.

"Yeah," I said, suddenly letting myself be honest with her and myself. "Too bad," she answered. "That's tough business, baby," she offered in a softer voice. "You got to watch out for yourself now," she counseled me.

Tanya seemed wiser than practically anyone else on the ward. For the most part, she kept her uncommon sense to herself, but when asked, she showed herself to be real and to the point. In that moment, she gave me a gift of validation for something unspeakable, not to be mentioned again.

Cindy was coming to our ward again. Something happened at Halloran, causing her to temporarily be transferred to B-1-North for a few days. When she arrived, I suddenly asked her to marry me. The idea of marriage was deeply embedded in my psyche from the religious influences in my life. Elgin was the least romantic place for such a ceremony. Still Cindy accepted my offer, and Bertie spread the word quickly to other girls on the ward. The girls decided to join me and Cindy in a wedding set for the following Wednesday evening, when Harris was on duty, not Magee. It was easier to get away with things on Harris's shift.

Bertie seemed to make it her personal mission to bring about a beautiful matrimonial celebration. She brought back two simple silver bands for us from town and had a frosted cake made with colorful decorations, including my name written on it. She had some excuse about why she only had my name and not Cindy's put on the cake. Bertie also brought bright flowers to put in a vase and some for our hair. She explained to Harris that the girls were throwing a little party for me because I had been sad lately. Harris bought the lie and settled into the office with her radio on.

Some of the girls kept an eye on the office and on the back door while others stood farther down in the hall with us, where we gathered by the small alcove. Cindy wore a white cotton dress with yellow flowers printed on it. I decided to put on my black velvet skirt and a white blouse. I wore the cameo necklace my mother had given me. Bertie took her position on my left side as we stood in front of Tanya who held a bible in her hands. The big metal door, with its tall outline, dwarfed Tanya's small dark angular frame. Jeri played her guitar and sang. Ann walked up next to us with Cindy on her arm until reaching me, then Cindy took my hand. Tanya opened the bible and knew exactly where to find what she wanted to read. She began speaking in a voice of unquestionable authority the words from 1st Corinthians chapter 13 verse 4-13. "Love is patient; love is kind; love is not envious or boastful or arrogant or rude…and now faith, hope and love abide, these three; and the greatest of these is love." Tanya looked up from her biblical text studying both of our faces and asked, "Do you Jan, take Cindy as your wife?"

"I do," I said.

To Cindy she asked, "Do you take Jan for your wife?"

Cindy smiled shyly, looking up at me, and whispered, "Yes."

"Then I declare youz married!" Tanya called out emphatically.

The black girls watching us standing together in a group, called out in unison, "Amen!" All the rest of the girls around us jumped up and down, laughing and hugging. Cindy and I began kissing.

"Oh yeah, an I forgot to say, y'all kin kiss!" Tanya uttered, realizing she didn't need to. She chortled loudly and walked away with the other black girls falling in around her as she strolled toward the big alcove to get some cake.

It wasn't long after that when Tanya and most of the other black girls disappeared from our ward. Generally, we were not told when or why girls left the ward. Sometimes we could get information and sometimes not. One day even my roommate Bertie was gone. I missed Bertie and our friendship. It scared me when all the black girls disappeared. I missed them and the culture they shared together that I could sometimes take part in. I valued their raw honesty telling it like it was. Most of the girls had come from Chicago's segregated South Side ghettos. Being with them opened up new awareness and understanding in me and, I think, also in them. Perhaps the administrators moved the black girls out to make room for a whole new group of white girls to come. Many of the new girls were from the suburbs near where my family lived.

A tall, thin white girl with thick glasses and long wavy auburn hair moved into my small dorm room. Her name was Martha. She was a little older than I was and lived in a wealthy part of the northwest suburbs of Chicago. Her parents originally placed her into the same private hospital my parents had considered putting me in. Her parents' insurance coverage eventually ran out, so Martha found herself in the Elgin garbage can with the rest of us.

Martha would not use the bathroom during the day when others might see her. She waited until night when all the other girls had gone to bed. As soon as an aide announced, "Lights out!" she would get up and go into the bathroom by herself. I don't know how she made it all day, but she succeeded in stealing some privacy at night. In the darkness after she climbed back into her bed, she told me her stories about getting into trouble for secretly drinking her parents' alcoholic beverages every day. Martha was a quiet, homely, bookish girl who began attending high school with me. Another new girl named Vicky also joined us. She was from the Elgin area and had gotten into trouble for using drugs.

Cindy was sent home. Her mother decided to take her back after she got angry with her husband and left him. When I heard that Cindy was leaving, I stood up in the dining hall and hugged her as her ward filed by. The aide from Halloran started to pull us apart, but Harris interrupted her and gave us a minute together. Then Cindy was gone. I flattened and folded my heart of love for Cindy over into little quadrants and tucked it away along with a stash of her love notes. I couldn't let myself feel too much about her being gone. My life in Elgin had no space for such emotions. I had to stay in the present with whatever was happening right then. Otherwise, I could fall into the abyss of an ever encroaching, all-encompassing sorrow I knew could swallow me completely. I remained a romantic but let go of Cindy. It would be seven years until I located and visited with her again.

Returning from school one day, I heard the usual sound of keys jingling as the tumbler twisted the metal latch out of the crumbling wall, allowing the tall metal door to swing open onto B-1-North. Harris appeared on the other side and closed the door after me, walking with me out of the small alcove. She inserted the appropriate key from her large cache of keys into my dorm room door. It swung open. This was the normal routine after school, so I could put my books and supplies away.

As I was holding my school books in my arms, I noticed a couple of girls over by the water fountain watching me. They stayed still and silent until Harris walked back into the aides' office. Intuitively, I stood still. Then Vicky stepped up to me and said, "The aides took your poetry. They have it in the office." I searched her face, trying to comprehend what she was telling me. Vicky was a new girl who wanted to befriend me. I had not taken much time to get to know her yet.

"What did you say?"

"Your papers, they found your papers in your room and they took them." Vicky repeated her words more slowly while peering into my eyes, waiting for my reaction.

I walked through the unlocked door into the small dorm with two beds in it, then spun around to the left and placed my schoolbooks on the beige metal dresser. Bracing myself, I walked over to my bed. Placing my hands on the thin plastic twin-sized mattress covered with two white sheets, a blanket and thin pale green bed cover, I pulled the mattress up off the wire weave beneath it. Nothing. There was nothing there but twisted wires in air.

I had been keeping my writing under my mattress for months, spreading it across a wider area as the volume increased. My mattress had grown higher as my writing continued to flood onto page after page. I didn't speak about what hurt or confused me. Instead, I wrote my feelings into cryptic romantic prose. This steady flow of ink to page had become my breath in an emotionally airtight reality.

I stood looking at the bed frame with its vacant outstretched wire. My eyes kept blinking; I was unable to comprehend the loss. Soon, I became aware of the sound of laughter through the usual din of human girl sounds. Vicky followed me, walking toward the office saying, "They've been in there laughing like that all afternoon."

My body moved with leaden limbs, slowly stopping in front of the aide station door. Inside sat Harris and Wilson together, smoking cigarettes and reading through a stack of my poems. They both looked up from their pastime and stared back at me. Silence. Then they broke into nervous laughter, looking at each other again. Wilson stood up and said, "What were you doing hiding all this junk under your bed? How could you sleep at night with all this foolishness under you?"

"Give it back! Give me back my writing," I demanded.

"You know you're not supposed to be passing notes in the dining hall." Wilson scolded me as she lifted one of the love notes from Cindy that was mixed in with the poems. Wilson's wide smile allowed her five-pointed star to glint from her front gold tooth. "Ok," she conceded. "You can have your papers back." Her broad brown hands began pushing the papers together. "What's all this writing about anyway? It doesn't make any sense. What could you possibly know about love?"

"I know it's what makes life worth living," I said.

Harris stood up and placed a handful of white and yellow papers onto the stack Wilson had pushed together on the desk. Then Harris lifted up the pile and handed it to me. I took the armful of disheveled papers from Harris' hands and walked back stiffly to my dorm room. Harris called after me from the office, "It doesn't mean anything, all that writing. It doesn't make any difference or change anything. You're just living in a fantasy." I didn't answer her or turn around. I felt the back of my neck and the skin on my face burning. The papers in my hands didn't feel like they were mine anymore. They felt soiled. My poetry was my safe place hidden away where I could go when I needed to. Now there was no safe place.

I gathered all my papers together and brought them with me on my next home visit. I convinced my mother to take me to Kmart where she bought me a tall, narrow grey metal file cabinet with two locking compartments. I insisted that my parents return my diaries they had taken the year before and placed them along with my poetry and love notes into the metal enclosure, turning the lock closed. I pushed that file cabinet into my closet and shut the louvered doors. The keys stayed hidden where I trusted only I could find them.

Something frightened me about the closet in my bedroom in my parents' house. I had to make sure the doors were closed before I could fall asleep.

Sometimes I dreamed that the doors were open, and I'd wake up and check to make sure they were closed. Something terrifying seemed to lurk behind those doors in the dark. I did not sleep well or soundly on home visits.

One night in late fall of that year, I snuck out of my parents' house to visit Jane. It had been a while. I made it across the highway to her house, but everything seemed unfamiliar and strange. Jane let me in, but she seemed like a ghost. Her house felt smaller like someone else lived there. We stayed together and held each other closely under the sheets of her bed while whispering about how good it was to be together again. Yet, something felt out of place.

When I left her bed and closed the wooden door behind me, I slunk downstairs and let myself out into the frigid air of predawn. Carefully I checked to make sure no cars were in sight before crossing the highway, as I moved swiftly toward the area where my parents lived. I slipped like a shadow down one cold quiet street after another. Still and silent houses crouched on gloomy haunches in rows with their windows blinded by drawn shades. Streaks of light crossed the fetid dark I clung to for shelter. Then I felt something like cold fingers on the back of my neck. I turned to look but saw nothing. I hurried on. There was another touch on the back of my calf like an icy serpent slithering underneath my pant leg. I kicked and shook my leg while trying to get to the yard of my parents' house.

Cutting across a neighbor's backyard, I saw it coming for me. There was an animal with dirty matted white fur, wild eyes, and teeth protruding from gums exposed through tightened black lips. The creature was staring at me as it slowly began slinking forward. I felt terror rise as this wolf-thing stalked me. I tried to be brave while walking faster. Don't run or it will chase you, I thought. I heard a low deep growl roll toward me like thunder. The creature came closer, snarling, its head twisting with saliva dripping from its mouth. Grab a stick and walk fast, but don't run, I told myself, looking for anything I could pick up as I continued to move toward my parents' home. I didn't see how I was going to get into the fenced yard before that thing attacked me.

Then to my left, I saw something more frightening, two more eyes staring at me. It was another one. "How can this be?" My mind raced as a black-furred, mangy-looking creature emerged from the shadows of a white stucco house. This one looked like the other creature but acted even more aggressively. It began to run toward me. I broke into a sprint that was powered by the sheerest of terror, longing to reach the gate before rows of sharp teeth tore into my flesh. In what seemed like seconds, and yet felt as though I was in slow motion, I stretched every sinew and muscle to catapult around to the back of the fence while visualizing an open gate as it materialized into my outstretched hands. Rushing through, I slammed the gate behind me. *Clang!*

Both dogs began leaping up as the rectangular frame of metal fence wire and pipe crashed closed. Running toward the glass patio door, I slid it open and leapt inside, pushing and locking it behind me as quickly as possible. I did not look back. The curtain swung behind me.

I quietly and slowly lifted my feet across the rug up onto a series of steps winding from the lower entryway into the upper hall that led to my bedroom. Passing my parents' door, I made it into my room. I closed and locked the door behind me.

It felt as if evil had taken animal form. How could such rabid looking creatures be wandering around in the perfectly coifed northwest suburbs of Chicago? What kind of dog would appear in the night out of nowhere? Two! My body trembled and shook for hours.

When I went back to the hospital, Ann told me about a dream she had with two vicious wolves, one black and one white. We both shuddered when I shared my experience with her.

We told John about it on the way to school. He seemed to know what had happened. "The hounds of hell have come after you," he told me. "You have to protect yourself now that they know where you are." He began making a series of intricately drawn talismans for me to place in my room and to carry with me.

My first inclination was to pretend that I didn't feel afraid or believe that I was being stalked by something evil, yet I wondered. I kept John's drawings and was grateful for his efforts. I did not try sneaking out of my parents' house again after that incident. I offered up a prayer to a God that might be listening and able to protect me.

New awareness began growing inside. I acknowledged the tangible threat that came from something that did not want me to know what I was beginning to decipher. From reading mythology, I understood that there are gatekeepers and guardians on the threshold of change. I had a choice to make. Would I shrink back in fear and remain as I was or expand beyond my limitations? I decided to step forward on my path of awakening, acknowledging there was a true evil born from the unnatural split between light and dark energies. Somehow, I knew there must be something larger than that heinous polarity, something that encompassed both light and dark into another way of being I had not yet experienced.

MARILYN

Taking a breath, I return to the present from my barrage of memories. John called yesterday from the town of Elgin on his new cell phone. "There are only two pay phones left in town," he told me, "and one of them is at the police station. You know I'm not going over there," he exclaimed. It was the first time I was able to call him back after missing his call. I mentioned to him that I was nearly finished writing my memoir about my experience at Elgin State Hospital.

He reflected on that time and told me that I was different from the other children there. He went on to say that I was the only one who seemed to understand real love. "The boys on my ward," he continued, "were only interested in sex in an aggressive way. The girls seemed confused and distant. I tested you and found that you were the one motivated by something else. You lived as though love was part of your very being. You were the only person who said anything kind to me after my father died."

I was grateful that John saw the essence of my souls longing to experience love and be a loving presence amidst the cruel chaos of our young lives. Witnessing the pain of others while experiencing so much suffering firsthand ignited my desire to become a possible solution to a ravaged reality.

While I was housed in Elgin, I touched the lives and bodies of other girls in an attempt to create a love that could outshine the abominable emptiness engulfing us there. This effort was fatally skewed by the complicated influences of our shattered lives. Jagged fragments tore at the fabric of what once was innocence. It was in the midst of such confused attractions that I found my heart opened in a more clear and resonant way with Marilyn. Something transpired in the hollow of disallowed love that has stayed with me to this day. I'm not sure how that happened.

I met Marilyn when I was first admitted to Elgin. She was on the Halloran ward. We were immediately drawn to each other. I hoped to get to know her better, but she was discharged and gone before that was possible. Instead, my affections found direction and blossomed in my relationship with Cindy. Cindy and I both learned a lot and grew in our exchange. When Cindy left the hospital, I didn't hear from her again. I didn't know how to contact her. My romanticism stayed current and kept me afloat in a situation of constant challenge and change.

I continued to attend high school during sophomore year. Coming back onto the ward one cold afternoon, I walked into the main alcove and set my books down on the table. Several of the newer girls on the ward were sitting around talking. I heard one of them mention Marilyn's name. I continued to listen while I opened one of my books and took out a pen. I stopped and turned. "Did you just say Marilyn Arrigo was here today?" "Yeah, she was admitted and then sent to Halloran," Vicky told me. I was disappointed I'd missed her and that the staff had not let Marilyn spend even one full day on our ward, but I joined in the conversation with all the girls excitedly talking about her. Even the new girls had heard of her. She was someone who left an impression on those she came in contact with. Her time in Elgin before I arrived seemed to be one of those special eras on the girls' wards at the hospital. I felt excitement at the thought of seeing her again. I was nervous when it came time to line up and go to the dining room. I could hardly wait to be near her.

There was something untamed about Marilyn that stirred my own quest for an unfettered life of love and adventure. Her dark eyes gave passage to some mystery I longed to be joined with. We wrote love notes to each other, passing them back and forth through the dining hall when she returned for a second time to Elgin. We managed to coordinate rendezvous where we would secretly descend a dark stairwell leading to a locked door at basement level near the dining hall in the Center Building. We tried to ignore large black water beetles that lingered in the small, dank corners of that stark, in-between shadow space.

Marilyn and I would stare into each other's eyes, talk in whispers, and hold each other close. An indescribable peace would fill my senses when I was with Marilyn during those stolen moments, out of view of the hospital world. Together we created a completely different domain that felt enchanted. We drank from lips full of promise, bending down in devotion, not hungering for anything. Each touch was a fulfillment unto itself, a whole. This elixir of mutual passion made me drunk with a secret joy. The world we created together was impossibly beautiful, in sharp contrast with our living situation.

It was different with Marilyn. She was sixteen years old and mature for her years. Marilyn met me with a love equal in passion, both tender and strong. I didn't have to convince or seduce her. She was willing to make the sustained effort to develop a bond of enduring love during the storm of life we both experienced at Elgin. While in her arms, my jumbled mind and fragmented heart found peace without effort or struggle. Every moment we exchanged was life giving. Marilyn spoke from her heart with clarity and was truthful with me. She seemed fully present when we were together and loved me in a way I didn't have to guess at or embellish. Some aspects of this love will forever remain a mystery. Why Marilyn took the form of perfect yet unattainable love is not clear.

This love had its bliss and its tragedy as the winds of time changed course. The aides on her ward discovered and punished her for her fearless love for me. Marilyn stopped showing up in the dining hall for days. Worried looks from other girls on her ward soon turned into messages that were passed down through a chain of connections. I learned that Marilyn was tied down and being kept hostage on her ward. She was given shots as punishment for her involvement with me. The staff must have discovered our notes. That defilement of Marilyn's life and our love lasted nearly three weeks.

The other girls from Halloran told me that Marilyn was shrinking into a bony skeleton of a girl. She was disappearing in a bed while continuing to refuse to deny her love for me to get out of it. I was heartsick. One day I managed to get outside near the area of her ward and throw a rock at the third floor window. I shouted up toward where it was partially opened, "I love you, Marilyn. I'll always love you no matter what they do to us!" One of the Halloran girls looked out through the window and nodded to me. I left hoping Marilyn either heard my call or would be told by the other girl.

I'm not sure what happened or who intervened. Marilyn was let out of restraints and allowed to come to the dining room just before she was discharged from the hospital. After school that day, I purchased a single red rose.

I stood up when Halloran ward passed by our tables after the evening meal. Marilyn stopped in front of me. I offered her the rose, along with my heart. She placed a gold ring with a horizontal, onyx cabochon, onto my left forefinger. We hugged tightly. I could feel how thin she was under her clothes. I was glad she was getting out of there, while at the same time, my heart was breaking.

Years later, John said, "I remember the day you gave Marilyn a rose. Most everyone stopped to watch. It was the single most loving act in four-and-a-half years of my watching what took place in the dining room."

There is a rare life-changing alchemy possible between two hearts if certain elements are combined together at the perfect time. Love can create a greater self than one felt capable of alone. Union with another can exist beyond the physical realm and open a vision that is not bound by romantic fascination or limited by the presence of everyday challenges. This loving emotional presence created in the past between Marilyn and me still shines brightly at the thought of her, despite years of change and lost contact. She awakened a part of me that has remained resilient. I trusted and believed her. I let her love in. That love took up residence as a part of me, helping me realize perhaps for the first time, I was worth loving.

My love for Marilyn grew stronger and caused more clarity and maturity to form over the rough reactive romantic girl I had been. I would soon leave the hospital with an enduring love and devotion for Marilyn. What would not happen was the two of us ever being able to live that love together outside the hospital grounds. I made a promise to love Marilyn without end when she left the hospital. She promised to return to me someday. We vowed to be together.

One day, soon after I had been discharged, Marilyn showed up at my parents' house. I rushed her up to my bedroom and closed the door. We embraced. I wanted to talk with her before my parents discovered her in the house. She asked me to come away with her. How I longed to join her! There she stood, barefoot, wearing an old t-shirt with blue jean bell-bottoms and only her full, wild heart reaching out through her extended hand to me.

She told me how she had run away from her family home. At that time she was traveling alone. While we sat on my bed, she told me about a situation she had with some guys who had picked her up while hitchhiking, along with another girl she met along the way. One of the guys took her into a room and tried to force himself on her. She heard the other girl scream from another room in the house and then a gunshot sounded. When the man pursuing her became distracted, Marilyn ran out. She didn't know what happened to the other girl. It haunted her.

I could not bear to run away again, especially after hearing of her narrow escape from harm. I had my own buried story festering away inside me, contaminating my response to the call for love and freedom. Instead I gave Marilyn all the money I had and the rest of my carton of cigarettes. We promised to write to each other. She left me in the summer of 1970. I never saw her again. I wrote to her and eventually reached her by phone when she was back at her family's house. Our opportunity to speak by phone was blighted. I was not allowed to make phone calls and was confined to the house. I continued to write to her and waited with great anticipation for her letters to arrive, but they didn't. I continued to wait for Marilyn, believing we would find our way to one another again someday. That's not what happened.

Just before I was eighteen and ready to leave home legally, I broke into the locked drawers of my father's large wooden desk in the basement. Inside one of those drawers, I found an odd collection of items that had obviously been retrieved from my garbage. Among them, I was horrified to find folded up bathroom tissue with line imprints of my blood from cutting myself. My father must have found these before Elgin or during my time on home visits. It felt creepy to me. Why would he save those? There was also a large packet of unopened envelopes with a rubber band around them. As I pulled the stretchy band away and turned over the first white envelope with black lettering on it, I recognized Marilyn's handwriting. There were the letters she had written to me over the years that I'd felt in my heart but had not seen. My grief and rage overflowed when I opened each letter and read her words of love and confusion about why I wasn't answering her letters. I tried to locate Marilyn after that, but she had moved on. The waves in the sea of my own life continued to grow higher and deeper.

My attempts to locate her failed until I was in my early twenties. By some strange twist of connections, I located a relative of hers who gave me her address in California. She was weeks away from getting married. Carefully I wrote out a letter and explained to her why I had not answered her letters. I told her how I loved her and had waited for her as we promised. We both had gone on with our lives, but I'd never forgotten her or the gift of love she gave to me in Elgin. I thanked her for her love. That love eventually bloomed into a tiny flower of self-love, a delicate violet in a chaotic swamp of pain. I didn't hear from her after sending that letter. I waited. Finally, I sent two dozen red roses to her address and wished her well in her new life.

DISCHARGE

By the time it was my turn to be discharged from Elgin State Hospital, the ward had changed tremendously. It was early June 1970. Ann and all the other old-timers were gone. Many of the new girls had come to the ward for drug-related reasons. They seemed apathetic. I lost my support in helping to bring stability to the ward. Violence began to disrupt the lives of those housed there. As the temperature rose, so did the angry, stressed temperament of the young population on B-1-North.

One spring evening, the only aide on the ward was in the small far dorm taking care of some crisis after lights out. A new girl ran under the Ping-Pong table and began screaming about some terror only she could see. I heard more screams coming from the big dorm and ran down there to find two girls holding Darcie, the tattletale, down on the floor while pushing safety pins into her breasts. Horrified, I confronted them and pushed them off of her. She looked up at me with startled gratitude and re-buttoned her pajama top as she got back into bed. The other girls disappeared like cockroaches when a light is turned on.

I tried to make a difference and help out, but there was no way to stop the flood of constant crisis on our ward. I watched as a new form of punishment was initiated on some of the girls who got into trouble. They were forcibly tied to a chair where an aide would cut off their hair in a short ugly ragged fashion while they screamed, cried, and begged the aide not to. This was a cruel method used to change their behavior. I thought it was a frightening thing to do to teenage girls who were already suffering from low self-esteem and multiple emotional wounds. The intention was to humiliate them and it worked. Crushing spirits came in daily doses.

A new girl named Deena arrived. She seemed too young and innocent for such a harsh place. I tried to warn her and give her the best information I could. She was one of the girls who lived out the warning we gave nearly every new girl, "If you aren't crazy when you come into this place, you will be by the time you leave." Deena slipped over that edge and got caught in the wheels that ground her down into something unrecognizable.

She would later be the cause of Puri's back being broken. That happened while I was an outpatient. On an outing, Deena jumped out of the back seat of Puri's car while it was traveling down a road in line with an oncoming truck. Puri saw from her rearview mirror that the door was opening. She realized the alignment of the girl's body tumbling out and swerved to keep her from going under the tires of the truck. She lost control of her car and jumped a curb, slamming the front of her car into a tree. Puri flew through the windshield.

Deena's skin was imbedded with gravel but otherwise she survived her leap intact. The other girls in the car made it through with no obvious injuries. Puri was never quite the same. I visited her in the hospital. She told me the pain was so great, her meditations and the medications they gave her did not ease her pain enough for her to function. It was hard for me to see Puri suffering and broken in that way. She had to wear a back brace for a long time after that and stopped wearing her traditional clothing, her sari. Instead she began wearing homely domestic western attire.

How did I get discharged? I think Puri had a lot to do with it. She spoke with my parents and encouraged them and Dr. V to give me a chance to live at home again. She explained to me the sequence of events that was to take place and what was expected of me. My sophomore year at high school ended in early June 1970. I was told I would be going to live with my parents.

Puri informed me that I was not considered cured because I was still demonstrating lesbian behaviors. My interaction with girls was no secret. She advised me that the conditions of my discharge were that I would become an out-patient of Elgin, living at home, going to school, and coming for my sessions with her every week. I wanted to get out of Elgin, especially after all my old friends and lovers had gone, and the ward had become such a tinderbox. The decision was made for me, and so I left Elgin State Hospital to the care of my parents and the rules of their home.

My reintegration into the outside world did not go well. I became disoriented by the life I was expected to live. I felt strikingly alone after living with other girls my age who at least had the experience of being cast out in common with me. In my parents' home, I was required to attend all church functions, which were numerous. The church environment was a hostile one for me. I was singled out as a bad girl, a lunatic no one would have anything to do with. I could hear the whispers behind my back. Some people pointed as they gossiped right in front of me. Many curious and disgusted looks came from parents and other teenagers.

My divergence became more obvious when I was not permitted to take the sacrament of bread and water. As the young priests passed the metal serving trays over me I told myself I didn't want it anyway. That action of exclusion belied the religious and family message of my difference from them and my unworthiness because of it. I sat silently. Wild sexual fantasies erupted in my mind like sparks finding gasoline as I sat through the long oppressive hours in church. God and Jesus began to take on malignant human characteristics.

My older sister Pearl returned from college for the summer. Then there were five of my parents' seven children living with them in that little yellow house. I was a stranger. None of us knew how to relate to each other. There was great tension between my parents and me. I was not trusted. I was not allowed to make phone calls or receive them, except from church members. Of course, there were no calls coming in for me except from those I was not allowed to talk to. When the phone rang, I would race to try and pick it up to find out who it might be and get a few words in before the call was forcibly hung up. If I left the house to walk to the corner convenience store, my mother followed me in her car and interrupted my attempts to use a pay phone or mail a letter. I was under house arrest, living with people who were afraid of what I might do. I'd lost all credibility and validity in society and as a family member.

During those times of painful isolation, I made art and wrote my feelings into my journal. I wrote poetry. No matter how I tried, nothing eased my growing desperation and loneliness. I began watching the new children's show, *Sesame Street,* on TV with my youngest brother, four-year-old Eddie. Behind a closed door in my room, I smoked my heavenly cigarettes. This was the one concession I won upon returning to my parents' house. Each cigarette helped me feel a bit sane amidst ambient insanity, until its fiery light was crushed.

I was probably released from Elgin for only a week or two before the clash of worlds collapsed my spirit and my health. Floating in the small three-foot-high circular pool my father put together in the backyard, I would look up at the clouds passing in the sky, watching for hours. One day I became excessively chilled. I went up to my room and shivered in my bed until dusk. No one came to my door. That evening I felt my body burning as though a fire was raging inside me. While my physical temperature rose, I tumbled into a deep emotional crisis. Everything inside and outside of me became exaggerated and distorted. Eventually someone knocked and came in. My temperature was taken. I had a 104-degree fever.

The fever lasted for days. I lay in an inferno with diabolical pressures that surged and swallowed me. Nothing was real anymore except darkness, sorrow, and pain. My older sister Pearl came into my room one evening and proceeded to tell me that I was being punished by God for my wickedness, and that I would be better off if I died. Sometimes I wanted to die but not to go somewhere else to continue to be punished for being me. I longed to go back to my true home, before I had been born, where I knew love was real. I didn't want to believe anything my sister told me; but her timing was perfectly destructive because I was already feeling lost and vulnerable. There was so little left of me to resist. I sank even deeper into disoriented loneliness.

What occurred to me when I began to resurface from the fevered fog was that I would be better off in Elgin than at my parents' house. In contrast, Elgin took on a glow from the bonds I had developed with other girls. It began to feel like a more appropriate place where I could be myself rather than being bound to a lonely, hostile, unforgiving world with my parents and their omnipresent dogmatic religion. There was no way I was going to be the daughter they insisted I become. I was a lesbian. I loved women. I was not interested in their religion that condemned and punished me.

Unknown to me at that time, the talons of having become institutionalized were sinking deeper and deeper into my outsider flesh. I had learned how to live inside Elgin and illogically reasoned that at least I would not be alone there. If I was going to be locked up anyway, I'd rather be with other girls my age. At that point, I was familiar with the world of Elgin and felt completely out of place in my family and the community I suddenly found myself floundering in. This began a distorted backwards quest for a place to belong, that caused me to take a razor blade and make some superficial wounds on my arm and then turn myself in. I did not cut deeply, partly because I knew I had promised Magee that I wouldn't, and partly because I really didn't want to die. I wanted to live but could not discover my opening or opportunity to do so.

I was re-admitted to Elgin State Hospital by my parents soon after being discharged. Immediately I learned that I could not go back to the same hospital. That time and era had passed. I had been discharged and expected to stay out and adjust to the outside world. My return was treated as a colossal failure. When the admitting physician examined me, he must have noticed I had a fever because he prescribed B vitamins and iron rather than Thorazine. He told me I was anemic. The aides gave me vitamin shots that seemed like punishment. I knew the routine and noticed the anger and disappointment in their eyes each day as I pulled down my clothing to let their sharp dart hit my hip or buttocks.

I was placed on constant mopping restriction and segregated from the other girls. When I wasn't mopping, which took hours each day, I was confined to a vacant room next to the aides' office. It was the same room where I had my arm stitched up once, but this time it was empty. That room became a sterile prison where I was kept in isolation.

I was not allowed to mix with any of the other patients on the ward. Solitary confinement was created especially for me. There was a big hand-written sign on a piece of paper tacked to the open door of the room. It read, *Anyone coming near this room or caught speaking to Jan will be put on restriction.* There were barely any words exchanged at all between me and the other girls I knew on the ward. They stayed away and cast looks of fear toward me when I was mopping.

Each day I would lie on the cool hard linoleum tiled floor of the little office, languishing in the twilight of a dwindling sense of humanity. Finally after asking, I was given a bible as my only permitted object. Opening it up to read only made me feel worse, so I kept it shut and used it like a pillow to raise my head off the floor. My fever continued to burn. I didn't know how long I could survive that way. I felt myself dying inside.

I was not allowed to see my parents, other members of my family, or even Puri anymore. Dr. Vico had decided to make me his special project. In a session with him, he told me he intended to break my spirit and destroy my flawed personality. He then planned to rebuild me in the way he thought I should be. I felt absolute terror being at the mercy of his authoritarian confidence. He planned to not only exercise control over my body and my outer life, but take over my inner life as well. My personhood was so unacceptable that it was deemed therapeutic to destroy it and make me into someone who would be more acceptable to society.

I felt myself becoming something less than human during that time of crushing isolation, humiliation, feverish sleepless nights, and constant adult criticism. I don't know how long this diminishing incarceration would have lasted or how I would have held up against the perpetual emotional blows or the physical deprivation had I remained there.

Only recently, while visiting John Johnson, did I hear more about this time period in Elgin State Hospital. John revealed to me that he had more drawings from his stay in Elgin. I asked his permission to copy them. While I was photographing each page of the different wards and rooms in the hospital, I noticed one picture of the Main Dining Hall that stood out. There was one table and four chairs with my name next to it drawn in blue like all the others, but then there was another table drawn in red pen with the date of June 1970. I asked John about this drawing.

"Was that when I came back to the hospital after being discharged?" John dutifully answered my questions.

"Yes."

"I don't remember eating or where I slept when I came back."

"Well," John offered, "They brought you into the dining hall wearing a hospital gown and restraints."

"Was I sitting alone?"

"Yes."

That was all the information I knew to ask. I needed time to let John's words and picture settle in, to see where they fit into my own recollections and awareness of that time. It wasn't until several months later that I felt ready to ask for more. When John called me on a new moon, I began questioning him again. "John, when you walked by my table was I looking at you or was I looking down?"

"You were looking down."

"Were there any other children in hospital gowns?"

"No."

"Where were the restraints?"

"They had them hanging from your wrists."

"What did they use the restraints for?"

"An aide brought you in, pulling you by the restraints. When I got back to our ward, I heard a staff member complain about what Dr. V was doing to you. She was upset that he planned to break you and rebuild you the way he thought you should be."

As soon as John said that, I knew he was remembering accurately. It matched the fragment I remembered of that time. I can only imagine what else was done to break my strong, independent spirit. Dr. V was free to enforce his form of segregation and humiliation, including my being restrained in a bed in the hall at night.

I can understand how the pain and suffering in my sick body along with the horrors of such treatment was enough to cause significant dissociation. No wonder I remember so little of that time. Dr. V's prescribed actions subdued me, while reinforcing a perpetual message of being deeply flawed. Shunned and shamed, I began to disappear inside myself.

Suddenly I was discharged again. I learned that Puri put her job on the line to get me out. She saved me. I was completely grateful and agreed to live by the rules of my parents' house and not act out or injure myself again. Nothing else was possible for me. I had to accept the situation, so I did. Eventually I was taken to a medical doctor who gave me the diagnosis of mononucleosis. He could not help me. Completely exhausted on every level, I knew I had to ride it out and rest. I wondered if I might ever feel better again.

A few years after I was discharged from Elgin, John told me Dr. V had been released from his position because of abusing children there. I read the article in the newspaper that John showed me. Dr. V had two "retarded" boys tied down in restraints for two weeks after they were caught masturbating. He had plenty of time to inflict other cruelties onto children before that point of being released from his position of unholy authority. I was glad to hear of one small note of justice in that world of woe at Elgin State Hospital.

OUTPATIENT

Soon after I was released from Elgin the second time, my parents packed up the blue and brown imitation wood Ford Country Squire station wagon and drove all of us back to our ancestral farm in Pennsylvania. I kept to myself and didn't say much to anyone. My uncle in New Jersey was a professional photographer and offered to take some photos of me for the modeling career he remembered I had once been interested in. With his boxy camera perched on a wooden tripod, he distilled images of me shortly after being discharged from Elgin.

Puri gave me a book written by a colleague of hers. It was *Notes to Myself: My Struggle to Become a Human*, by Hugh Prather. I also took Kahil Gibran's book, *The Prophet*. While visiting the farm I sat out in a field of grazing cows, reading and then writing my own notes to myself.

At fifteen years old, I decided to become a vegetarian as a spiritual practice in relationship with nature and to honor the lives of animals. Puri set an example by not eating meat. Neither did my paternal grandfather. I decided that this would be my way of life as well. After making this decision, I didn't know what to eat. My mother didn't know what to feed me. She seemed baffled and annoyed by my new diet. While my mother made meals for the family, I made my own. I began nurturing myself from other sources growing wild on the edge of my contained and controlled adolescent life.

Tying patterns of knots into black cords and strings, I created a macramé belt and wove thin leather strips into a tiny whip I wore hanging down from it. I felt I had been whipped into submission. Defiantly, I held onto the whip as though I might somehow control it by wearing it as a symbol of my ongoing oppression. A thick black leather watchband protected many of the self-made scars on my left wrist.

Although forbidden by my parents, I pierced both of my ears and put gold rings into them. I'd heard sailors did this as a symbol of surviving a shipwreck. For me, the wrecks in my life were about surviving the imposed imprisonment in Elgin, and afterwards, in my parents' house. I didn't understand then how hard or long that process of survival would be or the complicated process of freeing myself from the prison that replicated within my own mind.

When we returned from summer vacation to my parents' house in Illinois, I strung together a specific number of colored beads and hung them on cords stretched under the portrait I'd painted of Laura Nyro. Each bead represented a month of time until I would be eighteen years old and able to legally own my own body and my own life.

I continued to visit Puri every week for a session. Although Puri believed in the power of love and set an example of love in my life, she indicated that she did not believe lesbianism was a valid form of loving expression or a natural part of my identity. She tried to help me get in touch with my feelings. At that time, I didn't know how to fully laugh or cry.

I was an outpatient of Elgin State Hospital until I was eighteen years old. I was never considered cured of being a lesbian, although at sixteen years old I did take on a boyfriend. He was an acquaintance I had met through work.

I began working part-time at fifteen and full-time at sixteen years old, while I finished school at night. I asked Kent, an older boy I met through work, to go out with me. I told him my situation of being a lesbian under house arrest and that I would like to go shoot photography in nature and have some fun. I had become a salesperson of photographic equipment in a department store and wanted to develop my skills. Having an interest and talent with art and photography ran in my family. My maternal great-grandfather had been a professional photographer using his artistic skills to create a living for his family. My great aunt and grandfather helped their father with his studio. Kent happily agreed to go out with me under my conditions that he accept that I was a lesbian and planned to move to Chicago to live a lesbian life when I was eighteen years old.

Kent and I proceeded to have a wonderful, playful time together, going to movies, hiking, going out to eat pizza and fondue and other menu items that would fit my vegetarian taste. It was easy to be with him. A whole world opened up that had been previously off limits because I was showing interest in a boy, not a girl. I felt a new sense of freedom with unfamiliar and seductive privileges. After a year together, I slowly tried becoming intimate with Kent. I discovered the beautiful experience of sharing sexual intimacy with a boy who was my choice, in my timing and way. We felt happy together and for a moment, I swung toward the pattern I was supposed to take. It was so easy in that world with him, but it wasn't really my world.

Kent asked me to marry him, and I seriously considered it. We became engaged and set a date. He converted to my family's LDS, Mormon religion and all the bells began to ring, the sun was shining. But I did not marry Kent. We continued to spend time together and stayed very close, but my previous plan to live as a lesbian when I turned eighteen began to resurface. Kent told me to keep my engagement ring when I explained that I couldn't marry him. I knew if I did I would betray a part of myself and not be a true partner for him. I loved him, but I needed to be free to discover and express my truth.

Although we separated soon after I came of age, I've continued to carry some part of his love throughout my life. He gave me precious gifts, many of which I could not understand or fully receive at that time. His love and playful nature brought me joy and created a peaceful island of ease in the traumatic reality of my teenage existence.

Kent's care made me to feel more lovable and valued. He defended me in ways no one else ever had. He heard my stories and held me when I felt sad. He even confronted Sergeant Hastings, who turned out to be a neighbor of his and a friend of his father. Kent's father was a highly respected state police officer. Kent had even babysat for Sergeant Hastings' children.

One day Sergeant Hastings walked into the photography supply store where Kent worked. Until then, Kent had always greeted him in a friendly, helpful manner. This time when Sergeant Hastings asked for his usual supply of developing chemicals, Kent twisted his mouth into a disdainful frown while looking him directly in his eyes and said, "Sergeant Hastings, get out of this store!" Startled and then angry, Sergeant Hastings raised his voice demanding that Kent get him the chemicals he wished to purchase.

Kent would not back down in their standoff. Kent's boss emerged from the back of the store and came over, about to intervene. Then Kent clearly said in a most direct unwavering voice, "I know Jan and what happened to her. Now get out of here and don't ever come back!"

Sergeant Hastings' whole demeanor changed instantly to that of a man who was caught. He quickly spun around and walked out of the store. When Kent turned and spoke with his boss about what had just happened, his boss immediately understood that Kent had done the right thing. He could see the guilt written all over Sergeant Hastings face when he said my name out loud.

Sergeant Hastings and his family quickly moved out of the neighborhood, never to be heard from again. I was proud of Kent for standing up for my honor and preventing Sergeant Hastings from purchasing photographic developing chemicals he knew the veiled purpose of. I'm sure I wasn't the only vulnerable girl who was snared by Sergeant Hastings' debauchery.

Evan, my younger brother by two-and-a-half years, entered adolescence in a storm of incoherence. He suffered a breakdown when I was sixteen. After many battles in our younger years, we had done a good job of avoiding each other after I returned from Elgin to our family home. As a child, I occasionally took my anger out on him. Arguments could escalate into a wrestling match. I understand what Parker Palmer said about violence happening when we do not know what else to do with our suffering. Although I had learned to take a fair amount of teasing and demeaning treatment, it was hardest when I felt the contrast of my own position in the family juxtaposed with his. I loved my brother, but in him I witnessed our parents giving the love and favor I could not attain.

As a child, Evan gleefully accepted and utilized the privileges afforded him because of his gender and birth order. That was his world, his normal. He was the hoped-for boy after three girls in a row. He immediately had a lot in common with my father. They had similar personalities.

When my oldest brother Brian was born, my father was in the army, stationed in Germany during WWII. When Dad came back from the war he struggled with his two-year-old first-born son for my mother's attention. There was one time in particular when he lost his temper with baby Brian's crying. My mother later confided that my father's quick temper flared. He broke two of the wooden bars on the drop side of the crib by shaking it so violently until baby Brian was silent. All of the six siblings that followed used that same crib my father had repaired. No physical damage was done to Brian, but the two of them never bonded. Fortunately, for my younger brothers sake, my father was ready when his second son arrived.

I know how hard it was on me to become the oldest child living at home when we moved from New Jersey. I can only imagine how it must have disoriented Evan to become the oldest of the last three after I was sent to Elgin.

In 1971, I saw Evan becoming a man. He grew taller and his voice lowered. Oddly, I would find Evan wandering in the hall upstairs talking gibberish about God speaking directly to him. Once he came into the bathroom before I closed the door and began telling me how much he loved me in a way that made my stomach tighten. His eyes didn't look right. I wondered what was going on with him.

Evan grew worse. He stayed up all night wandering the halls chattering away to the spirits he seemed to be engaging with. He had become a midnight prophet. He tried to enter my room, but I locked my door and pushed my dresser in front of it. I'd seen kids like him at Elgin and didn't want him startling me.

My parents didn't know what to do. They barely had me in check and then when Evan entered his teens, he went down for the count. They took him to various doctors and even spoke with Puri. Puri suggested that Elgin would do him no good and could actually harm him. Soon he was shipped out to the private hospital my parents once told me was too expensive for me. I was stunned. I was glad that Evan was doing better and making progress quickly there, but I couldn't help acknowledge the different attitude of saving Evan verses controlling, and I felt, dumping me. I tried not to let it bother me. Evan had lost his mind and the hospital was helping him find it with therapy and some medications like lithium. I tucked my hurt away and carried streaks of shame deep inside my cool exterior. Some deeper part of the little girl in me wondered if I might be completely unlovable by my family.

My brother Evan defied the odds by using his opportunities and my parents' love and support to grow up. He became a devoted church member holding the priesthood, a successful businessman, and loving husband and father. I am grateful to him and his wife for raising five healthy, happy children who can enjoy the benefits of feeling loved and supported by their family and church community. His daughters benefitted from having his love and protection.

Evan gained tremendous benefit by maintaining a deep spiritual faith bonded to the structure of the LDS religion. I am proud of my brother today, while at the same time acknowledging the harsh contrast I faced as his sister. The conditions of my childhood required tremendous patience, a quality I was not inherently good at.

Month by month, I continued to count down the beads that took me closer to my eighteenth birthday. I wanted to get away. Tension built between my mother and me as I grew older and closer to moving out of her control. Once I came back from work and discovered that she had found and destroyed a collage I made that included artistic nudes of women. It hung in my room behind the door. She couldn't see it when the door was open.

On another evening, my mother burst into emotional flames and started screaming that she was going to kill herself. While my father was sitting in the den next to the kitchen watching TV, my mother stuck her head into the oven. She was screaming and crying, but she neglected to blow out the pilot light so gas would escape. If she were serious, she would have done so in privacy. I don't think my mother really wanted to die that night. She couldn't figure out any other way to express her pain or ask for the attention and support she needed.

Shrill cries filled the house as I ventured out of my cave of a room to see her dash from the front door into the street. My father ripped himself away from the TV in time to run after her as she went screaming through our tidy little neighborhood. Those same words I'd heard at fairly frequent intervals most of my life came bursting out of her broken heart through her shaking sobbing voice. "I'm only a slave! No one loves me. I'm going to kill myself!" I felt sorry for my mother's pain. At the same time, I unknowingly etched it onto my own heart, in ways that would later play out unconsciously with others.

I developed qualities of devotion when caring for people in need that I'm sure was born from my experience of my mother's attempt to care for me when I was in trouble. Sometimes her care took on elements of fanatic obsession. I didn't like or understand her erratic yet painstaking attention to keep me as her daughter during that time when she could have let me go. My mother listened to Puri and opened her mind and heart as best she could. She was determined to love and care for her children as her church and culture expected. My "illness" brought attention to me as the identified patient of our dysfunctional family. My mother took Puri's counsel seriously and tried to learn more about how to parent her children. As bad as it was, I'm sure my life would have become far more wretched had she not done so. I learned to appreciate my mother's sacrifice and attempt to hold her family together when I was old enough to see her position more clearly.

While growing closer to the age of eighteen, I continued to plan my departure into what I thought would be my freedom. I pushed away from all that my mother represented. I felt she abandoned herself in order to be an acceptable daughter, mother, wife, and church member. She was as creative and brilliant as her brothers, a gifted artist, yet she accepted her relegated role as a caretaker. My opportunity to live a different life, truer to the core of who I believed I was, began to rise above the dim horizon that was my life with my Mormon family in the sterile northwest suburbs of Chicago.

With my saved income, I purchased a new wooden conga drum. The first day I brought it home I began beating on the stretched calfskin drumhead with my open hands. I found a rhythm that I continued to play for hours until after sunset. Without interruption, I drummed into the dark. I could feel the heartbeat of the drum awaken a deep inner knowing inside me. I felt at home within the vibrations connecting me to a greater pulse of life. As I let myself shift into an altered awareness through repetitive movement and sound, I was able to ride into a presence of pure being. When I finally exhausted myself, I felt completely at peace. I turned on my bedroom light and saw that I had played until my hands bled.

I bought a ten-year-old white VW Beetle from a church member for $400. That well-used vehicle was so badly rusted the road could be seen through the passenger side floor. It reminded me of a Flintstones mobile, but it ran like a dream and provided me reliable transportation to work and to visit a young black boy named Gregory. I had befriended him when a church MIA (youth group) teacher took a group of us over to visit him. After that, I continued to go there on my own.

Gregory had been shot in the back of the neck by a stray bullet from gang warfare. He was at a city pool near where he lived in the Robert Taylor Homes housing project on the south side of Chicago. Gregory was twelve years old when that occurred. The injury paralyzed him from the neck down. He was sent to be cared for in a nursing home out in the suburbs near where I lived.

I visited Gregory every week for over two years until his death the month before I turned eighteen. Kent also developed a relationship with Gregory in the last year of his life. Kent went with me to attend Gregory's funeral on the Southside near the high-rise housing projects. Kent's father, the state trooper, drove us there and waited outside for us, fully armed.

Gregory died under suspicious conditions. It happened in the middle of the week. After work, I suddenly felt an inner tug and drove over to the nursing home rather than waiting for my usual Friday evening visit. I was pulled there by deep concern and a sense of longing. I walked into Gregory's room to find him dead in his bed with his respirator machine unplugged. Days earlier, he had expressed fears to me about the lack of care he was given.

A swing arm lamp fell down onto Gregory the week before. When I visited that weekend, Gregory smiled and didn't complain even though he had a third degree burn on a large area of his forearm. He told me about how he cried out for help again and again as he watched and smelled his skin burning. No one came in time to interrupt the severe injury.

One day when Kent came to meet me, he overheard a couple of aides talking outside Gregory's room. The service attendants were expressing an opinion that Gregory wasn't ever going to get better or amount to anything. They complained that he was a drain on taxpayers' money and on their services.

I was grateful for the friendship Gregory and I shared. His joyful presence made a difference in my life. When I found him dead, the look on his frozen face was of fear and shock. He was a great kid, full of hope, love, and humor. Normally he had the biggest smile on his lively face when he saw me enter his room. I wished I had gotten there earlier.

His death reminded me of the unfairness of the world and how people could be thrown away like garbage, just because they didn't measure up to some arbitrary value system. His still eyes stared out past me as I looked at him lying there, my own life colliding with his death in that moment.

There were nothing but roadblocks when I tried to investigate the true nature of his death. I felt in my heart that someone with the power to do so simply decided to unplug him from his life source. While I was enjoying a brief respite from my own struggle in the world, my young friend slipped away. I cannot claim the joy of my liberation without speaking for the other children that touched my heart and were lost. How was I so fortunate and blessed to have found my way? It has become my task to remember those who marked my path, creating a map from all of our stories.

1958   1972

Gregory Spencer

Gregory Spencer Memorial © 1972 by J. M. Seis

MOVING OUT

While working full time and going to school during those years following my discharge from Elgin, I was planning my escape to the city as soon as I was legally capable. I believed it was my truth and my right to live a life of woman-oriented love. Even though I had developed a genuine love for Kent, a stronger passion burned inside me. I knew I wanted to be with a woman. I was deeply grateful for my experience with Kent but knew that it was different for me. I was a lesbian, and loving Kent didn't change that.

I found ways to maintain a sporadic connection with Jane, visiting her whenever I could. She also attended night school. A thread of our romantic involvement stayed alive. I knew by then that we would never, and yet always, be lovers. I accepted the mystery of both her profound presence and invisibility in my life. We maintained an intermittent secretly lover-like relationship for many years. Her constant but inaccessible love was a butterfly of emotion frequenting the passion of my young heart.

Puri was a consistent caring influence in my life. My mother drove me to my hospital sessions each week until I was old enough to drive myself. I wasn't exactly sure how to trust and open up to Puri. It took years for me to utilize the awareness and skills Puri painstakingly tried to teach me. Her influence and efforts eventually culminated into my having a greater capacity to feel my feelings, including my grief and my joy. I grew to love and respect Puri.

B-1-North was closed soon after my discharge, and the girls there were moved to a newer building. Puri told me that all new girls were required to have a spinal tap as part of their tests on admission. I was horrified by the idea of such an invasive and potentially painful procedure being done on the new young girls. My recollection of the doctors there was of rampant incompetence. I considered Puri an exception but working in any capacity at Elgin State Hospital was basically the bottom of the barrel professionally.

One Saturday Puri arranged to pick me up in her car to take me with her to the Hindu temple in Chicago. Once there, I was immediately drawn to the colorful ornate images and statues of Hindu gods and goddesses. I soaked up all that Puri told me about them. It was incredibly different there, more moving than any religious experience I'd had before. I could feel a living spiritual presence in those gods and goddesses. It fed a hunger I didn't realize I had.

While driving back in the evening's twilight, Puri let slip a comment about something that happened when she was a student in Hyde Park. Although she was not completely specific, I followed the clues in her innuendos to imagine her as a young college student being attacked by a man or men who sexually violated her. She blamed herself for what happened, calling herself stupid for being out at night alone after working late at the lab. I didn't say much in response; I listened. At that moment, I understood why she had not been able to talk with me about what happened when I ran away.

Becoming a woman was fraught with dangers. Trapdoors could suddenly swing open, swallowing up independence, authenticity, and individuality. There were so many secrets held beyond those closed, hidden portals. In that instant, I witnessed a part of Puri that was not free. An unspoken warning became imprinted in me through her missing words and obscure meaning. There was an undeclared war being waged that had no clear beginning or end. Women were expected to remain unarmed and silent. As women, we were responsible for being targets. Each woman would be accountable for her own plight if she were hit. Freedom was sacrificed in exchange for the hope of safety. Coming into this awareness made me even more determined to become a free woman-loving woman.

On May 13th, 1972, I drove myself in my little VW bug to Chicago for the first lesbian dance held at the University of Illinois, Circle Campus. I learned about it through the underground newspaper, *The Chicago Seed.*

Linda Shear sang songs and played piano while women gathered around and danced together. I didn't realize then that it was the first out lesbian concert in the United States. That concert occurred at the moment of my emergence. I was excited and scared to be in a group of real lesbians. Most of them were much older than I was.

A masculine-looking woman in the bathroom gave me the title "jail bait." I heard the term "bull-dagger" used for the first time. It was a little scary and yet invigorating to be there. I went home with two issues of *The Ladder,* the first nationally distributed lesbian magazine published by the Daughters of Bilitis, the first lesbian rights organization in the United States. Soon after I found a book called *Lesbian/Woman* written by Dell Martin and Phyllis Lyon. That book, along with *The Ladder,* opened up a new world and made me feel connected to others who identified as women who love women.

I finished high school at night in the month of May 1972, while I worked full-time in the day. It would be six more months until the last bead was pushed over to the other side of the string stretched across my bedroom wall. In November of that year I was legally (but not emotionally) an adult. I prepared to move to Chicago.

Emboldened by graduation and my nearing eighteenth birthday, I began taking the train to Chicago regularly to attend CLL meetings, (Chicago Lesbian Liberation). I met other women there who were engaged in political activism. Two of them were my age. I aligned myself with a political consciousness movement for social change. I was finally living my dreams.

I told Puri and my parents of my plan to move out. My parents had their bishop come over and talk to me in an attempt to discourage my move into what he called "the den of iniquity," where he said I would "be damned to hell forever." I swore at the bishop as I stood up and walked out of that room where he sat as a male religious authority figure, making his decree like a curse on my life.

I was no longer willing to be forced to submit to hate-filled, fear-producing beliefs. I was a woman who believed in love or what I thought was love. My time had come. I was part of the love generation, carrying me toward the life I had been dreaming of for four long, tedious years.

It was hard for me to say goodbye to Sharon, my youngest sister. I'll never forget the sad look in her eyes as I was preparing to go. I wanted to protect her from the mocking and teasing that was now focused on her. When I turned on my father and challenged his behaviors toward me and my mother, he turned his attention to my younger sister. He made fun of her weight and food consumption. Evan had learned to be a teaser as well. Sharon was an easy target. She was sensitive and quiet. She cried easily. I stood up for her whenever I could, but I was not fully present as a teenager in that house. I regretted not doing more for her and hated to leave her there to face the twisted family dynamic alone. It wouldn't be long until she reached adolescence. Sharon was smart. Fortunately, she found solace in her studies and in playing the cello. I was the rebellious older sibling whose influence perhaps helped her to not choose that path.

I moved to Chicago when I was barely eighteen years old to live my life as a lesbian. At first, I believed that I was finally free. But my sacred shining hope could not hold up to the incredible challenges I faced. All those formative years of being a patient of Elgin State Hospital and under house arrest in my family home made me ill-equipped for adult life in a city. The pain and trauma that had occurred created gigantic sinkholes inside of me, ready to open and swallow my dreams. What happened during my time in Chicago became the next click in the wheel of change. My effort to be independent instead brought an end to who I was. A chaotic dismemberment occurred when I thought I might finally be free. Like a caterpillar, I had to dissolve completely before I could begin my true journey of rebirth and transformation.

PART III

WHEEL OF CHANGE

CENTER BUILDING

The Center Building at Elgin State Hospital gradually emptied out during the years I was an outpatient. It was completely shut down around the time I left to live in Chicago in 1972.

I went to visit Puri again a year after I moved from my parents' home. She was in an office in a different building. The old brick Center Building continued to stand like a frozen specter, a megalith of an ending era in the history of mental health. I recognized adult patients once housed there for decades as they began showing up on the streets of Chicago. Many of them were homeless. It was strange and sad to see familiar old mental patients from Elgin roaming aimlessly about. It felt like we had all spilled out into another time and place with Elgin strings attached to our very souls.

Something kept drawing me back to the hospital grounds. I was haunted by a feeling of unbreakable connection I couldn't seem to resolve, no matter how far I got from that time and place in my life.

In the summer of 1986, I was thirty years old and preparing to move away from the Midwest with my new passionate lover. Lucia was a twenty-one-year old athlete. We were enjoying a magical, intensely intimate time together. Before we left for the west coast, I asked her to accompany me to the place where my childhood completely ended. I struggled to find closure with my experiences surrounding that time. I didn't feel capable of starting a new life with her without putting better closure on my past. I needed her as my witness.

We drove out to Elgin and saw the old abandoned Center Building still there. It was dotted with broken windows and looked as though it was filled with ghosts starring out with vacant eyes into forever. We parked the van in a large empty lot and walked in on foot. Two security guards rolled by in their car, but we managed to avoid them. We ran around to the back porch where I looked through the windows into B-1-North. One door hung open, exposing a stairway to the ward above. I twisted the rusted metal handle of the door to B-1-

North, but it was frozen. A security car drove by slowly and we both ducked down behind the porch.

My heart was pounding and suddenly I wanted to run away from there. Lucia stood up and discovered a broken window above another window. She climbed up like a monkey, swinging her muscular legs over the sill and easily squeezing her body through the opening. She signaled for me to do the same. I was stunned and couldn't move. Was I going to break into the place I once wanted desperately to get out of? Something inside me shifted. I grabbed a brick and some pieces of wood from a broken place on the porch and set them against the side of the wall, then stepped onto them. I pulled myself up with my arms. Lucia grabbed me from inside and helped guide my body through the rough opening.

I got down and put both feet onto the floor of what was once the coatroom. The place was decrepit with crumbling walls and peeling paint. It was filthy with dust and dirt. Hangers and a mop bucket were skewed on the floor. I felt disoriented and could hardly take in what was happening or fully realize where I was. I walked out of the coatroom into the hall and stood still, looking at the empty aides' station and remembering Magee, Wilson and Harris —seeing them in my mind's reflection in contrast with the emptiness in front of me. B-1-North was abandoned and dilapidated. I was puzzled by seeing old-fashioned menstrual pads with the ends that are designed to tie on a strap, strewn all over the floor in the hall by the bathroom. I walked into the main alcove and stood staring into the space where I had shared so many experiences with other girls.

Then something happened to me. Inside I unfroze. My body melted into a fluidity of movement with the intangible. Lucia stood watching my apparent transformation as my voice became more resonant with sounds and words flowing through my lips. I began singing a song of love and honor to all who had been there. I danced with the souls that had fused with B-1-North in Center Building. My arms extended and my torso swayed like a tree in a slow storm as I sang a song of freedom. My knees bent as I turned in graceful embrace with something coming through me. Then it stopped. Lucia's eyes grew wide as she looked at me, obviously stunned and moved by what had just happened.

Knowing we had to get out of there, we quickly returned to the coatroom. After climbing up and out the window back onto the porch, we waited. A guard drove by in an automobile. We darted off the porch and ran around the building until we could get to our van and drive away.

"What happened to you in there?" Lucia asked me.

"I'm not sure," I said, grateful for the opportunity to sort it out. "I felt as though the spirit of all the girl's trapped in there formed a circle around me. That song came from the color of our souls, our innocence, the beauty of our perfect selves remembering. I was singing us home."

I had gone back to Elgin State Hospital to find something of myself that had been lost there and discovered many other spirits waiting. Lucia and I moved to California soon after our experience in Center Building.

Five years later, John Johnson sent me a letter. Even though we had not been in contact for many years, I still had the talismans he had drawn for me tucked away with my special papers from that shared time at the hospital. He told me what was happening in Elgin. There were plans to tear down some of the buildings. Soon after hearing from John, I visited the Midwest and saw a high chain-link fence erected around Center Building with signs warning people to stay away. The materials that had been used in the building were determined to be toxic, full of lead and asbestos. It was strangely gratifying to see the place I had lived so many searing moments of my life surrounded by red warning signs with the words, *DANGER, DO NOT ENTER*. (Or you may never be able to leave, even when you think you have, I thought.)

A few years passed. John sent news about packs of vicious rats that had inhabited the tunnels for years, attacking construction workers as they started tearing the building apart. I thought of the spirits of those who lived and died in Elgin State Hospital inhabiting those rats, biting and clawing to hang onto the grounds and buildings that were the only memorial to their forgotten and disposed of lives. Despite the wrath of the rats, Center Building with its Annex, B-1-North and South were completely demolished in 1993. As synchronicity would have it, I moved back to the Midwest from California that same year. I drove to Elgin, once I was back, and witnessed the end of Elgin State Hospital as it had been for more than a hundred years.

When I visited Elgin in 2008 on my way to live in Florida, I noticed a large mound of dirt at the site where the Center Building once stood in front of the two tall smoke stacks. For me, at that time, the mound marked a site of reclamation where the earth was taking back into her bosom what had been separated from its source. Like an ancient ancestral burial mound, it quietly acknowledged those who carried some of the shadow of humanity into obscurity. Is it possible to bring this shadow to light so it does not take form in another way in another generation? Hasn't it already taken form in our prisons and wandering homeless? This is the bridge I cross, seeking my own liberation by writing my story, yet hoping to connect the dark separated from light into a circle of wholeness for all, especially for those who have been disenfranchised.

I can imagine bringing a community of healers and spiritual people together in ceremony around this haunted hill in Elgin. I would suggest a shared intention to sing and dance for the souls of the lost and broken there. The strength of our unity and compassion is a balm for the living as well as the dead.

It takes a community to heal collective wounds bound in toxic emotionally-charged, physical environments. When I crawled through a broken window into B-1-North in Center Building before it was torn down, I could only sing for my own soul and the souls of those girls I crossed paths with. I started something that writing this memoir continues. I can imagine more songs and ceremonies to help heal the fragmented souls and traumatic imprints left on the grounds of Elgin State Hospital, as well as similar places.

A few years after I visited Elgin in 2008, I gained permission to take a group of my apprentices to Mendota Mental Health Institute in Madison, WI. The buildings resembled those I had experienced as a child. The same architect, who designed Elgin State Hospital, designed Mendota using the Kirkbride plan. Mendota was founded before Elgin in 1860 and is still operating today.

There were more than fifty effigy mounds on the land created by early native people before the development of Mendota. Indigenous sacred grounds became the place where modern inhabitants contained those considered insane, safely away from the city.

A storm blew in early morning on the day I planned to teach. I heard rumbling thunder and the patter of rain on the roof. While I was still groggy and barely awake, an enormously bright white light filled my bedroom. At the same time, a deafening crack, that sounded more like an explosion, shook the entire house. The electricity went out. I grabbed my flashlight by the bed and carefully ran downstairs. My friend, who hosted my classes, came down from her bedroom. We looked around to see if we could discover any damage in the house. She checked the circuit box and flipped a couple of switches that returned the light.

When the rain died down, we went outside and discovered a tall walnut tree near the house had been struck by lightning. The trunk was still smoldering. Lightning shattered one side of the length of the tree sending shards of wood in a direct path from the tree right into the ceremonial fire pit. I noted the significance of this occurrence. Lightning is associated with the initiation of a shaman.

As the students began to arrive, we invited them outside to experience the raw power of nature and to bring positive energy to the tree. They took some of the shards of wood to place in their medicine bundles. Many years later that tree is quite well with its lightning scar still visible.

Preparation was important before my students and I embarked on our outing to Mendota. The lightning was an auspicious creation energy inspiring all who gathered. These were my advanced apprentices who had been studying with me for several years. We were nearing the completion of our classes together. They had been through many initiations with intensive training in order to create a shaman's altar, a medicine bundle, known as a mesa. Creating a mesa in modern times and culture is an adaptation from ancient Peruvian shamanic tradition. A mesa is activated through initiation rites at sacred sites and through direct transmission from shaman to shaman.

What makes a shaman powerful is his or her ability to use energy consciously for specific purposes that are intentionally healing for themselves and others. I learned about the creation and use of a mesa from my teachers and while on yearly pilgrimage to Peru. One use of a mesa is to efficiently metabolize and consciously interact with energy. The lesson I was teaching my students was on intentionally creating and then directing a particular type of vortex in their mesas.

Developing a torus, in a mesa, accesses one of the most elegant, natural methods of moving energy in and out of the Middle World we live in. Often the intention of a shaman is to move stagnant energy where it belongs, either in the spiritual realm above or more often to the dense earthy world below. After my students had practiced and grasped the concept of activating a torus in their mesas, we joined our mesas together to create a community torus.

The shaman's mesa as well the shaman themselves become a vortex of change and transformation. The power of a shaman's mesa as well as our ability to connect our power as a community helps metabolize large fields of disrupted energy and bring that energy into more harmony.

When the time was right, we caravanned out to Mendota. It was a grey, misty, partly rainy autumn day in Wisconsin. After arriving I needed to walk around and listen to the spirits. I invited my students to do the same. We each went where we felt drawn. One woman began playing her Native American flute. Others sat and meditated. Some walked over to look at the ancient effigy mounds still remaining on the property overlooking Lake Mendota. Before we did our ceremony, it was important to ask permission not only from the hospital authorities, but also from the land itself with the inhabiting spirits of the land.

I felt drawn to walk around the last standing original building that had once been a medical hospital for the asylum. A familiar sensation came over me as I ambled closer to the old brick building. It felt familiar, holding a combination of comfort and pain, protection and danger. Being on the grounds of Mendota plunged me right into my own personal traumatic bond with Elgin State Hospital further to the south in Illinois. I found myself singing to the spirits I sensed still trapped inside those abandoned rooms and hallways in Mendota. I sang to my own child within me, who recognized this familiar atmosphere.

Suddenly I heard a deep throaty hooting of a great horned owl. I slowly and deliberately walked around the building in a clockwise direction. "Ho ho-ho hoooo" cried the owl four times as though deliberately timing its call to my walking a circle of four directions. As I reached the door of the building, the owl fell silent.

When I rejoined my group, we created a circle and sat down in a cleared area surrounded by tall, old trees. Opening our mesas, we prepared for our ceremony. "What did you hear, see, and feel on this land?" I asked them.

"I felt a spiritual presence like that of native people who once lived in this area and did their own ceremonies here. I felt as though they were aware of us and starting to gather around us." Leo responded.

"It was Lu Lu's flute." Polly piped in. "After she started walking around playing, everything began to wake up, or maybe I slowed down and tuned in enough to perceive what was already here."

"The energy definitely feels thicker and more dense." Yvonne offered.

"Let's create intentional sacred space by calling in the directions." I suggested. We all stood up and intuitively joined together asking for healing for the land and the spirits of the land, including all creatures. Our prayers went out into the four cardinal directions, above and below, gathering the power of intention into the center where we stood in the Middle World.

Then we sat down and began rattling, ringing bells, and focusing on getting the power of a vortex spinning in our own mesas. Eventually, we joined our separate individual mesas into a greater mesa. After many times practicing together, we were able to sustain a large vortex for a short period of time, intentionally sending stagnant maligned energy to the Lower World. We also created a spiritual portal to the Upper World for lost souls to return home. A part of me felt completely merged with the enormous natural energies we were accessing. This was about being in service to a greater harmony of which all creation is part. By consciously activating a configuration common in all of nature, we believed we were able to amplify movement and change. Shamans' ceremonies can be seen as an active form of prayer. By creating a community torus in our mesas, we were in service and, at the same time, in surrender, "Make me an instrument of Your peace. Thy will be done. Heaven and Earth are one."

We could feel it when we slipped back into ordinary reality. We completed our ceremony, cleaned up, and returned to our workshop space. I felt lighter after our ceremony and knew I had also been holding a piece of my experience of Elgin State Hospital in my heart. The ceremony was intended to help the spirits of the land and all creatures at Mendota Mental Health Institute, but I sensed that we were also being changed by our ceremony. Without realizing it, my students had helped me receive a personal blessing, releasing more of the ghosts I'd been carrying and unable to liberate on my own.

I've participated in so many circles of healing in my life for various reasons. I've taken groups to Peru, Bolivia, and Chile to sacred sites on pilgrimage annually for many years. I've watched students of the mysteries hungrily soaking up energy in the power spots of the earth, but isn't the earth one body, one earth? Isn't one human life experience connected to the mundane, to the great and the tragic in all human experience? That is what the circle of life means to me. All life is connected and interacting all the time.

This memoir takes the form of a community ceremony when I make it available for others to read. As a *Ceremonial Memoir* ™, I am intentionally creating a vortex of energy to release what is stuck and maligned, back to the belly of the mother earth where it metabolizes into usable energy again. In the great torus of creation, what is let go of to the beneficent dark of the earth, allows more light to flow in from the universe, creating balance and harmony here in our Middle World.

Since I was a little girl, I have carried a dream in my heart, a vision of human beings' greatest potential becoming manifest. I've had the gift of vision, where I can see and mirror others' shadow and light. From this gift, I envision a world where shadow is acknowledged, while love and respect become the currency driving the economy of our soul's purpose. I am driven to live this dream to the best of my ability, a dream of being accountable for cleaning up our mess and collectively giving birth to new consciousness. Is this an impossible dream? My heart, brimming with stars, somehow already knows the way home.

DREAM

Some dreams are more than dreams. Some reflect light and others absorb dark. It happened one night in 1969 while I was on a home visit from Elgin. I dreamed that I opened the left louvered door of my bedroom closet. Hanging from a clothes hanger was a naked girl's body, upside down, dangling by her knees. Her arms lay oddly positioned on the floor beneath her. Looking closer, I noticed that her arms had been cut from the armpit all the way through the flesh and bone. Her severed arms were still attached at the top of her shoulders by the sheerest layer of skin. Then I recognized my own face on the girl in the closet and immediately knew that my father was the cause of her being there.

Abruptly I woke up covered in clammy perspiration and felt my body preparing to vomit. I could not move. I sat frozen in my bed, staring out through the darkness. A pale glow from streetlights nearby cast shadows on the closet doors. They were closed. I pushed back the covers on the bed and lifted my body up. I hurriedly walked out of the bedroom into the hall and over to the bathroom. Turning on the lights and closing the door behind me, I sat down on the cold toilet seat and hung my head between my trembling legs.

That dream soon submerged, mixing among other unconscious parables, but was never completely forgotten. Since that night I have made sure to keep my closet doors tightly closed, especially before going to bed.

Throughout my life, dreams have served as signals and guides for me. Some dreams portend, while others review important times of my life. This one exposed a mysterious unwelcome truth lying beneath the strata of my ordinary awareness. It showed me in no uncertain terms that I had become dismembered.

I studied Greek myths as a teenager, gleaning symbolic meaning and universal aspects of human experience from them that could apply to my own life. When lost, I searched through myths, seeking to understand their underlying code. The ancestors' left maps within their myths I could apply to my own life journey. It would be many years until I would begin to unravel more of the mystery of finding the hidden dream body of myself, hung upside down with severed arms. At that time, my severed arms dream was not yet understood with the depth and meaning it would reveal later in my life.

PACT

In the summer of 2008, all but one of my siblings, along with their children and grandchildren, gathered on our ancestral land in Pennsylvania. I had seen most of them at two different weddings a few months before. It was unusual for my siblings and their families to gather together three times in less than a year. Toward the end of my stay, my father came up to me after nearly everyone else had gone. I was packing my suitcase, preparing to leave the next day. My father does not speak often. His health has been declining. He made a special effort walking toward me hunched over with age, his bushy graying eyebrows raised. I stood near the doorway of a small bedroom upstairs in their home across from his bedroom with my mother.

He told me that he loved me and that of all his children, I was his favorite. "Although we've had some difficult times in the past, that's all behind us. You're my keystone child," he finished saying and gave me a hug. Three months later when my mother called near my birthday, he asked my mother to hand him the phone. He told me again that he loved me and stated flatly that he'd never hurt me. He insinuated that we had had some bumps in the road, but that was over now. I was silent at first taking in what he said, and then I told him that I love him. I do. That's true. What good does it do to tell my father that I have been dragging corpses most of my life, unable to bury them?

In 1992, I brought my parents a book by Melody Beattie on co-dependency and a video of John Bradshaw, *On the Family,* about the effects of growing up in a dysfunctional family. My mother watched part of the video carefully with great interest, but my father didn't like it and soon turned it off. He controlled the TV remote and also, to a great degree, my mother.

While visiting, I asked my parents to listen for one hour as I spoke to them about some of my experiences as an adolescent. At that time, I took full responsibility for my life and my healing but wanted them to know something of what had happened to their daughter while in their care. My father listened and didn't say much afterwards.

In that hour, I broke the silent family pact to not know what I know and not feel what I feel or express it. For years afterwards, my father would suddenly start pounding on a table and even have tears in his eyes, saying seemingly out of nowhere, "If anyone ever tried to hurt any of my children, I would have to dispense instant justice!" Those words burned into me at the time. I wondered, wasn't I one of his children? Didn't someone or something hurt me? Why is what happened to me so untouchable and unknowable? I had become untouchable and unknowable to my family. In those distant yet emotional statements from my father was wrapped a tiny but tremendous life-giving love that I just couldn't figure out how to unwrap and take into me.

I have forgiven my father for not being able to understand the miracle and the catastrophe of my life while he was in the role of being my caretaker. I've asked him to forgive me for hating him and fighting with him all those years. I know he cannot see or understand how shards from his sharp anger lodged deeply into my child heart and cut chasms through my search for love and my capacity to provide for myself in the world.

His rejection and condemnation, along with the loss of his protective presence and demonstration of love and belief in me during my youth, became an absence nothing else could fill. I know it is time to let go of my father as he continues his journey toward death. I honor the love that is there, but at the same time I have difficulty digesting the words and intentions he has chosen to share. What the young part of me needed to hear from my father was, "I'm sorry I wasn't able to understand you or the situation you were in. I was unable to be there for you when you needed me. Please forgive me for lashing out at you and blaming you. It was never your fault. I love you. I'm sorry you had to go through all of that pain feeling so alone."

I would reply, "I understand that you did the best you could with what you knew and how you were raised. I know in your heart you never meant to diminish my value or crush my spirit. I forgive you. I accept your love." I would tell him, "I love you, Dad. I set you free. I need to set myself free too. I wish for you a good and peaceful death and for myself a better chance at life." I know my father loves me, not more than his other children as he said, but maybe in a more complicated way than his other children.

"Leave the past behind," my oldest brother gently suggested to me last week.

This morning my yoga teacher told me, "This is the moment, now, there is no power in the past." She continued to encourage the group of us stretching in the beachside sand of Biscayne Bay by saying, "There is only love and fear, Breathe in love, exhale fear."

Through the audio in my car I listen to Eckhart Tolle saying to not think about the past; but my past is thinking me. If I don't claim it and name it, have my say, I feel its unnamable power will replicate without mercy, a complex perennial misfortune, driving me into my grave. It already has repeated numerous times. I must find a way to consciously change this series of malefic replication from early painful seeds. The quality of my life depends on getting to the root.

As I gather parts of my child self from the Underworld, I am discovering ways to integrate as I forge a new path of healing. These are the places where I lost myself.

On the Wall

There is no light in the morning,
The sun was taken from me,
The shadows hide the tears
And hide a stolen image
Called friend.

(J.M. Seis, Jan in Elgin State Hospital, 1969)

The Dark Mother is part of my solution for tracking the deep root of misfortune left inside me from my childhood. She helps me excavate my unconscious, bury the dead, and discover hidden treasure. Her embrace of my human experience is inextricably woven into the fabric of earth. As long as I am alive, I am not separate from my female body or the natural world that my body is created from. The Dark Mother is a matrix of unconscious connection to all that is of the earth, and being in a body. Her great circle encompasses destruction and creation giving birth to the light of my awakened self.

I first discovered her in the dark, when I was alone and afraid. It wasn't my biological mother I found comfort in as a child, but some vastly opaque presence that felt maternal, at the same time as deeply mysterious. She was not distant in the Upper World like the masculine presence of God, Jesus, or what I was told was the Holy Ghost.

Somehow, I remembered her love when I entered this world in my current lifetime. I wrote letters to a mother I imagined as a loving witch of the night. This was the only form I could conjure as a ten year old that expressed the metaphysical loving connection I sensed deep inside me.

The Great Mother in her dark form is a holy spiritual presence, completely available when I am explicitly human. She is an archetype of divine feminine power in its most utilitarian form.

I'm sure it was the Dark Mother's encouragement of love through Laura Nyro's voice, when I was languishing in despair, as a young teen locked up in Elgin. She was there in the shouted command for me to get up when I lie dying in my hospital bed from the gash I had opened in my arm. This Mother is a subtle, profound comfort waiting in the shadow of life's cruelties, offering a promise of return. Her arms lifted me when I was sexually assaulted. She held my essence in pure love when my body was being brutally stolen.

All Her darkness is made of the most vital life-giving, mysterious forces of the universe. I only need surrender and flow deeply within Her vast black enigma, until I pop out into the brilliant flowering of everything else. There is my redemption, not in human terms, but in the true journey of my soul in this body, in this lifetime.

In my experience, I find that the past and the future are not stagnant or linear but are continually flowing within the present. All moments exist as a living dynamic essence in the circle of time. Time is now and now is tied to all time.

So here I am fishing in the circle of time with my hook sharpened on the rough losses and painful longings of what is considered past but has continued to wriggle out into the present. Here the same energies and themes become the challenges I face as well as the gifts I harvest. Those difficult repetitive themes don't go away. If pushed far enough, they become an unwanted and often unrecognizable reflection in the lives of those around me. Unhealed ghosts are passed from one generation to the next. Unspoken messages are sent out and received constantly in an ongoing interaction amidst all life. We are all connected and what we do or do not do, affects our world. The Dark Mother lives in the unseen domain within the depth and breadth of human experience.

Each day while twisting and stretching into yoga postures, I am aware of wringing out old unresolved grief from my cells, while at the same time remembering an essential joy. This mid-life body tells a story my mind attempts to turn into words. Stories have power in them–the power of death and also life.

As a young girl, the symbolism I found by reading old tales and myths provided a map for being more awake in the present. Stories from oral traditions continue to connect me to the strength and wisdom of the ancestors. I rely on divination from spontaneous, unfolding symbols in nature. These seemingly random occurrences are loaded with underlying meaning. I could not have survived and found my way in life, without having developed an acute sensitivity to listening to the spiritual voice of All That Is.

FAIRY TALE

As a child, I was both fascinated and frightened by Grimm's fairy tales. My parents had a book I would leaf through, stopping to stare at the intricately detailed color prints of characters in the stories. As an adult, I find personal meaning in the Grimm Brothers' folk tales gathered from old European oral traditions. Today these stories take on archetypal qualities and demonstrate aspects of our collective unconscious that help me unravel patterns in my own life and relationships.

I remember one story of *The Handless Maiden*, where a father mistakenly sells his young virgin daughter from his garden behind the house where he lives with his wife. He agrees to give her to an evil one, thinking the evil one is asking for his tree in exchange for great riches. Caught in a bad bargain, the father eventually succumbs to the demand that he sever his own daughter's hands. The father cuts her hands off. In the story, the daughter survives through the purity of her falling tears, expressing her grief and loss. She then begins a journey apart from her family and the ordinary world. I can relate to this story, as a story of shamanic initiation and the necessity of leaving ordinary reality in order to discover and access spiritual gifts.

Through the story of *The Handless Maiden*, I am aware that I too have lived in the world without arms or hands, unable to reach out or participate in an ordinary way. I have lived apart, trying to find my way home, wandering in a wilderness for forty years searching for wholeness and freedom. In that strange undefined realm, I first learned how to give others the love I was searching for. I then needed to learn how to become love itself.

Like the old ladies in Elgin State Hospital I was once horrified by, a young part of me became locked inside an invisible world. I was unable to run away, even while it appeared that I never stopped running. When a door opened, I exited, yet inevitably I found myself trapped again in a similar way. I struggled to survive in this other world between worlds as unexpected angels of grace and mercy came to assist and instruct me.

I lost my worldly appendages at a young age, along with certain qualities and capacities of independence in a fast-paced, competitive world. I have lived outside of that belief system. The worldly arms and hands I attempted to graft on to participate in ordinary reality, swiftly fell off again. Instead, I developed other skills and abilities that are of a mystical nature. These have become my wings.

I believe I can bring the most silenced and shamed parts of myself home into the center of my own heart, connected to the heart of earth, bridging separate worlds. I know it is possible because it is happening. My life is brimming with miracles occurring especially during the darkest of times. I am alive despite tremendous odds. I am a miracle of love, striving toward a greater purpose, a destiny resonating in my bones that I am committed to fulfilling regardless of how long or difficult the effort. I am guided by vision, a light that no darkness can extinguish. I regularly experience spiritual ecstasy.

In no way could I have imagined climbing mountains in Peru on spiritual pilgrimage, when most of my life was filled by chaos and loss, along with chronic illness and disability. I have given and received real love. My personal quest for understanding has allowed me to peer beyond the staged set of ordinary life, experiencing a creator's brilliance and depth, hard to express in words.

Recovering my wholeness involves gathering knowledge and wisdom and then giving it away to others in order to grow. A constant stream of people have quietly come to study and work with me over the years. Yet no one, not even I, can fully grasp the source of power that flows through me on their behalf. I've learned to trust implicitly the mystery that often comes to me in the guise of a mythic mother presence. She is with me when I work with clients. I am devoted and in service to being an instrument of Her healing.

A healer's gift can be born of brokenness where hope and compassion enter and gestate in the ravages of isolation, rejection, and humiliation. Threads of light break forth from jewels in the dark, seeded and cultivated in myself and in those who've come seeking my assistance and guidance on their journey. As a gardener of the soul, I have learned ways to transmute poison into medicine.

I've studied with medicine people and mystics from all over the world, primarily focusing on the ancient Americas' way of healing. People of the earth have created techniques and processes that mix the spiritual world of nature into the ordinary, through measured dose and timing. I have received direct healing through the earth, including with wild animals and spirits of nature and from people of the earth.

I was drafted into full-time service in a community I helped to create in 1995 and have continued to learn, teach, and serve in a wider community ever since. It is not my religion. It is my way of life. But it all began long ago as a child. It was innately part of who I was and still am today. The giant crevasse between my early and later life that I've now spent years trying to bridge is an illusion. That feeling of separation is slowly collapsing with the writing of this book.

During my visit with my parents in 2008, I noticed my grandfather's book in the basement. It was an 1872 copy of *German Popular Tales and Household Stories,* collected by the Brothers Grimm. Coincidentally, this edition was printed the same year Elgin State Hospital was established.

My maternal grandfather was quite different from my paternal grandfather. He was a joyful, smart, independent-thinking, musical, and pious man. He was tall and thin with one short bowed leg he kept balanced with the other in a specially made high shoe. He often coughed and cleared his throat from constant asthma in his injured lungs after a long bout of pleurisy when he was a young man. In his attempt to find a cure, my grandfather, then confined to a wheelchair, took a train to Utah to see if the desert air could save his life. After quite a while, in desperation he was inspired to concoct his own remedy that included turpentine and poured it directly in the drain tube in his chest and into his lung. His self-made cure nearly killed him. After the initial violent reaction, his lung began to mend. Eventually he returned to Pennsylvania walking, no longer disabled and deathly ill. He also returned as a baptized Latter Day Saint who then converted his father to the new religion.

My grandpa was the only man in my childhood whom I felt completely safe with. When he picked me up and carried me as a sleepy young child from the back of his Oldsmobile into the house, I relaxed into his arms with total trust. As I write this now, a glint of my grandfather's love and safe arms carries me through his book. Here it was sitting among dozens of old dusty books where he left it decades ago in his basement office in the room with the furnace. I am grateful for this old sooty book with memories of my grandfather's love falling out of its broken binding.

I immediately opened its delicate discolored pages looking for the story of the *Handless Maiden*, but the book fell open to a different page. The initial words felt like a warning of danger jumping out at me from the story of *The Robber Bridegroom*. I knew I must read it.

The tale begins with a miller who had a beautiful daughter whom he wanted to marry well. He promises his daughter to a man he believes is rich. The daughter's intuition signals her that something is wrong. She wants to avoid the bridegroom's invitations to visit his home but eventually goes, following a trail of ashes he has left for her. When she enters the house, a bird in a cage cries out the words, "Return, fair maid, return to your home: T'is to a murderer's den you've come." The girl wanders through empty rooms until she finds an old woman in the basement who warns her again and offers to save her life by having her remain very still and hidden for a period of time.

During the young girl's hidden time, she witnesses a terrible fate occurring to another girl dragged in by a band of robbers. The robbers pay no attention to the poor girl's cries and give her three glasses of wine, one white, one red, and one yellow, after which she swoons. The hidden bride shudders and trembles to witness the fate of the poor girl.

One of the robbers sees a gold ring on the poor girl's finger and takes a hatchet to cut it off. The finger flies off and lands right in the lap of the hidden bride. She stays still as the robbers try to find the finger with a gold ring. The old woman intervenes, convincing the robbers to look during daylight and eat a meal she makes for them. The old woman mixes a sleeping potion into the meal and the robbers fall asleep. The bride and the old woman escape by following sprouted seeds and beans the bride had earlier laid along the path.

When the day comes for the wedding, the bridegroom arrives to collect his wife. She sits silently with her father and his relations and friends. Eventually the bride speaks after the bridegroom's prodding and begins to tell everyone about a dream she had that is the exact experience she encountered in the house of the bridegroom.

When she finishes her tale about the dream, she produces the finger with the ring. The robber bridegroom jumps up pale as death and would have gotten away except for the guests who grab him and take him to the judges. Soon after, he and his whole band are condemned to death for their wicked deeds.

When I finished reading the story of *The Robber Bridegroom*, a whole panorama opened up inside me. The story illustrated how I too had entered a dangerous place that my father and mother had agreed to send me to for my own good. I knew that it was unsafe in Elgin, but it was also unsafe to be born a girl in the world as it was. Eventually, in contrast to the violence I experienced in the outside world, Elgin became a cage of adaptive safety as well as a cauldron of change.

Looking at the symbolism of this story, I think of how the bride finds her way to the bridegroom's house by ashes. Ashes often symbolize the dead. Here could be the path of the ancestors leading to a life she is destined to enter through the actions of her father and the absence of her mother.

In my own life, the experiences of my parents and my ancestors before them became part of my path. The gifts as well as the burdens, including unexpressed grief, rolled down like an ashen carpet under my baby feet as soon as I was able to walk.

When a bird in a cage cries out a warning, I imagine the bird as the intuitive part of a woman. In the folktale, the bird is a part of nature imprisoned inside an otherwise empty house. This can be the fate of women who allow themselves to be kept in a cage of society's expectation to control their nature; their sex and their bodies.

Elgin was my cage where I experienced an initiation. I understand how the story's caged bird is aware and serves as a messenger at the threshold of an initiatory experience. Although exploring the house is dangerous, the bride continues as though knowing she must. She uses her intuition to find her way to the essence of a hidden truth.

Intuitively following the trail of my memories led me to discover my essential self, buried in the rubble of an unacknowledged battlefield. I have not found any magical process of healing that precludes walking through the original pain to its source to reclaim what belongs to us. By doing so, lasting change and profound healing can occur.

In order to transform, the bride must descend to the basement or into the darkness of a lower realm of consciousness. This descent can also represent the journey of taking form in a woman's body. The bride is a symbol of innocence and the soul incarnating into physical life. The descent is also an entry into the collective unconscious.

In the basement, the bride finds an old woman who can make food and medicine and who knows the way out of danger. I sense this old woman represents an ancient wisdom all women can access by entering these lower realms. In my experience, I find that we do not discover this resource until necessity compels us to go deep. This realm is the domain of the Dark Mother archetype. In this darkness, the wretched fate of the poor girl is witnessed.

The poor girl is ravaged by a band of male thieves who take what they want of her, destroying and dismembering her in an effort to claim something precious, symbolized by the gold ring. The gold ring on a severed finger flies into the lap of the hidden bride, who is a virgin, undefiled.

Is not one woman's defilement and dismemberment also unconsciously felt and carried by other women? Sex is power. Sexual violation is dismemberment. I believe the poor girl, the old woman, and the bride are all interconnected. In some ways, they portray the triune aspect of the Divine Feminine, sometimes seen as the maiden, mother, and crone. Yet I believe the mystery of the Divine Feminine is much greater than that trilogy. The virgin and the poor girl highlight the split of light and dark, virgin and whore, valued and exploited. The split between the dark and the light of the feminine is held and made whole by the ancient healing wisdom of the old woman, the Dark Mother, an aspect of the Great Round.

In the story, the bride embodies a symbol of transforming consciousness. She must become still while an ancient grandmother concocts an alchemical solution through purification in the cauldron of change. It is within a defined time of darkness that the old woman can work her magic and influence the course of the unfolding events.

In the classic initiatory process of being separated from source and then reunited, the bride is saved by her silence and stillness in the dark. What a profound message to remember while going through our own transformations. The bride is then able to return to her family and community by following the sprouting seeds that she planted earlier along the path.

There is value in silence and stillness. During my childhood, there were times when I needed to be still in order to survive. I am in stillness now while writing this story. Seeds germinate out of stillness in the dark. What was planted of value in my early life becomes the awakening awareness guiding me back to the family of humanity. Return is only possible when the season of darkness and stillness is complete.

There is a similar process of initiation employed by engaging the path of the medicine wheel and the labyrinth. A season of silence and stillness lives in the North of the medicine wheel. After the chaos of change and endings in the West, I too have often become impatient for the birth of the new in the East. But without "the between time" of the North, the birth to come in the East is not possible. Any premature leap into the East only drags unfinished endings into the next round of manifestation.

In the Grimm's story, the bride waits until the appropriate time and chooses a mythic form, a dream, to tell the story of the lost girl. She brings a broken and violated part of a woman back up to the surface of ordinary reality in an attempt to obtain justice and gain the support of her community. All of the characters in the folktale hold an aspect of relevance that reflect a woman's journey of descent and return encoded in the story.

Initiation can be quite different for women than it is for men. Women are not as prone to taking the iconic, individualistic hero's journey as Joseph Campbell so eloquently described. Women can experience a death and rebirth through a descent and reemergence that involves the body and nature, as well as collaboration with community. These are the aspects I've learned on my journey of initiation accompanied by the Dark Mother archetype.

As I continue to search for meaning in my story, I find these patterns and symbols hold a universal truth. In my work, I seek to sift out systems, cycles, and meaning in others' lives. I help them discern their pathway and timing through their experience with what stops them but creates an opportunity for metamorphosis. I continue to make a map of my own journey as I assist others in theirs.

The Robber Bridegroom and *The Handless Maiden* present mythic patterns of an initiatory process. As I sit writing a story from a time of darkness in my own life, I see how I have again descended to a lower realm, like the bride in the story. I have witnessed violence toward a poor girl, my younger self. I can accept that I have had to go through a process of initiation. By listening to my intuition and the voice of ancient wisdom in the dark, I know when to wait and when to escape.

Through this book I am bringing the golden ring along with my dismembered self back into the present and into the society in which I live. This golden ring represents the light of love in my soul that cannot be stolen or lost. It is the key to the locked door I could not find a way to open in the past. I am retrieving this indestructible circle of brilliance that is much greater than one lifetime. By doing so, I find my opportunity for liberty and the promised victory of coming home. A guiding omnipresence of love has signaled to me as though by sonar, a way and a reason to live all these years. Listening to my own silenced story, feeling my feelings and grieving my losses with others, and myself, has uncovered my inner resilience. I follow these sprouting seeds guiding me to a greater destiny than was ever possible before. Liberation becomes unstoppable.

TIME

When I moved out of the Midwest to Florida during the writing of this memoir, a curious experience began unfolding inside me. Something happened that is quite difficult to explain. I seem to have crossed paths with a parallel reality.

After I moved to the subtropics, the warm Atlantic seawaters claimed me and facilitated a return to a core self. Here by the great sea of my birth, I awakened to another part of me that fragmented off a long time ago and yet continued on. Although I have experienced and participated in a number of ancient mystical practices on my path of healing, I had not encountered this variation of regaining a broader sense of self. There have been powerful changes from my previous spiritual processes, but this experience was different. This was an intersection with a reality that might have been mine.

Each morning as I walked out onto the shell and coral-littered sands to greet the waves for my morning meditation, I became aware of an internal homecoming. I encountered the presence of another self. This was the feeling and essence of a person I might have been if I hadn't moved away from New Jersey in 1967.

The essence of this other reality was a strange sensation I allowed to occupy my awareness without really thinking. If my thoughts moved too near, the immanence would recede. Because of this, the first several contacts went unnoted and washed back out to sea without a trace. I doubt this phenomenon could have occurred at all if I had not been completely emptied out from the life I had been living and stripped of the identity I had worn.

After so many endings and so much letting go of who I had been, I was open and had no resistance to a distinct being that began seeping into my present. Perhaps it was an inner self I was unconscious of that was surfacing into my awareness, given form by my imagination.

To create a story from this indescribable experience might be a distortion, but without a story it would not be told or hold any relevance. My experience with an alternate self seemed directly as a consequence of writing this memoir. Some part of me must have needed to know this other self in contrast to the person I had become. On some level, I needed to know who I might have been and to join with the resources and essence of that other reality. In an effort to explain this internal mystical process, I will spin what I've experienced into a fable.

Once upon a time, I began developing a beautiful relationship with the subtropical Florida waters of the Atlantic Ocean, where I met with a woman who was somehow familiar–but a stranger. The other woman had all the characteristics of someone who had lived well and utilized many privileges and opportunities offered to her in her life. She had suffered some challenges, losses, and tragedy, but she had not been torn away from the core of the life she was born into. Her arms could reach, and her hands could grasp worldly opportunities.

Morning after morning on the dawn-splashed sands, I had the impression that two middle-aged women walked together arm in arm talking about their lives and listening with rapt attention. They behaved like separated twins who had unexpectedly been reunited.

Receptive to the unfolding story, I continued to collect bright shell fragments from the shore of my imagination. The other woman retired to Florida after living in New Jersey and working in New York City. She decided to purchase a home after vacationing in Florida for many years. Using her creative skills, she had become successful by worldly measure. She married and gave birth to two children who grew up and went into the world on their own. The female presence that seemingly walked beside me had not been broken away from her extended family and community.

This parallel self had not gone to Elgin State Hospital. We may have been one when I climbed into a tree as a child, clinging to the branches in a storm, seeing various patterns of life's possibilities blowing ahead me. But she split off when I said "yes" to the offered quest to understand the depths of human experience that includes suffering. By traveling through that abyss, I discovered many things including how I could become a bridge for sacred harmonies to return as soul essence on behalf of others.

Instead, my other self had walked the familiar path my siblings and ancestors walked. She had not been taken away, separated out, torn apart, and put back together again. She had walked a more traditional and seemingly safer path. She was the possible part of me that was not broken and had the opportunity to live her life in a more ordinary manner. I could feel this presence inside me, unfamiliar and yet familiar at once, projected onto the screen of my mind like a living fairy tale.

During my first winter in Florida, this subtle familiar female presence revealed a fear I shared about financial stability and sustainability. She seemed concerned about losing the value of her investments during the world financial crisis of 2009. I marveled at what it must be like to have social and financial security and then lose it. In my altered state of consciousness, I shared with her about the spiritual path I have taken through uncharted territories and the wonder of how it has provided for me in the most unlikely ways.

The woman I might have been was intrigued and wanted to know more. She had realized in midlife that she was missing something but wasn't sure what that something was. She longed for the faith and inspiration I've been guided by. She was interested in my spiritual map born from walking through a pathless wilderness, where I refused to cut down, claim, or fence the magnificent wonder of this extraordinarily interconnected landscape.

I wanted to discover more about this other self's worldly skills and how she had achieved wealth and credibility. It was as though she began imparting knowledge by joining with me. Our intersecting paths gave me a sense of the resources of two separate realities combining into greater accessibility from both. I imagined what it might be like if I was truly confident and competent, engaging in a more worldly life with more ability for abundance. Joining with her into a greater self could facilitate my development of the essential hands and arms necessary to function more fully in ordinary life.

Believing in the unbelievable and allowing the mystery to inform each moment, I have folded one path into another so that the possibilities and resources of these separate realities might join and become accessible in the present. Here in the in-between time has emerged an awareness of a self I did not become, that was hidden beneath the surface of my potential. Now the selves of my past, present, and future can dance together in the light of new promise.

In the reflection of an alternate self, I was able to acknowledge that I might have lived an ordinary life, but my soul chose not to. Being in the stillness of the North of the medicine wheel during my initiatory transformation, I needed to recognize the other self that split off in order to better understand the significance of my early decision.

Swiss psychiatrist, Carl Gustav Jung, brought the concept of the greater Self, with a capital "S" into public awareness early in the twentieth century. He illustrated the self as a dot, representing the ego, with a circle around it. He referred to this as the unification of the conscious and unconscious self. This symbol is also used to represent the sun. Jung combined four quadrants into the circle with a dot to further express the individuation of the Self. Jung's map of an integrated Self is also represented by the medicine wheel and in a mandala.

My timeless Self stands between who I am now and all my possible, probable realities. It is who I was before I was born and who I am becoming beyond this one lifetime. This is the greater Self I originally wrote this story to engage with, and whom I trust will return, incarnating from form through formlessness to form again.

In the process of writing this memoir, layers of how I adapted and presented to the world have peeled away. I find myself naked and still, in a holy place of divine union. Walking through the past has yielded unexpected seeds that I am learning to plant, cultivate, and grow in fertile ground. I've found a tool for transmuting poison into purity, where brilliant flashes of freedom can come hovering to drink from the ever-changing flower of wholeness.

I've been on a quest lasting decades, searching for my home I knew well enough to miss. I've found it within me. When I teach my apprentices, I look to my own life and to the lives of others for inspiration. Through this time of healing and change, I've learned that it is not those who rush around assuming authority and behaving as though they have all the answers that I wish to follow or emulate. The mastery I am most inspired by comes from those who can be calm in the question, and humbly not know, in order to awaken and dance with something of greater awe that cannot yet be put into words. In this place of ecstatic openness, I discover how imparting and receiving wisdom becomes effortless. The truth I've learned is, true power involves surrender, surrender to something greater than the temporal self.

ARMS

I finished writing the main body of this memoir in February of 2010. That summer I went to Peru again on annual pilgrimage with a group of spiritual seekers and students along with my medicine woman friend from Chile. Four days before I left to fly south, my father fell. Since my mother could not lift him, she called my nephew nearby and then dialed 911.

The ambulance came and took my father away to a nearby hospital. They were unable to run the tests they wanted, so they moved him to another hospital eighty miles away from his home and my mother. I spoke with him by phone and asked him how he was feeling. I assured him I would rally my siblings to come help. I told him I love him and he said he loves me. That's the last time I spoke with him. He died while I was at Machu Picchu at the precise time I was at the Temple of the Condor. There was a moment when I stepped off toward the edge of the temple and lifted my arms, feeling a rush of ecstatic energy flow from my feet up through my body and arms into the sky. I didn't consciously know about my father until later that evening when I received an email from my eldest brother.

I had a dream thirty-six hours after my father died. In it, I was visiting a piece of land my parents used to own. They often spent time on that forty acres of rural Midwest land to restore themselves. My mother was an avid gardener and had enlisted my father's assistance in creating an especially fertile garden where they grew many delicious vegetables. In my dream, I was standing near the garden on the land that had become mine, when a friend pointed out something in the garden. I walked over closer to see what it was.

There in the garden was an area that was dug up in the midst of flourishing life. Two whole arms, as though from a teenage girl, were lying on top of the black hill of fresh fertile earth. My dream body thought, "Oh yes, this is a crime scene, not yet finished."

When I woke up and spoke to my roommate, she suggested it was my arms returning to me from my father leaving and meant that both of us were letting go. When I wrote to tell my advisor, who had encouraged me all through the process of writing my memoir, she kindly pointed out that the dream was yielding to me the potential to finish the work of discovering what had happened in my life. She reminded me that it was an "incomplete crime scene." I knew instantly that what she said was true. And so, I persevere in the work of writing until this puzzle is solved and my essential arms are reattached. I am already embracing this incredible life more fully since coming this far on my journey of wholeness.

WHEEL OF CHANGE

I have finished writing this book, but the story is not over. Today is Yom Kippur. In the Jewish tradition, it is a day of atonement—a day of reparation for injury and harm, reconciliation between creator and created. The Latin origin for the word atonement denotes unity, *onement*, returning to the source. Perhaps the concept of "sin" is about those acts, frames of mind, beliefs, and experiences that separate us from the Divine unbreakable Self. My process of atonement is through this journey of return, revealing what has been hidden, remembering what has been dismembered.

During midlife, I discovered burdens I could not carry alone. My embodied pain became tangled up with humanity's exiled fear, separation, shame, loss, unexpressed grief, wounds that do not heal and sorrows that personal tears cannot wash away. Along this journey I discovered that some wounds and losses don't belong exclusively to one person's experience and can't be completely resolved in the ways most often utilized. They must also be addressed at the level of the collective, through community.

In the late 1980's and early 1990's, I participated in many spiritual and shamanic workshops with knowledgeable teachers. I felt power there. I did not see the people who had profound moments in the workshops anchoring their new awareness in practical ways in their ordinary lives. The workshops sometimes inspired discord in relating to their loved ones when returning home. There was such a difference in awareness and no clear way to share what the participant had just gone through. Those who found sustenance for their spiritual life often needed more workshops to feed their hunger and reignite their passion for life. I felt this in myself and decided to try an experiment.

In 1995, I planted the seeds of my personal healing experience into the garden of a Midwest community. For thirteen years, I devoted my life to service by facilitating spiritual community gatherings. At that time, I joined together with others to create a shamanic educational non-profit organization called "Pachamama Inc."

Pachamama Inc. served as a structure to hold our stories of meaning and truth we needed to hear and tell. Our organizations events provided a proving ground where we attempted to create a cohesive spiritual community within the chaos of modern life.

As a practitioner of spiritual healing, I found the power of community could provide different benefits than a one-on-one session or a teacher-student workshop. I witnessed profound healing occur when individuals were seen and heard in a safe, sacred space, a space of self and other, held within the context of a spiritual community. A sustainable spiritual belief shared by a group connected to the natural world provided fertile ground for spiritual action to take root.

After co-creating and working within this community environment for some time I felt I needed to find a way to provide deeper healing directly to the part of myself that was lost during my teens. As it turned out, the community where I was in a leadership position could not provide this service to me, although we may have wished for that possibility. A series of events occurred that helped me realize I must experience something beyond what I had helped to create.

In the process of my continuing journey of healing, I developed a writing genre called *Ceremonial Memoir* ™. I did this in order to identify and activate an ancient spiritual tool that can expand personal stories into a universe of lights in the dark. As we address collective wounds carried by individuals and groups of individuals, writing becomes a vehicle to connect us globally. Being willing to see and hear each other changes everything. Writing in sacred space allows the solitary experience of expressing a personal story to take on the potency of a greater circle of shared intention. What may have felt like a personal dead-end can become an illuminated pathway. A maze becomes a labyrinth. Personal stories become maps of inspiration for others to find their way.

My memoir is a dialogue when it affects others, inspiring part of their story to surface. It's no longer about me; it's about you, and it's also about us, and our world. My burden is lighter and my ability to transmute suffering becomes potent medicine. This is a path of transformation beyond the personal that can connect to a new kind of future, which I hope to discover with those who also seek to understand the mystery.

Writing is healing. After writing my stories into this book, they no longer belong to me. I have to let them go. I offer them as a ceremony amidst our greater human story. I did not protect myself by keeping secrets. I became lost in a great pool of darkness, and yet darkness became my teacher, gave birth to me like a mother. I felt completely alone, but I was not alone.

I made a vow as a child connected to a greater creative essence I held onto as a tree. The tree of my childhood was rooted in this world, but it also reached down into the unseen darkness where it could draw sustenance and thrive. That tree of life I held onto through the storm is now branching out into a universe of possibilities.

Our ancestors have given us the medicine wheel. I acknowledge this holy configuration in the center of my heart as a holographic compass. It is the enduring structure I have used to organize my story and own it. Here the Central Axis, a Tree of Life, makes it possible to come home to the true self in a balance of shadow and light.

Although there are many ways to represent the medicine wheel as the great wheel of change, I use a circle with a cross inside, as a symbol of the crossroad of spirit and matter. Four primary elements create life on earth and form an initiatory four-fold path. The earth, air, water, and fire are our bodies, breath, emotions, and spirit.

In the center of the wheel there is a place where the paradox of unity and separation meets life in the present moment. Spirit and matter, above and below, future and past, all intersect with now. I am a timeless, formless soul inhabiting a temporal body, creating a crossroad of choice. Life can be experienced as a cross of suffering as well as a circle of transformation.

The Center provides an access point where I ascend and descend, as though by a ladder, into other realms of consciousness. It is here that I grow wings and establish a trusted relationship with the Divine and my mirrored greater Self. Anything and everything seems possible, but then comes a return and an all-important reintegration with the physical present. I have climbed that ladder and experienced the embrace of pure unconditional love that transforms chaos into meaningful order. Translating that experience into ordinary life has become my work.

After all I've become aware of on this strange and perilous journey that is my life, I have also learned that it is not my life. It is our lives. My infinitely small earth life exists within an enormous matrix of creation more mysterious and grand than I have the ability to fully comprehend. Who knows what might be possible from the choices and changes of our present moments as they refract through time and space?

I complete this portion of my story and place it into the South of the medicine wheel. Longing for completion in the Center, I shift my attention to writing the West, the North, and the East stories. These form a map of my life, as I attempt to research and diagram a terrain of consciousness.

I wanted to write a different book, but my silence about this early time cost me my voice in other areas of my life. Finally, something moved inside and allowed this silenced voice to speak. The time was ripe. I listened and I wrote. Secret demons gnawing at my heart all of my adult life sprouted wings, turning into sudden angels.

Thank you for your willingness to explore my *Ceremonial Memoir* ™. Perhaps you may be inspired to write and tell your light and shadow stories by creating a sacred space and allowing hidden truths to emerge. I hope so because you are a beautiful miracle, no matter what has or has not happened in your life; and so am I. Together our light and dark unite within the circle of humanity. The community of love we create together becomes our home on this blessed earth.

We don't receive wisdom; we must discover it for ourselves after a journey that no one can take for us or spare us.

Marcel Proust

FAREWELL

Mother didn't notice when I pushed the screen door open and ran outside the house and down the steep grade of green grass sloping slowly toward the sidewalk. I turned right and continued my pace along the cement walkway as it curved gently toward the big street I was not allowed to cross. Reaching the end, I waited and watched cars go by, looking to my right where dark asphalt in its glorious blackness climbed up the hill and made a "T" with an even busier road.

Turning my head to my left, I said aloud, "There it is!" A big green and white bus came into view and soon stopped in front of me. I angled my head up as this suited man and that suited man stepped down onto the pavement. One dropped a smoky cigarette and crushed it out with his foot. Walking away I saw sparks glow cherry red and sparkle across the ground, then disappear.

"Daddy." I uttered when I saw his face. A smile widened once he saw me. His thick, black, plastic browline glasses with silver wire under each lens framed his hazel eyes, suddenly growing brighter. "Let me carry your briefcase," I begged him with my small hands reaching toward his.

"Oh no, it's much too heavy for you" he replied, but I put my hand on the other side of his wide strong hand, grasping the brown leather handle to carry it with him.

"I can do it with you, Daddy." And so I carried the case with my father all the way home and up the steep driveway to the light-colored walk, stepping up to the front doorstep and inside.

"Maribel, I'm home," my father called up to my mother who came out of the kitchen into the split-level living room, holding my little baby brother in her arms. "My good little girl walked me all the way home", he said to my mother as she disappeared back into the kitchen. Then he let go of my hand and walked upstairs.

I called up after him, "I love you, Daddy…I love you."

Rest in peace, mother and father of this life. At last I'm coming round the circle to home. Over and over, I have chosen to love, then, now, and always.

To J.M. Seis, My Adult Self,

All I ever really wanted was a home and a family. In the past, I responded to the insanity around me as a child in distress. I was never "crazy."

I fulfilled my assigned task of taking out the emotional, psychic garbage of my family. I helped release the refuse of a generation and a belief system that crushes lives and souls. I am the privileged witness who recorded the stories and kept them safe until the day I could finally tell someone who would believe me. You believe me. Today is the day. I am free to love and be loved. I am home. I don't feel a need to run away or run to something or someone else anymore.

In the past, all I wanted was to give and receive love, but love was something I learned to look for outside of myself. When I was in love, I turned other people into a kind of deity. My God was love. I created a romantic storm of feelings to color the harsh realities of my life. I believed I could accomplish my potential and go through hell unscathed, if I was in love and someone truly loved me. Now I know you were always there in the deepest part of me shining a light for me to come home.

You didn't blame me for all the things that happened to me. I finally believe that those painful experiences were the violence and cruelty of a world out of harmony with itself. The shame I've carried is not mine. I let it go.

There is nothing to prove or defend. I am at the center of human experience where my true lineage is part of the Tree of Life. Rooted by living consciously on earth, I am reaching up to embrace a family of stars, turning light into food. No more hunger. Only peace. I join all the ages I've been and will be because I'm not separated from my body, the earth, or my whole Self anymore. I believe in a divine creative presence of unconditional love. I've discovered this love because of you taking all this time and effort to sort my essence out of the rubble.

> I love you and need you,
> I am you,
>
> Jan, Your Inner Teenager

Let me fall if I must. The one I will become will catch me.

Baal Shem Tov

AFTERWORD

It took nine months to write the first draft of this book. During nine years of rewriting and editing, I attempted to bring together very different parts of my self and my life that have been divided, even absent. I descended into hell again and again combing through the wreckage in order to salvage essential parts of a dismembered self. By writing, I have purposely built bridges to cross into new more integrated terrain. I didn't feel this book was finished until I found peace with these various experiences in my life. Different parts of my consciousness needed to come together as an inner family held by love, mutual understanding, and respect.

How can the shaman, teacher, healer, who others come to with such hope and trust be standing side by side embracing the exiled, beaten and plundered girl of my youth? How could I not embrace her? She is my hero and I am hers.

The truth is I have to accept that I may never completely understand what it means to fully integrate all these different experiences and aspects of my life and my self. I am finally willing to accept that there may always be missing links and odd indefinable aspects of who I am. Some experiences in my life will probably always have sharp edges requiring care for how I hold them. I think what matters most is that I have created a space to embrace with gratitude all that I have lived and am yet to live, and that's enough. I am enough, already, right now. This book is finished, the door is unlocked and open at the intersection of my soul experiencing life. I offer my life experience for the benefit of others. May the ceremony continue through memoirs to come.

Blessed Be. Amen.

APPENDIX

My life is my message.

Mahatma Gandhi

THE MEDICINE WHEEL

Throughout this book, I use the medicine wheel as an underlying structure. I intuitively placed a circular symbol at the beginning of various chapters. Sometimes the cross in the circle rotates or the wheel changes color (in the color edition) denoting a significant shift within my life at that time.

Although the meaning and use of the medicine wheel varies according to the era, geographic and cultural influences, it is an enduring instrument of transformation. The wheel as a circle is as vast and dynamic as an ocean; its defining cross has helped to guide the ship of my existence toward greater coherence.

In the center of the wheel are two intersecting lines. The vertical axis, embodying what is timeless and spiritual, crosses the horizontal axis of the temporal and physical. These paradoxical polarities create dualism as a cross, within holism represented by a circle. The cross can be seen as a tree of life and death, where light and dark spin creation's web into countless manifestations. The spinning wheel becomes a torus connecting the threads of all worlds while weaving endless strands in and out of time and space.

I have woven my coming of age story into the direction of the South of the medicine wheel encapsulating the element of fire. Pain and passion culminate into a choice whether to convey my history through continual suffering or through transformation into inner peace and service. Fire changes density into light. In its mysterious processes, we can remain ash or rise into spiritual realms of new awakening.

In this modern usage of the medicine wheel, I am associating the South as a place in time when we go through a foundational experience that marks us. It can be viewed as an initiatory rite, a time of descent and or ascent into a different realm than we had previously been aware of.

As I place my life into the four directions in a ceremony of healing, I redefine how I carry my stories. I live my life as ceremony and write it as *Ceremonial Memoir* ™. The writing itself is a ceremony. Reading this book becomes a participation in the ceremony.

After completing this South edition, I intend to continue writing the stories of the West where there is chaos and endings, the North, a place of wisdom and stillness, and the East where the light of new vision is born. These are the cycles of creation I align with and use as my spiritual compass.

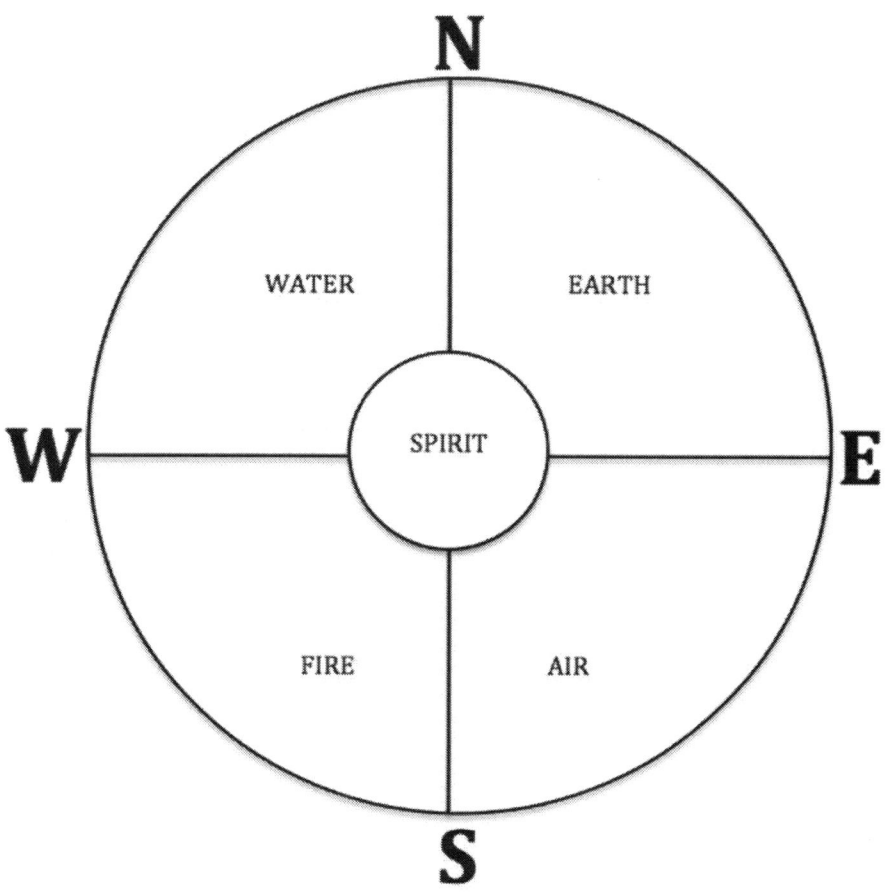

DARK MOTHER ARCHETYPE

The Robber Bridegroom, Grimm, Jacob and Wilhelm. Grimm's Fairy Tales.
John B. Gruelle, illustrator. Margaret Hunt, translator. New York: Cupples &
Leon, 1914. Public Domain.

The Basilica of Our Lady of Copacabana, Bolivia. Lower dark and upper light Madonna's. © 2013 by J. M. Seis

Archetypes exist as universally present patterns and symbols. The Dark Mother is connected to the unconscious mind and the primal experience of being in a body connected to nature. She is present in birth, death, sex, survival, pain, loss, grief, suffering, joy and transformation. Her nature is cyclic.

As part of the collective consciousness, she expresses her influence through many forms and has many faces. The Dark Mother is known by countless names including Kali, Hecate, Isis, Astarte, Inanna, Diana, Demeter, Quan Yin, and the Virgin of Guadalupe/Tonantzin. She is often depicted with dark skin. Symbolically she is a smoky mirror reflecting shadows into light.

I have threaded the essence of the Dark Mother archetype throughout my story because she is an unseen presence of constant unconditional love and guidance in my life, especially during times when I have suffered. I learned of her through experience. Any explanation I could give would be inadequate. When I refer to her directly, I may call her by different names including, Dark Mother, Madonna, or Virgin.

The Dark Mother is part of the Great Mother archetype, having both shadow and light aspects. She was once experienced as whole, but over the last two thousand years or more she has been completely divided, with her dualistic parts given lesser and greater importance depending on which aspect is acknowledged and by whom. Both men and women are greatly influenced by this overriding belief structure.

My adolescent self collided with and became lost in the divide between what has been interpreted as good and evil in women. Writing this *Ceremonial Memoir* ™ gave me a method of reuniting my shadow and light, allowing me to carry my experience of being female into a more balanced and integrated Divine Feminine archetypal belief system.

EMBRACE YOUR DARK
TRANSFORM YOUR LIGHT

THE USE OF THE WORD SHAMAN

The word *Shaman* (SHAH-men) is believed to have come into widespread use from a mispronunciation of the Tungusic language by nineteenth century German anthropologists publishing their research on the Evanki tribe in Siberia. The word shaman became Westernized and used generically to describe someone who shifts their consciousness in order to access helping spirits and information in the natural and spiritual worlds. This information and energy is primarily used for healing and service in his or her community.

I would never describe what I do as that of a *Machi* or a *Paco*. Each culture has a different title of respect for their medicine men and women. Although initiated in Chilean and Peruvian shamanic traditions, I reserve respect for those who are carrying a direct lineage in their bloodline and healing practices. I am deeply grateful to those who kept these traditions and practices alive and shared them with others including those outside of their culture. It is an honor to use what was given to me as a gift, a tool, and a responsibility. I understand that our world desperately needs this healing medicine.

Front Door Small Alcove B-1-North, ESH 1970

Bathroom B-1-North, ESH 1970

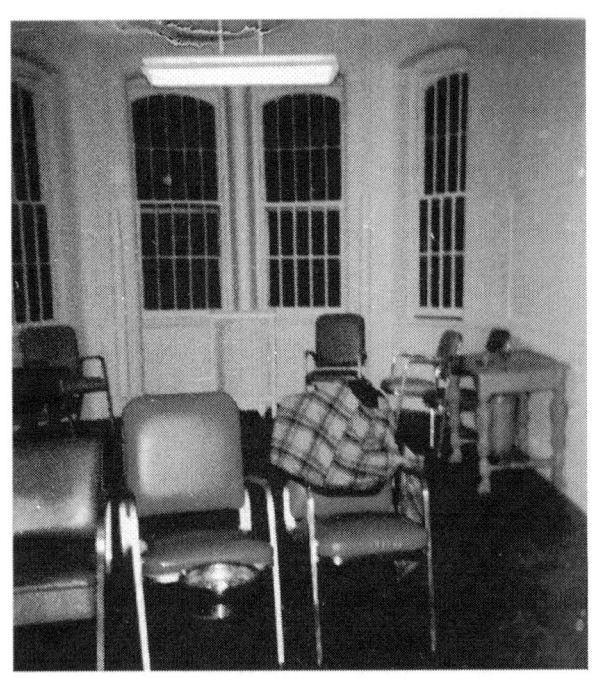

Main Alcove B-1-North, ESH 1970

Hallway B-1-North, ESH 1970

Far Dorm B-1-North, ESH 1970 (Student Room)

Dining Hall B-1-North, ESH 1970

Annex of Center Building ESH 1985

Annex Plaque ESH 1970

Photos taken in Elgin State Hospital © 2008 by J. M. Seis

Elgin State Hospital B-1-North, Sign, 1985

Elgin State Hospital B-1-North, Porch, 1985

Elgin State Hospital B-1-North, Back Doorway, 1985

Elgin State Hospital B-1-North, Building, 1985

Photos taken at Elgin State Hospital © 2008 by J. M. Seis

Alcove Window Outside B-1-North, Elgin State Hospital 1971

Alcove Window Inside B-1-North, Elgin State Hospital 1985

Inside B-1-North, ESH, Main Alcove from showers 1985

Inside B-1-North, ESH 1985

Photos taken at Elgin State Hospital © 2008 by J. M. Seis

Alcove Window B-1-North, ESH 1971

Entry into Center Building Annex 1971

Center Building, Elgin State Hospital 1971

Photos taken at Elgin State Hospital © 2008 by J. M. Seis

Elgin State Hospital Behind Center Building by B-1-North, 1971

Photos taken at Elgin State Hospital © 2008 by J. M. Seis

MAIN BUILDING, NORTHERN ILLINOIS HOSPITAL FOR THE INSANE, ELGIN, ILL.

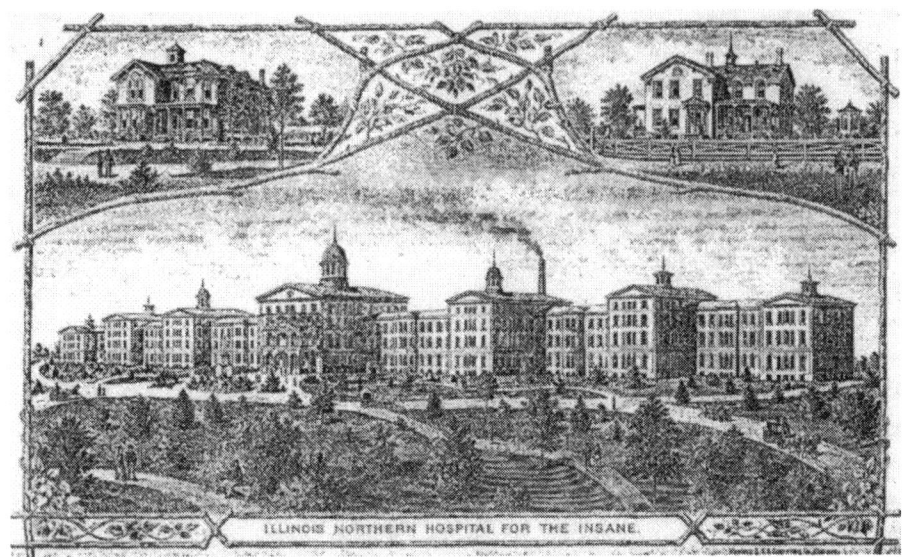

Brick Found, Center Building Mound and Smoke Stacks © July 2008 J. M. Seis

FIRE ZONE

BURR

790

RECOVERY IS OUR VISION

WELCOME TO
ELGIN MENTAL HEALTH CENTER
EST. 1872

PLEASE OBSERVE THE FOLLOWING RULES WHILE ON GROUNDS:

1. IF VISITING, PLEASE HAVE A VALID I.D. READY.
2. SMOKING IS PROHIBITED ON GROUNDS EXCEPT IN DESIGNATED AREAS.
3. POSSESSION AND/OR USE OF ALCOHOLIC BEVERAGES, DRUGS AND FIREARMS IS STRICTLY PROHIBITED ON GROUNDS.
4. OBSERVE ALL POSTED TRAFFIC REGULATIONS, INCLUDING THE POSTED SPEED LIMIT OF 20 MPH.
5. ENSURE YOUR VEHICLE IS SECURE AT ALL TIMES. DOORS SHOULD BE LOCKED AND WINDOWS CLOSED.
6. VEHICLES PARKED ILLEGALLY OR LEFT OVERNIGHT CAN BE TICKETED AND TOWED AWAY.
7. CAMERAS ARE PROHIBITED.

Thank you for understanding and for your cooperation.

Burr Ward, Elgin Mental Health Center © July 2008 J.M. Seis

1961 © J. M. Seis

Photo Booth in Elgin © May 1969 J. M. Seis

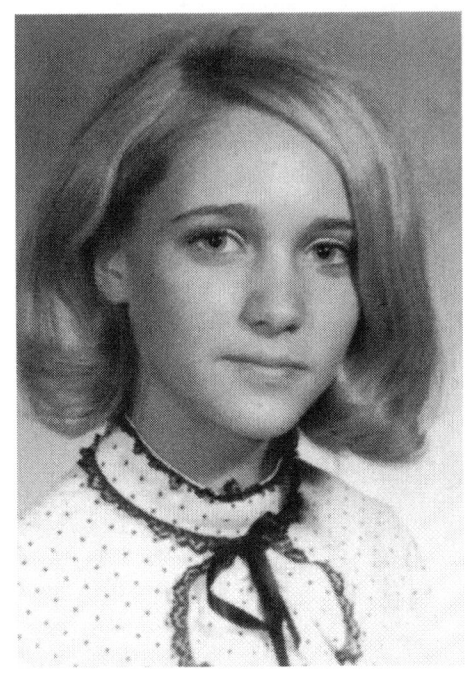

Elgin Sophomore © September 1969 J. M. Seis

Summer New Jersey © 1970 J. M. Seis

Summer New Jersey © 1970 J. M. Seis

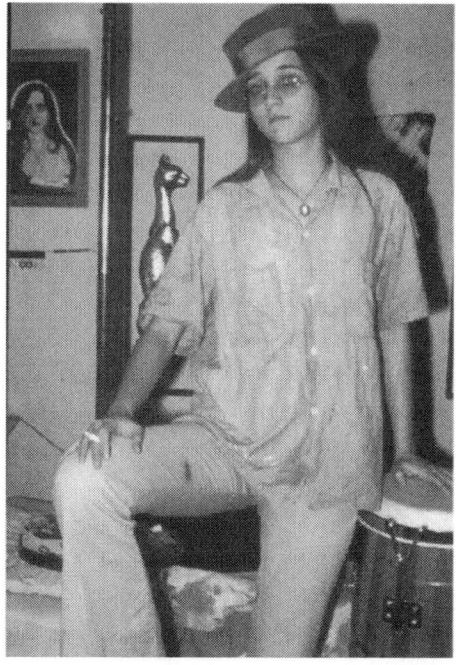

Laura Nyro Painting and Conga Drum © 1971 J. M. Seis

Puri at Elgin State Hospital © Fall 1970 J. M. Seis

Sillustani burial/rebirth towers Peru © 2009 J. M. Seis

Machu Picchu Temple of Condor © 2010 J. M. Seis

Machu Picchu Altar to Putukusi © 2011 J. M. Seis

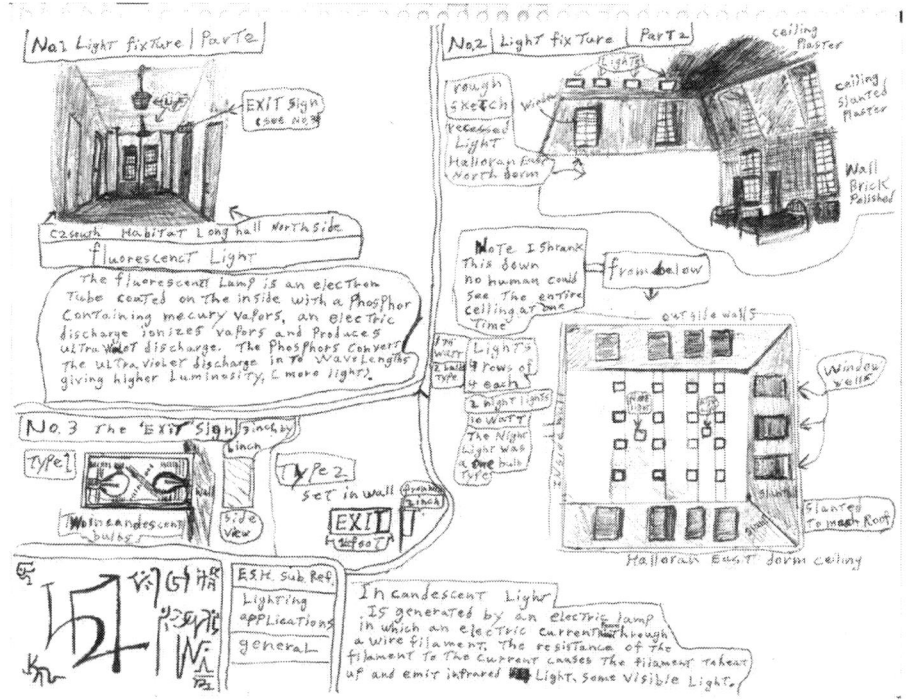

John Johnson's art while in Elgin State Hospital 1968-1972 © J. M. Seis.

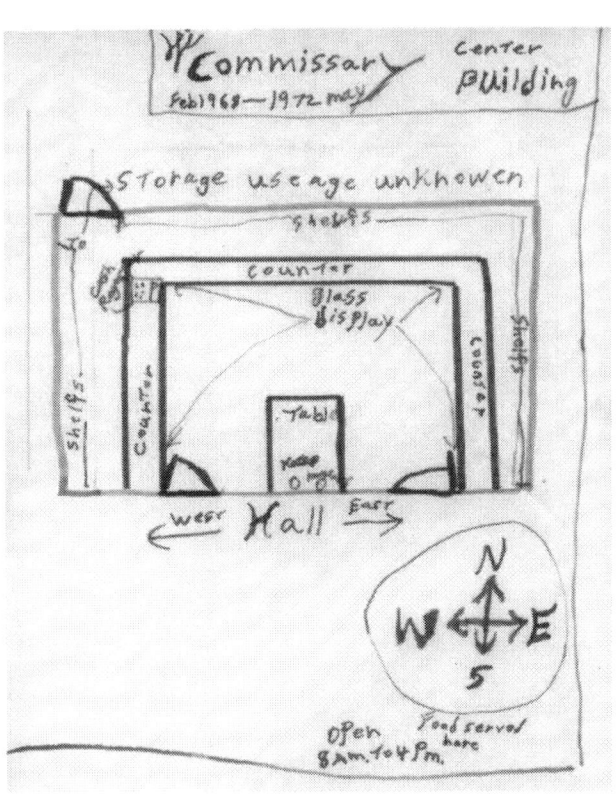

Commissary
Feb 1968 — 1972 may

Center Building

storage useage unknown

shelfs

counter
glass display

counter

shelfs

shelfs

counter

Table

Rose O met

← West Hall East →

N
W ← → E
S

open
8 am to 4 pm

food served here

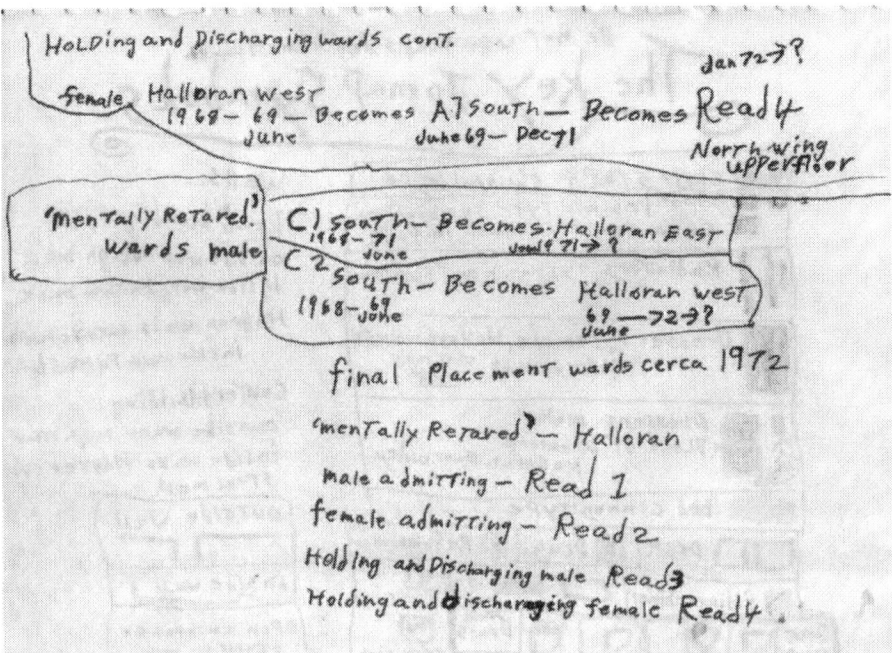

Holding and Discharging wards cont.

Female Halloran West
1968 - 69 — Becomes A7 South — Becomes Ready
June   June 69 — Dec 71   Jan 72 →?
                                                    North wing
                                                    upper floor

'mentally Retared' C) South — Becomes Halloran East
wards male 1969 - 71   June 71 →?
            June
C2 South — Becomes Halloran West
1968 — June 69   June 69 — 72 →?

final Placement wards cerca 1972

'mentally Retared' — Halloran

male admitting — Read 1
female admitting — Read 2
Holding and Discharging male Read 3
Holding and Discharging female Read 4

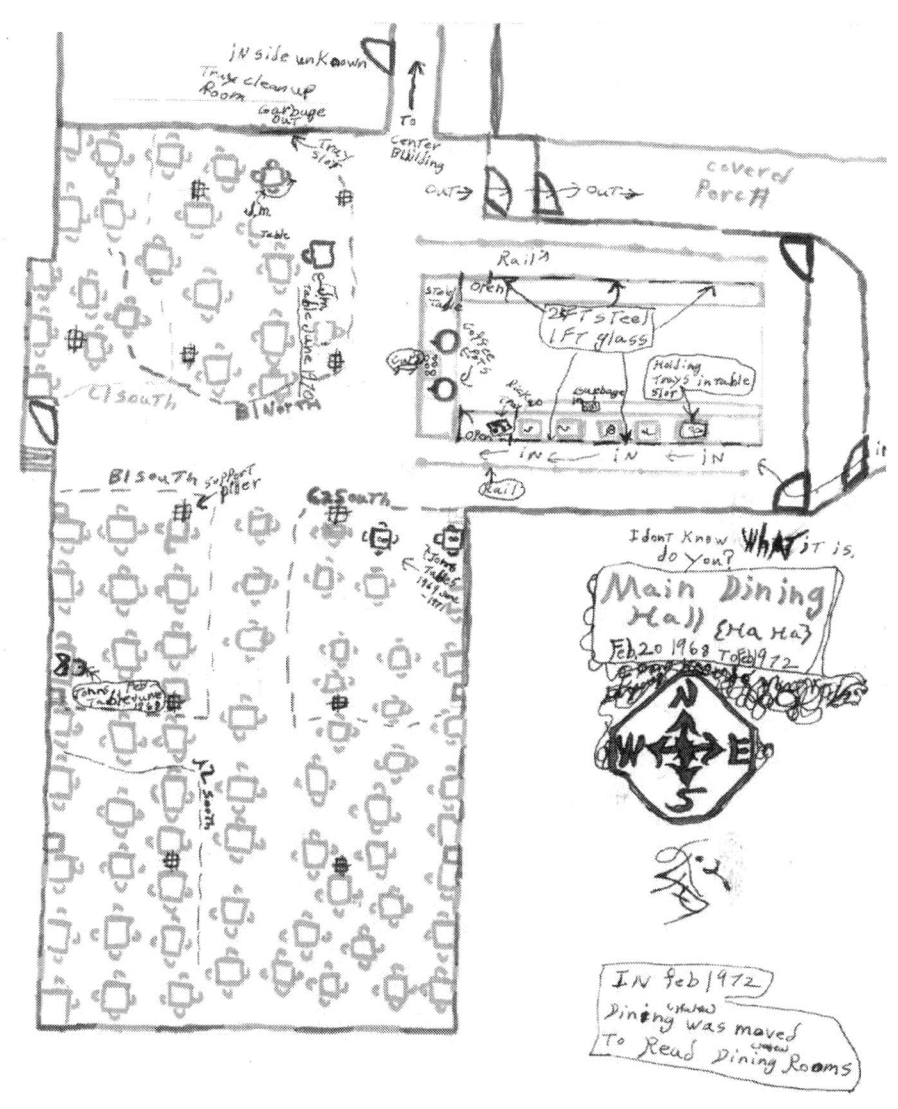

John Johnson's art while in Elgin State Hospital 1968-1972 © J. M. Seis.

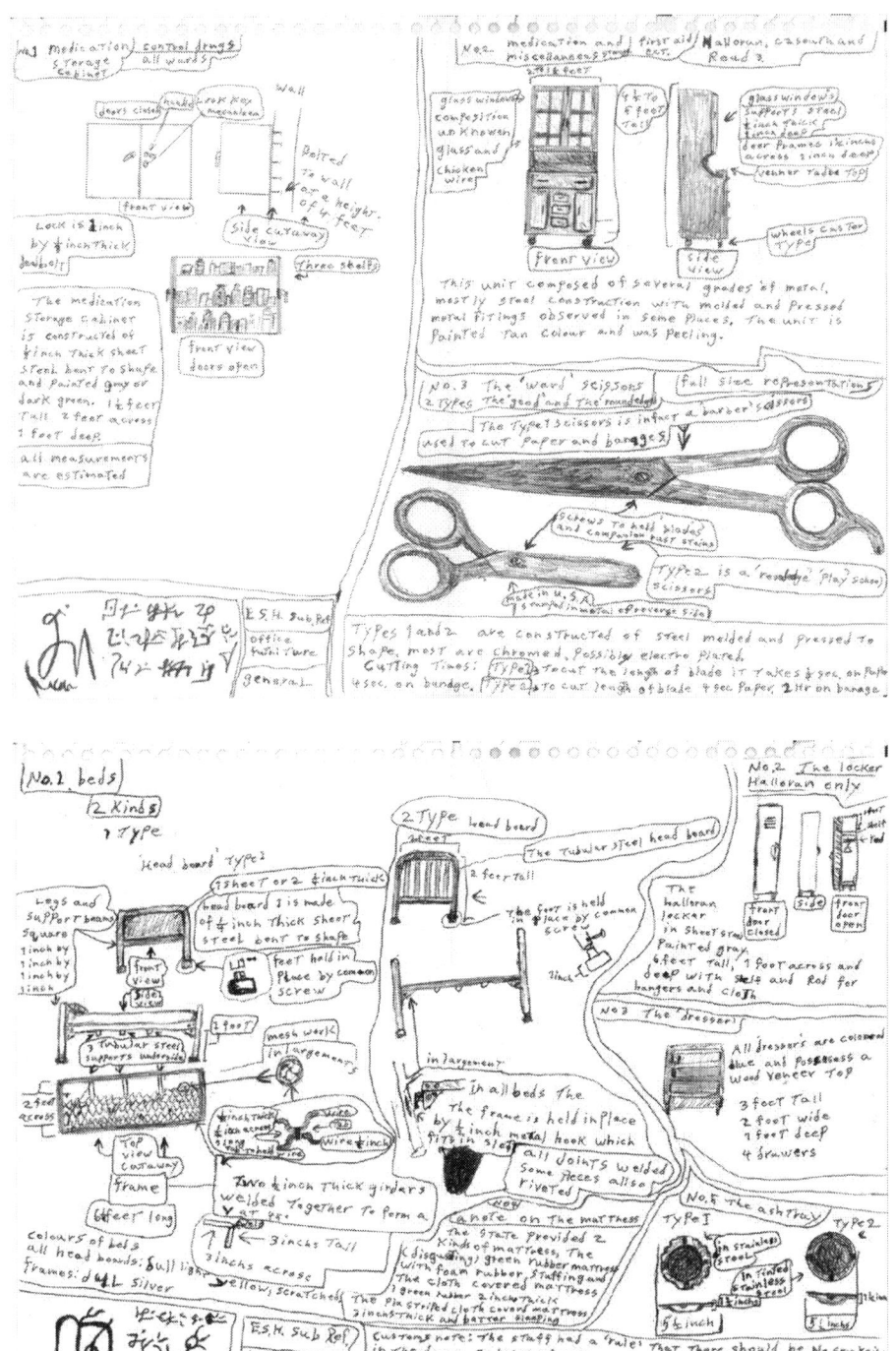

John Johnson's art while in Elgin State Hospital 1968-1972 © J. M. Seis.

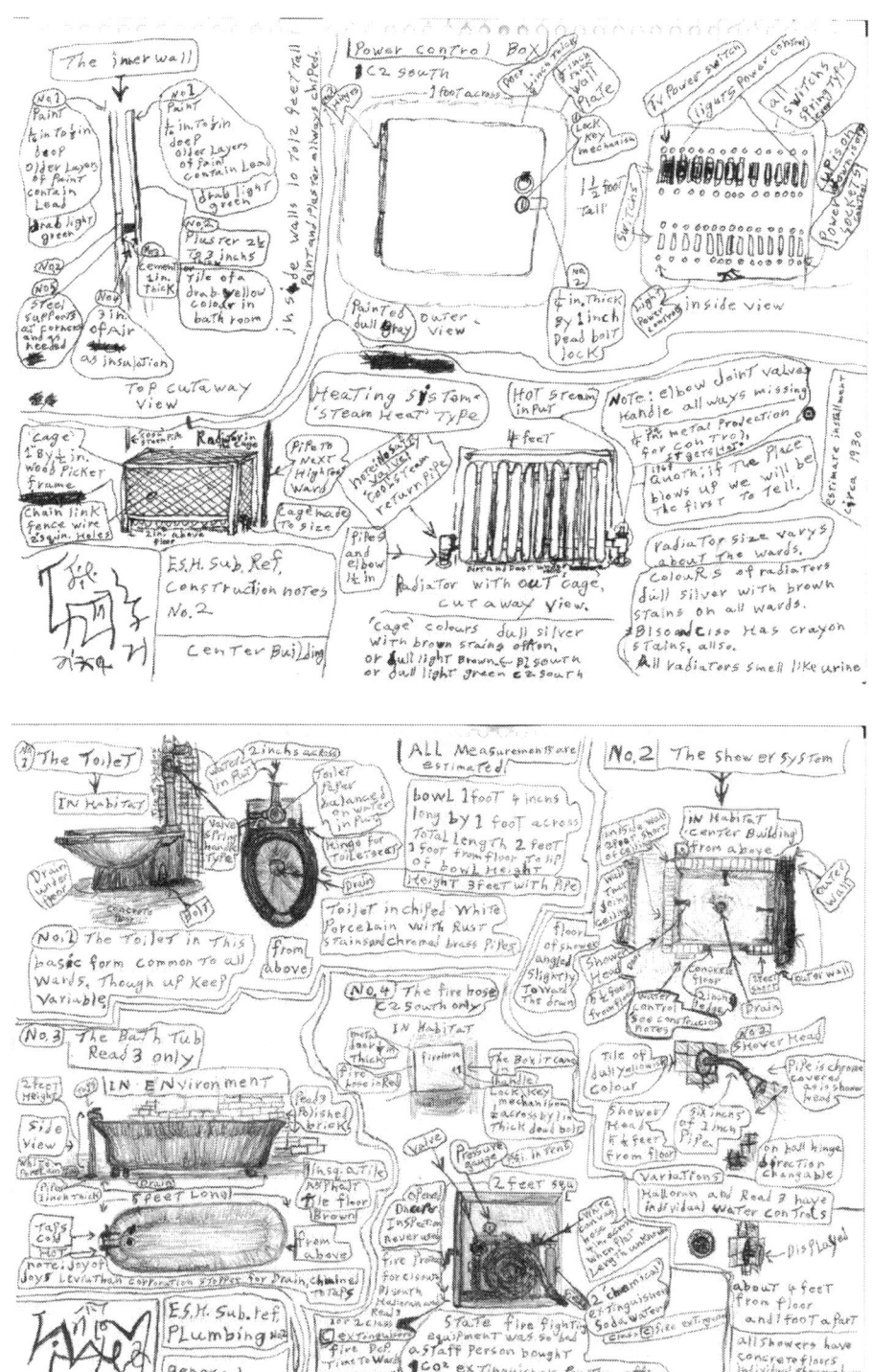

John Johnson's art while in Elgin State Hospital 1968-1972 © J. M. Seis.

John Johnson's art while in Elgin State Hospital 1968-1972 © J. M. Seis

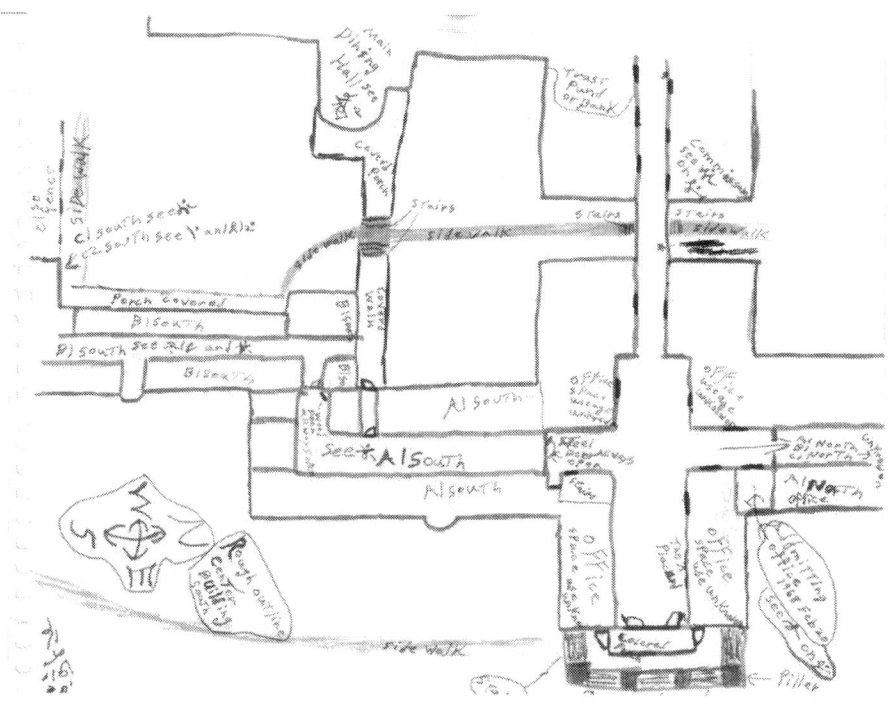

John Johnson's art while in Elgin State Hospital 1968-1972 © J. M. Seis

Honoring My Teen "Jan's" Poetry from 1969-1971:

Ideas on Love
Love is the flowing and whispering of
all myth and dream that touches the realness
of truth, and moves the presence of separateness,
into living, touching, heart, mind, and hand,
one to the other,
where no door can separate
nor clock disintegrate.

Present
Our hearts entwine with future,
let us kiss our ever present now
before the tomorrows
forget us as one,
before the forevers
leave us undone.

Wanderer
catch me
as you rove on,
hasten to pull forth
this leaden being
that I might be free as those around me.

Wanderer cries
as he passes by,
neither can I take you
or cause you to be free,
freedom's held within the mind
not within a key.

A Lover
You can have love
yet no lover,
or have a lover
yet no love.
I feel grateful
that I now have the two
in one
as you.

Sappho
A woman, of fair eyes;
hair cascading down in rivers of softness
upon her subtle breast.

I gazed from the brush as she in quiet splendor
neared the edging of the sea and knelt.
Woman, I cried.
Why go forth alone to the sea,
where among the throne of life
to kneel so humbly?
What whispered thoughts prays your heart?
I spoke in the silence of my own.

There sang the song of all birds in one voice,
there collected the coral foam and crystal spray,
in one woman's form.
There knelt the bliss of all nature accomplished,
perfect and natural.

And I with thieving eyes stealing wealth
without consent
fighting my trembling body as it neared the earth
in which to grasp the silken sand seeds
and weep for losses I should not claim.

God take mercy
condemn me not for my body
and desires inhabited therein.
Be it a curse from days unseen?
Be it damnation or tempts to stray?

Here in a body at which men gaze,
my spirit longs for the reflection.
There in the knelt form lies my quest,
dare I proceed as my heart calls?
I must or forever weep in the dark abyss.
I go now, I leave this shallow coverage,
but how my heart does quake and shiver
to my bones.

"Woman, fair woman, hear me now."
I neared the perfect one.
"Woman, oh woman of such quiet,
see my eyes, they are not crazed,
feel my heart, it is warm and full of life,
touch my hand, is it not real?
and such is my soul,
alive and tender towards your own."

No movement, nor did she speak
but silent watched my eyes with hers,
glistening from the wake of a golden moon.

Ah, to take leave of fear and gaze fixedly
upon this golden one,
to partake in such awesome splendor as this.
Here an eternity of peace lies within
the iridescent blue of sensitive eyes.
"I love".

I spoke no more than that.
My body was taken in through her open robes

And cradled by her
against the silken warmth of tender flesh,
arms and arms, kisses on silence, tears of salty sea.

I love.

Marilyn
I gaze into your soft eyes
brown and filled with tenderness,
I feel the warmth
of your voice and touch,
I can taste your sunshine
my mind open and ready
to accept your glisten and splendor.

Your spoken wisdom
roams through the meadows of my mind,
I touch the silence of your hair,
it flows freely as rivers through my fingers
and I find my strength scattered.

I wish to bury my face
in the white of your shoulder
and cry soft tears in my joy.
Cradle me darling,
let the stars gaze over our twoness
and heaven drop its soft dew
upon you in nakedness
sleeping innocent as a child
within my arms.

Inspiration
I'm dead
busted
broken headed
sear eared

and empty bedded,
gay, afraid
shy enslaved,
intelligent when I'm not too busy being
- stupid –

Many have passed through
few stayed,
I've been to harm and back to safe
but I really can't say
which was more inspiring.

Petition to Smoke
Between prison doors
of an educational farce,
people are thrown to and from
illusions of freedom, becoming entanglement,
pushers peddling
knowledge, dope
and discipline.
It's insanity complete
without escape
kindness unknown.

With all the hassles anyway
while scrounging after what we need
running from stern narrowness
of unmerciful minds,
crying out in hidden tears
from increased aggravation.

I don't like so many people here,
mirrors of emptiness
pass and bump,
they'll never know my name
while still I live four years with them.

This whole world has intensified,
madness claims one out of four,
swept under the carpet and ignored,
but aching still like unhealed sores.

With so many heads in different spheres
the loneliness, the lack of peers,
there are times when I prefer to sit
maybe just for five minutes
amidst the shadow of peace.
I light a cigarette and watch the smoke curl
forgetting for a time,
the problems of the world.

Someone to Need
someone to listen
to bear by your side
through all the groans and wailings
while laboring with life.

Truly we search
seemingly endlessly
for that touch of warmth
that timeless summer of rejoice
where all arms are two
reaching solely in purpose
of encompassing you.

We dance through life
dragging cumbersome burdens
frantically hiding them
calling it past,
while its deathly hold
still clutches the throat
and dares to speak its name
shattering glisten and frailness
causing a crisis within the soul.

I know,
it is felt in the deepest core
reminding of loneliness,
alienation and hopelessness.

There is still time
people to know,
but there is one mystery
needing to be delved.
The hidden self
Must open.

With the Sun
Crusted aching
upon the cold edge of night,
clinging to its fast and razor wings
frozen to a hope that couldn't be,
but my life exists
its holy glory and damnation
lies swinging in such chancy winds,
the terror of one moment
leads to the rejoicing of another
fleeting –

Time groans agonizingly around my senses.
What am I doing here?
What have I done?
The passage of another dream slips sweetly,
slowly,
yet quickly, painfully away!
And I didn't even catch hold of its slippery tail
before I heard the birth of another
shifting among the winds.

The sun woke up the morning
but I did not,

Instead I was swollen,
bursting, propelling in furious bright
fantastic surges of energy and light
with all my might
I began
and ran
and fell in love
with the sun,
not needing to prove myself any further,
to anyone.

I'm a Poetry Writer
blues chanting
winsome melody type dreamer
with courage to survive.
But fears enough to make me hide,
always looking
and reaching, sometimes trembling
toward that which I need and desire.

I'm not crazy though many will say so
and laugh out loud
at the dreams I've spun,
but you can see
it can only be
me and myself alone
to stand for my right
to live, believe, and be free
even walking into hell filled caverns
because I would not conform to be someone
that wasn't just whole-spirited me.

I live
and love
and am
quite gentle at heart,

asking very little but of peace
and sweet caresses
from underneath
this whimsical encounter,
my loving, ever ending
beginning
life.

ACKNOWLEDGMENTS

I know what it takes to write a book, or more importantly, who it takes. I could never have accomplished this arduous task without many people supporting me along the way.

Something stirred in me when I enrolled for a Ph.D. in psychology at Saybrook University. After completing the application, they wanted an identity statement. While answering their question of what my prior experience and interest in psychology was, the beginning of this book erupted. I didn't send what I wrote to the new university, but rather to my advisor in the Master's program at Goddard College where I was already enrolled. She read it and told me, "This is what you need to be writing." And so I must first give my deepest thanks to **Ellie Epp**, who encouraged me and listened to the girl inside me, finally tell the story she had been carrying alone for such a long time. When I saw Ellie shed a tear after reading my story, I could hardly believe anyone cared that much. Ellie's tear dissolved decades of denial and invited me to become a part of humanity as a whole person.

Thank you:

Merle Saferstein, for your endless hours of editing. I am so deeply grateful for your presence and love, your support and constant encouragement. You guided me through the critical later stages of this project. It was you along with my writing sisters at Gilda's Club, that became the cocoon for my craft of self expression to mature and my shaman self to become more ordinary and easier to understand. **Miriam Hall**, for your extraordinary time and attention. You used your expertise to organize my narrative into a more cohesive ordering. **Rebecca Jamieson**, you heard and understood the deepest level of my story and helped clear the way for better writing. **Lise Weil**, for reading and editing in 2009 and again in 2017. You kept pushing me to put more of my shamanic experience into the story until I finally did.

Many Thanks for Editing Support:

Carolyn Kottler, for your meticulous line editing. **Sally Voorheis,** for using your English teacher skills on my behalf, and liking the book so well you didn't want to stop reading it or give the marked manuscript back to me.

Thanks for reading and support:

Sandra Ingerman, for being capable of reading my story about my childhood while continuing to hold me in love and respect as a shamanic practitioner. You helped me bridge divergent worlds. Thank you for giving me my first human experience of receiving Soul Retrieval, and teaching me to become a better practitioner and teacher. **Louise Clough,** my dear friend from far away and long ago who took the time and care to read an early rough draft and encourage me to keep going. **Sharon Gerrity,** for your amazing emotional support. You've had the capacity to know and love me as a teacher and practitioner as well as a dear and trusted friend. I know this is a hard book for my friends to read, but you had the heart and stamina to read it twice! **Linda Thomas** and **Jeanette Hipskind** for loving, listening, and being my steady support team all these years. **Dr. Sameet Kumar** who gave me a masculine point of view after reading an early draft. You saw and affirmed the power of the shaman in me amidst a terrifying health challenge while rewriting this memoir. In my greatest darkness since Elgin, you reflected a path of light. **Julie Klein,** my dear writing sister, author, and friend. You cared so much as you read my story that you kept calling me to ask if I was all right. I'm doing great, dear.

I thank all those who took the time to read my draft and give me feedback including Mary D. Ramsay for encouraging me to write this story and for being my first editor. Thank you Kristen Penn for listening to the unfolding story as I wrote it.

I offer my gratitude to those who shared their homes with me during the last writing years, (including those I house-sat for) so I could keep my focus on writing and healing. Thank you to those who hosted me teaching classes and offering sessions in their area. Much love to my *ACA Twelve-Step, Fellow/Sister Travelers.*

I am grateful for the energy of the Pachamama and sacred Apu's, (mountains) of the Andean spine of the America's. This wisdom and knowledge from the earth continues to operate through my heart and through my mesa (shaman initiated medicine bundle/altar). I entered this chapter of my shamanic initiation when Q'ero Elder Don Manuel Quispe, Kuraq Akulliq, transmitted the rites of his shamanic lineage to me in 1995. I'm grateful to Luzclara for our many magical years of working and traveling together.

So many people were supportive of me during the writing this book in both direct and indirect ways. Please know how grateful I am to all of you. This has been a powerful accomplishment as a personal and community healing ceremony, where each reader is a part.

Invictus

Out of the night that covers me,
Black as the pit from pole to pole,
I thank whatever gods may be
For my unconquerable soul.

In the fell clutch of circumstance
I have not winced nor cried aloud.
Under the bludgeonings of chance
My head is bloody, but unbowed.

Beyond this place of wrath and tears
Looms but the Horror of the shade,
And yet the menace of the years
Finds and shall find me unafraid.

It matters not how strait the gate,
How charged with punishments the scroll,
I am the master of my fate,
I am the captain of my soul.

William Ernest Henley

J.M. Seis, MA. has dedicated her life to awakening consciousness through personal healing. She is a teacher and shamanic practitioner specializing in Soul Retrieval. Being a medicine woman requires breaking out of the ordinary. Medicine people may become awakened by overwhelming experiences that separate them from the collective, even casting them out for a period of time. A process of interacting with non-ordinary reality takes place that can include merging with an essential, supernatural presence, causing an extraordinary personal transformation. Once returned to ordinary life, medicine people, also known as shamans, are compelled into service for the benefit of their family, community, and the earth.

For more information visit:
greatmotherpress.com greatmotherpress@gmail.com
www.facebook.com/ceremonialmemoir

Made in the USA
Las Vegas, NV
09 December 2022